The Armies of the
French Revolution

To Jean-Pascal Tranie.
Thank you for your friendship.

The Armies of the French Revolution

Uniforms and Equipment

Paul L. Dawson

FRONTLINE BOOKS

First published in Great Britain in 2025 by
Frontline Books
An imprint of Pen & Sword Books Limited
Yorkshire – Philadelphia

Copyright © Paul L. Dawson 2025

ISBN 978 1 52679 233 4

The right of Paul L. Dawson to be identified as
Author of this Work has been asserted by him in accordance
with the Copyright, Designs and Patents Act 1988.

A CIP catalogue record for this book is
available from the British Library.

All rights reserved. No part of this book may be reproduced, transmitted, downloaded, decompiled or reverse engineered in any form or by any means, electronic or mechanical including photocopying, recording or by any information storage and retrieval system, without permission from the Publisher in writing. NO AI TRAINING: Without in any way limiting the Author's and Publisher's exclusive rights under copyright, any use of this publication to 'train' generative artificial intelligence (AI) technologies to generate text is expressly prohibited. The Author and Publisher reserve all rights to license uses of this work for generative AI training and development of machine learning language models.

Typeset by Mac Style

The Publisher's authorised representative in the EU for product safety is Authorised Rep Compliance Ltd., Ground Floor, 71 Lower Baggot Street, Dublin D02 P593, Ireland.
www.arccompliance.com

For a complete list of Pen & Sword titles please contact

PEN & SWORD BOOKS LIMITED
47 Church Street, Barnsley, South Yorkshire, S70 2AS, England
E-mail: enquiries@pen-and-sword.co.uk
Website: www.pen-and-sword.co.uk
or
PEN AND SWORD BOOKS
1950 Lawrence Road, Havertown, PA 19083, USA
E-mail: uspen-and-sword@casematepublishers.com
Website: www.penandswordbooks.com

Contents

Acknowledgements		vi
Introduction		vii
Chapter 1	Clothing the Soldier	1
Chapter 2	1791 and All That	25
Chapter 3	*Levée en Masse* and *Demi-Brigades*	47
Chapter 4	*Demi-Brigades d'Infanterie de Ligne*	59
Chapter 5	*Chasseurs à Pied*	105
Chapter 6	The *Légère* is Born	125
Chapter 7	*Cavalerie*, *Carabiniers* and *Dragons*	130
Chapter 8	*Dragons*	185
Chapter 9	*Hussards*	220
Chapter 10	*Chasseurs à Cheval*	253
Chapter 11	Conclusions	278
Bibliography		282
Notes		285

Acknowledgements

Over 20 years ago, I made my first visit to the Château de Vincennes, the home of the French Army Archives. A place I have come to know intimately in that time, and the 'holy grail' it keeps within its walls of millions of documents from the 1^e *Empire* (French Empire). My 2 or 3 annual pilgrimages to 'worship at the shrine of archive research' came to a juddering halt in March 2020. My writing stopped, and this book hit 'the buffers'.

Without Yves Martin's unfailing support and friendship with his most generous assistance in the provision of research material and illustrations this book would not exist.

I am also indebted to Sally Fairweather for her assistance with, and photographing of, archival material at the Archives Nationales and Service Historique de la Défense Armée du Tére in Paris. She has accompanied me willingly on my pilgrimage to Paris over 20 times, and spent hours and hours photographing archives and developing 'Vincennes Back' from standing for hours at a time photographing records. Without her help, friendship and dedication, this book would have taken years longer to write.

Hans Karl Weiß, Martin Lancaster, Ben Townsend, Terry Crowdy and Robert Cooper must be heartily thanked for their encouragement of this book and my research: their support and critical input to my thinking have kept this projecting progressing for the last 7 years. I hope gentlemen that the finished thesis lives up to your expectations and the thousands spent on air flights, hotels and dedicated patronage of Le Drapeau in Vincennes has been worth it.

Bertrand Malvaux is to be heartily thanked for allowing me to use images of his extensive collection. Bravo Sir!

The long-suffering staff at Service Historique de la Défense Armée du Tére in Paris need to be thanked for answering questions and locating items of research that have made this book possible.

Paul L. Dawson,
Paris, 5 May 2025

Introduction

A future marshal of France arrayed his men along a narrow ridge – they were mostly volunteers (*volontaires*), inspired with patriotic fervour against the regular army (*armée*) of Old Regime Europe. Among the mass of French blue coats were white coats – those professional soldiers (*soldats*) who had served the king and now served the people. General François-Étienne-Christophe de Kellermann's victory at the Battle of Valmy in 1792 shocked the world. It saved France and was the starting shot in almost 15 years of war, that witnessed France's resurgence and then demise.

In order to understand what happened next, we have to understand the army of Louis XVI. The King's Army we remember served the young Republic of France until new year 1791: its training, institutions, officers (*officiers*), men, clothing and equipment all lingered beyond the death knell of Louis XIV's (Louis the Great, the Sun King) military machine created in the late seventeenth century.

This book seeks to explore the army of Louis XVI and its transition into a citizen army, that of *sans-culottes* (civilians from poorer social backgrounds who became militants during the French Revolution in the late eighteenth century) and *demi-brigades* (military formations used by the French army following the French Revolution).

The data for the book is gathered from the vast archive holdings of the Service Historique de la Défense Armée du Tére in Paris. It is here in the library we find the printed text of the regulations and the archive boxes of the army. From the thousands of inspection returns we are able to flesh out how the regulations were put into practice.

I do not seek to present every regiment (*régiment*), due to both word count and the time needed to consult over 300 archives boxes – over 60 days' work in Paris – and the financial implications of that, but to give a flavour of how the regulations were implemented. As with the modern-day armed forces, the clothing that was issued to a 'squaddie' was done so on a regulated basis, each item being described by a series of 'dress regulations'. Each item of clothing had a specified duration period. A uniform coat (*habit* – single-breasted coat with long tails and cut away at the front to expose the vest worn underneath) had to last 2 years, a bearskin 20 years and a pair of breeches (*culottes*) a matter of months.

Every year a regiment would be inspected and the condition of the clothing assessed. A return of all the clothing to be struck off/disposed of was made and the appropriate number of new items ordered. Clothing and equipment needing repairs was also logged, as was how many items had been repaired since the last inspection. A soldier was responsible for the repair of his own clothing and any associated costs. Likewise, if he lost items, he had to purchase replacements – in many ways a soldier ended up paying to be in the army when these deductions were taken into consideration. It was very much 'make do and mend' by the time the cloth items of equipment were coming to the end of their service life.

These inspection returns are a fantastic resource for outlining what a regiment actually wore rather than the theory based on the regulations. The two often did not agree in practice. The regiment's clothing and equipment was overseen by the regiment's clothing officer. His work was overseen by an inspector general. The lieutenant clothing officer had to oversee the purchase of all items of equipment and clothing for the *sous-officiers* (sergeants, *fourriers* – company clerks – or sergeant majors) and men. Officers provided their own uniforms and equipment. The regimental council (*conseil*) oversaw that the items purchased on the regiment's behalf were of good quality, that they matched the regiment's specification and that the cost of purchase was as agreed in the contracts (*marches*). All receipts had to be lodged in separate account books that were overseen by a commissioner for war. This was to ensure that officers did not pocket money from the regiment obtaining contracts. The specification for each item of uniform was recorded in a register of uniforms (*registre de tenues*). The commissioner for war was to ensure that items purchased matched this register. All deliberations of the council in obtaining contracts for clothing and equipment from contractors were to be recorded so that the commissioner for war could see how and why a regiment chose a certain contractor. The council of administration (*conseil d'administration*) each year, acting with the clothing officers, drew up a store's inventory of the regiment, as well as gathered the parade states of the items of equipment and clothing issued. All clothing had a specific lifespan. Each time an item was inspected it was classed as either new, in need of repair, due to expire or expired and in need of replacement. From this data, the clothing officer was able to report the total number of items needing to be replaced or repaired. The contracts for repair of clothing do not survive, but the minutes drawn up by the council of administration do.[1] Under the terms of the regulations of 1791, the war administration supplied the regiments directly with broadcloth, woollen twill (*tricot*) and worsted twill (*serge*) to make *habits*, jackets (*vestes* – sleeved waistcoats, with a low collar; cut to have a V-notch at the centre front), knee breeches (*culottes* – knee breeches made from doe hide or sheepskin in the cavalry, and broadcloth in the infantry and artillery) and garrison or fatigue caps – off duty caps (*bonnets de police*).

The war administration also provided grenadiers' bearskins, ammunition pouches (*gibernes* – pouches for cartridges, usually carried on shoulder belts called *porte-gibernes*) with belts, *sabre* belts and musket slings.[2] The regimental council of administration was responsible for shouldering the cost of producing the clothing and equipment in house as it was made by the regimental craftsmen, as well as the provision of lace for trumpeters, gold (*d'Or*), silver and worsted lace for rank and service stripes, the *epaulettes* (ornamented shoulder boards with fringe worn by officers and elite troops) for adjutants, the lace for the *bonnets de police*, hats (*chapeaux*), plumes – decorations made of feathers, usually worn rising from the front or side of a *schako* (military headdress), hat or helmet – shoes, socks and underwear etc.[3] Therefore, each regiment was responsible for the clothing of each man in the regiment with no reliance on external contractors.

Cross belts, *gibernes*, haversacks (*havresacs* – cowhide backpack in which the soldier kept his personal belongings and spare items of clothing) and other one size fits all items were mass produced. Shoes came in 3 sizes, so did *chapeaux*, other items of headdress (*schakos*, *mirlitons*, helmets etc.) and the cloth parts of the uniform. This allowed for standardisation and, thus, ease of production. Ideally, each conscript was to receive his issue uniform and then have it fitted to him by the regimental tailor – this perhaps seldom happened unless a regiment was on garrison duty. Leather items were ordered from manufacturers, as were metal fittings like buttons. Headdresses were also out sourced. If made in house or bought in *marches* would be prepared for agreement by the regiment's administrative council, who would oversee the work and inspect the quality of the workmanship and materials. Each regiment, it seems, kept a sealed pattern for each item of equipment, which was the established model to be copied by suppliers.[4]

It is from these records that I have written this book: the preservation of such documents in archives is sporadic. Hence, my text is biased towards the end of the Revolutionary epoch.

x   The Armies of the French Revolution

Painted post epoch, this image of French soldiers at the battle of Valmy gives a flavour of the eclectic dress of the French Army during the Revolution.

Chapter 1
Clothing the Soldier

The purpose of a uniform was to turn a civilian into a soldier: the individual became a 'cog in a machine'. The uniform was both a mode of restriction but also of distinction: it set the soldier apart from the civilian, and created a form of collective identity and exclusivity. Uniform was representative of a number of debates in France that linked clothing, appearance and social rank. Uniforms drew directly on contemporary civilian fashions, as a means of fashioning the soldier and officer in line with contemporary ideals of masculinity and taste: dress was a symbol of rank and its relationship and significance in the presentation of self. The dress uniform, the *habit*, was cut to follow contemporary fashions, made in super fine broadcloth for officers. The colour of the uniform reflected the politics of the nation with the adoption of national colours of red, white and blue as opposed to the white of the *Ancien Régime*. Changes in civilian fashion dictated that the looser-fitting clothing of the mid-eighteenth century was replaced with a leaner, tighter-fitting uniform, resulting in a longer and tighter silhouette. This new silhouette resulted in cheaper and more practical uniforms.

Fashion dictated that the mid-blue hue of an officer's uniform became almost blue-black. By the later 1790s, sober shades became popular among fashionable men in reaction to the foppish and extravagant dress of the *incroyables* (fashionable dandies who wore flamboyant and very colourful clothing) of earlier years. There was nothing in regulations to indicate this change in colour or if it was deliberate policy, yet it is undeniable that original officers' *habits* are strikingly different in colour to that of the soldiers, and surely represents civilian fashion regulating military aesthetics.[1] It would be civilian fashion that drove the Bardin Regulation – Napoléon Bonaparte instructed Major Étienne Alexandre Bardin to standardise the uniform worn by the *Grande Armée* – as much as practical: the dark blue double-breasted tail coat by 1812 was almost a civilian uniform for men from the middle and upper classes, which was militarised into the *habit-veste*.

Being issued a uniform, as we noted, indoctrinated the civilian into the military world. It gave him both a sense of pride and purpose: cleaning and maintaining your kit was (and still is) one of the primary occupations of a soldier when not on parade. The life of a soldier, as well as his appearance, was defined through differing degrees of control. It was contingent on at least the superficial acceptance and adoption of these codes. Furthermore, adherence to the code is theoretically regulated and constructed by an identifiable hierarchy, enforced through differing degrees of punishment. Cleaning kit and taking pride in one's appearance and the discipline this activity gave the soldier, as well as looking and feeling like a soldier generated *esprit des corps*. In her examination of uniforms held at the Musée de l'Armée in Paris, Alison Matthews David (2003) reveals

2 The Armies of the French Revolution

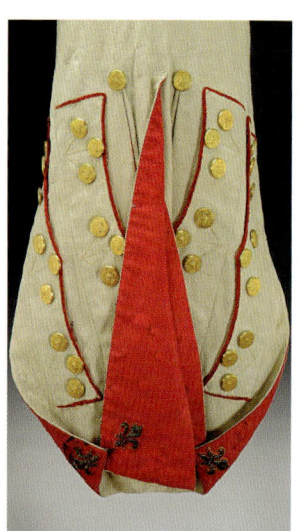
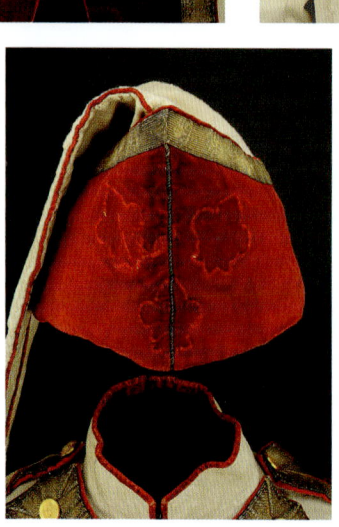

Clothing the Soldier 3

An incredible uniform of an officer of the *Régiment du Colonel-General* according to the regulations of 1786. The lavish use of gold lace, velvet facings and *gilt* buttons all show the flamboyance of the army of Louis XVI in his last years before the Revolution tore France apart. (*Collection and photographs of Bertrand Malvaux*)

that nineteenth-century French military officers often had their uniforms tailor made to incorporate discreet interior embellishments, such as luxurious silk lining.[2]

Such modifications allowed a clandestine expression of self. This type of modification may never have been seen by anyone else and served to reinforce one's unique and self-controlled identity within the regulated world of identify and appearance. We see regimental discreet changes to regulations from inspection returns, where regimental colonels sought ways of making their regiment not part of the uniform as a whole. The assumption of visual uniformity ignores the historical, social and economic contexts in which uniforms actually operate. As our study of regimental inspection has revealed, uniformity in reality compared to theoretical perfection is commonly compromised by miscommunication (for example, the misinterpretations of specifications, possibly purposefully to create a regimental uniform rather than that specified by the state), conflicting motivations, multiple manufacturers, channels of command or material restraints (like unstable dyes or shortages). Such factors may lead to a variety of effects: substitutions or deficiencies in uniforms, varying levels of strictness from uniform enforcers, necessary adaptations to new contexts and individualistic alterations. Because of their bureaucratic nature, uniform codes do not always quickly or easily respond to environmental or contextual shifts. Individual wearers, therefore, find ways to adapt uniforms when necessary. Realities of shortages during times of war and deterioration on the battlefield, often require creative compensation, which, in turn, affects uniformity. These caveats all mean that official regulations must be tempered by how regiments responded to them, which is the *raison d'être* of this text.

Regulations of 1786

The uniform, *habit*, of Napoléon's *Grande Armée* had its origins in the 1660s. Over time its cut and form evolved into the garment we recognised today. During the eighteenth century, the *veste* was the everyday jacket of the solider. The *habit* formed the soldier's top coat, being cut so that the tails, which were normally hooked together, could be opened out, and the *revers* (lapels) could be buttoned over, giving the soldier a bad weather garment. In general, the *revers* were normally folded back to show the facing colour, as were the skirts of the *habit*. As fashion changed, the *habit* became ever more tight fitting. Thus, the need for a top coat arose.

The regulations of 1786 and 1791, and the amendments of 1787 were the starting point for *habits* used in the first half of the *1ᵉ Empire*. Each man was measured and the clothing made so as not to encumber his movements:

> The *habits* and *vestes* will be cut in the proportions of the height and the size of the men, & kept sufficiently easy so that the Soldier can make with ease the movements which he will be ordered to carry out, without being constrained in his movements in case seams are torn; to effect this, the chests will be kept very wide, and the back of the *habit* and the *veste*, from one sleeve to the other, will be sufficient, as will

Clothing the Soldier 5

An incredibly well-preserved sleeved waistcoat made from silk, typical of those used by officers before the Revolution. (*Collection and photographs of Bertrand Malvaux*)

the circumference of the garment, to allow free movement. The measurement will be taken for each man on the chest, the shoulders being drawn back and the chest lifted; & to take the measurement of the back when the arms will be crossed over the chest. It will be observed that the cuffs must be buttoned easily throughout their length; the three buttonholes below will not be opened. The length of the coat will be such that with the *revers* buttoned across, the bottom edge of the tail will reach three *lignes*[3] from the ground, the man being on his knees.[4]

Under these regulations, the *habit* was slightly altered from 1779: the collar was now standing, and the cuff was to be closed by 3 buttons and not 4. The tails were still cut full, and the *revers* still closed over each other. The sleeves of the *habit* were lined in linen, and the body in *serge*. This was still very much an eighteenth-century coat. By 1800, the *revers* would no longer fasten over one another, and the tails could no longer open out. Fashion dictated that the loose-cut *habit* of the eighteen century became tighter fitting – this also saved cloth. By 1810, 2 *habits* could be made from the cloth allocated to make 1 *habit* in 1786!

Epaulettes

To mark out the status of grenadiers, under the regulations of 1786, grenadiers were issued with red broadcloth shoulder straps piped white – the same shape and form as the straps for fusiliers. The strap was 2 *pouces*[5] wide, interlined with linen and lined in cloth the colour of the *habit*. Red fringed *epaulettes* were authorised on 1 April 1791. These regulations give no width measurement for the *epaulette*, and state that the shoulder board was made from scarlet broadcloth lined in cloth the colour of the *habit*, the fringing was 2.8 *pouces* long. There were 4 layers of fringing passed around the end of the strap. The *epaulette* attached to the *habit* with a button at the collar and passed through a lace bride at the shoulder. Under the body of the *epaulette* was a long tab called the '*sous patte*' – the shoulder belt (*baudrier* – a broad belt worn over the shoulder that would support a sword or other item) passed between the tab and the *epaulette* body, meaning that when the cross belt was taken off, the *epaulette* remained attached to the *habit* and did not become lost.

Fusiliers continued to wear simple shoulder straps through to the end of the *1ᵉ Empire*. The shoulder strap was fastened at the shoulder by a button placed next to the collar. The part at the shoulder was cut into a 3-pointed *escutcheon* and sewn to the *habit*.[6]

Vestes

Under the uniform coat, the *habit*, the infantryman wore an under jacket – period terminology calls this a *veste*.

The decree of 1786 stated the following:

The under jacket will be cut long enough to embrace the hips well, and the bottom button completely covers the waistband of the *culottes*; the front buttonholes will be made in goat hair, & will be reinforced with a band of linen to line the opening of the buttonholes; the buttonholes of the pockets, the right pocket of which will be open, will likewise be goat hair; the length of the *basques* [skirts – tails on a coat or skirts on a jacket], counting from the last button, will be six and a half *pouces* [176mm], & it will be lined with linen; the sleeves, which will usually open underneath, will be sewn to the jacket, except at the front.

The under jackets of the Corporals, chosen men & Soldiers, will have small collars & cuffs of the distinctive colour, according to the facings of the *habit's revers* and cuffs … The collar of the jacket will be straight like that of the coat, but only nine *lignes* [20mm] in height; it will be lined with white cloth which will overlap at the edge, & will end a *pouce* from the edge of the front of the *veste*. The cuffs will be two *pouces* [50.8mm] high, & sewn on the sleeves, which will open four *pouces* [108mm] above the hand, & will close with two small buttons, one placed on the facing, & the other on the body of the sleeve.[7]

The entire garment was made from broadcloth, with linen lining. It was cut like a *habit* i.e. it had centre back seam and arm *syce* seams (the seam on the back of a coat or jacket, which curves around to the arm hole). It was quite literally a single-breasted jacket worn under a top coat i.e. the *habit*. The garments for *bas-officiers* (sergeant majors, *fourriers* and sergeants – later known as *sous-officiers*) – had no sleeves.

The front was cut so that it had a short 'skirt' at the front so that the top edge of the front pockets was on the natural waist, and the pocket flaps themselves and the front of the *veste* extended below the waistline and over the hips. The front tended to dip down towards the centre front, with a V-notch. It was worn as the everyday jacket – the *habit* functioned as a 'top coat'. The most unique feature of this garment was that the sleeve cap of the arms alone was sewn to the body of the *veste* – the underarm seam was left open. This allowed for a better fit under the *habit* and allowed greater freedom of movement in the shoulder.[8]

Gilets

In times of war, in cold weather, the soldiers were allowed to wear a waistcoat under the *veste* – period terminology calls this a *gilet* (sleeveless, straight cut-waistcoat without tails, closed in front with a row of 12 small uniform buttons sometimes referred to as a *gilet sans-manche*).[9] It was made from *tricot*. The button stands were interlined with linen and lined in twill. The front panel and back were made from linen.[10] The front was cut as before, with pockets at the waist and shallow *basques*, the back was cut like a waistcoat i.e. it had under arm seams joining the front to the back, rather than an army *syce* and centre back seam. At the centre back was a large triangular gusset that ran the full vertical length of the back of the garment. This allowed the *gilet* to be adjusted to fit by the means of tapes.

In finest scarlet broadcloth, these officers' breeches (*culottes*) are typical of those worn by army officers prior to and during the Revolution, albeit in white for the infantry. (*Collection and photographs of Bertrand Malvaux*)

Headdresses

For headdresses, the regulations of 1786 allowed a felt *chapeau* and a *bonnet de police* to be made from materials recovered from the old clothing.[11]

Bonnets a Poil

Colloquially known as the beehive, the most characteristic feature of the grenadiers' uniform was their tall *bonnets a poil* (literally fur hats). Adopted for grenadiers under the decree of 1 November 1789,[12] their use was confirmed with the decree of 1 January 1791. The grenadiers were allowed both a *chapeau* and a bearskin. Under the terms of the decree of 1789, the bearskin was to be made in the proportions of the decrees of 1767 and 1775. The regulations of 1767 stated that the bearskin had a natural leather body

Clothing the Soldier 9

A fusilier of the *Régiment du Colonel-General* wearing the uniform according to the regulations of 1786.

A grenadier of the *Régiment du Colonel-General* wearing the uniform according to the regulations of 1786, which only came into use from November 1788. In 1791, the lace was ordered to be stripped off such luxurious uniforms. (*Collection KM*)

that was boiled to make it hard. The front was decorated with a copper plate bearing the royal arms. The bearskin had a red plume on the left side worn above a white pleated linen cockade. The back patch of the bearskin was made from broadcloth the same colour as the regiment's facing and ornamented with a white lace cross. The white cords, made from worsted linen, terminated in a pair of *raquettes* (round or oval decorations, knotted from worsted cord).[13] No dimensions are given we note for any part of the bearskin.

The regulations of 1791 stated thar the bearskin was to be 13 *pouces* tall. The bearskin was to have a yellow metal plate in front, with a flaming grenade motif at the centre – we note no dimensions were given for the plate itself, and, therefore, were the same dimensions as those of 1767. The bearskin had white cords, and the rear of the bearskin had a red patch with a white lace. A red feather plume was worn from the left side – no mention of a cockade or the size of the plume.[14]

The dress regulations of 1799 stated that the *bonnet a poil* had a leather carcass, which was to measure 352mm tall over the fur following the contour of the bearskin, and 231mm wide. The carcass was covered in bear pelt. A leather sweat band adorned the bottom. At the top rear of the bearskin was the back patch, some 162mm in diameter. It was quartered blue and red, and decorated with a white lace cross. In full dress the bearskin was adored with scarlet worsted cords. The knotted portion of the cords was to be 921mm long, the tassels to be 88mm long, and the *raquettes* to measure 115mm deep by 74mm wide. At the front of the bearskins was a copper plate. The copper plate was to be embossed with the flaming grenade, the plate measured 137mm tall, 205mm wide at the base and 135mm wide in the middle.[15]

Bonnets de Police

The first *bonnet de police* or off duty cap was introduced in 1767. This was called a *pokalem* and copied the polish-style clothing. The top was formed from a large disc of cloth, gathered into a headband. The headband had a cloth plaque at the front bearing the regimental number and also had a second piece of cloth sewn to the headband, which could be lowered down to provide ear flaps and a neck guard. The ear flaps passed through 2 slots in the headband and were button together as detailed in the regulations of 1786:

> Each *sous-officier*, corporal, appointed man, grenadier, *chasseur* [literally means 'hunters' and was used for mounted men – *Chasseurs à Cheval* – as well as foot soldiers in light infantry units and the Imperial Guard] and fusilier, will wear a *bonnet de police*, which will be made with the off-cut material when cutting new clothing and the best pieces of debris from old clothing; and the amount of cloth allocated will be adjusted accordingly by the estimate below; this cap will be of broadcloth, lined with canvas, and made in the shape of a *pokalem*.
>
> The front will be adorned with a patch made from broadcloth, in the middle of which will be sewn, for the grenadiers a grenade, for the *chasseurs* a horn, and for the fusiliers a *fleur-de-lys*, in the same cloth as the facings of the uniform, and of the same heights and dimensions as grenades, horns and *fleur-de-lys* [emblem] as on the

An officer of the *Régiment du Colonel-General* wearing the undress *surtout* as outlined in the regulations of 1786. (*Collection KM*)

A grenadier of the *Régiment du Roi* wearing full dress respecting the regulations of 1786. (*Collection KM*)

habit; this patch and the turban of the *bonnet de police*, will be trimmed with a piping in the said facing colour.

The turban will be trimmed with a strip of cloth in the distinctive colour.

The turban can be folded down to cover the soldier's ears in cold and rainy weather, and will be attached under the chin with hooks and eyes.

More details were added in the regulations of 1787. In essence, the crown of the cap was made from 4 pieces of broadcloth sewn together with the seams all piped. The turban folded down, almost like the Bardin issue, and fastened under the chin.

Chapeaux

The traditional headwear of a French soldier was a felt *chapeau*. The regulations of 1786 stated the following:

> *Sous-officiers* & Privatemen, both of the Grenadier companies, as those of *Chasseurs* & Fusiliers, will wear a hat, cut round, of three *pouces* & a half at least deep in the crown, & of four *pouces* six *lignes* in the brim, edged, in the manner called 'à Cheval', with a black wool edging nine *lignes* wide; the brims will be raised with fastenings, in the usual way, & that of the left side will be held by a black loop, attached by a small uniform button.
>
> The hat will be cocked in the manner that the front corner might be shorter than the others, sufficiently raised, & a little turned to the side of the button; the fastenings of the back brim will be placed high enough for preventing its deforming. If will be trimmed with a white dimity cockade, in round form, & of three *pouces* six *lignes* diameter; the top of the crown, in war time [*sic*], will be trimmed with a perceivable iron skull piece.
>
> Each company of Grenadiers & *Chasseurs*, will be distinguished by a round tuft of wool, the height of which will be two *pouces*, & which will be carried above the cockade; that of the Grenadiers will be scarlet; that of the *Chasseurs* will be green; the Fusilier companies will also wear in the same manner tufts of round & flat form, six *lignes* thick & twenty *lignes* in diameter, which will be of the colours affected to their companies; namely: in the first battalion [*bataillon*], royal blue for the first company; salmon pink for the second; violet for the third; & crimson for the fourth. In the second Battalion, blue & white for the first company; salmon pink & white for the second, violet and white for the third, & crimson & white for the fourth. The two Adjutants, the Drum Major, Armourer & Musicians, will wear the tuft in white wool, as being attached to Headquarters.
>
> The hats will last two years, & they will be replaced in consequence each year by half of the complement.

Legwear

Tight-fitting knee breeches (*culottes de peau*) were common everyday wear in the eighteenth century. The regulations of 1787 describe the *culottes* being made from *tricot* and lined in linen. They were broad fall i.e. the front fall extended from 1 outside leg seam to the other, and was fastened with 5 buttons, the central button was 1 of 3 buttons that closed the centre front opening. The legs were cut so as to envelope the knee, the knee band and buckle sitting below the knee cap. The legs were fastened around the knee by 3 or 4 buttons, along with a knee band and buckle to keep the bottom of the leg closed. The knee band, in order to reduce the bulk around the lower leg, did not pass all the way around the lower leg. The knee band was 34mm wide and made from *tricot* backed onto linen and was 81mm long, of which 54mm was left free from the knee opening to pass through the copper buckle, which had an iron tang. The opening at the knee was 162mm. Unlike the *habit* and *veste*, the buttonholes were sewn with linen thread and not mohair as on the former. The *culottes* were worn over the soldier's underwear and stockings. The waistband sat above the natural waist. The *culottes* were adjusted to fit at the back by means of a gusset and a tab and buckle.[16]

From 1786, the *sous-officiers* and soldiers were allowed knee breeches made from nankeen or whitened linen as summer dress. These were paid for by the men from their pay. It was not permitted for the men to wear a mix of linen or *tricot* breeches, instead the entire regiment had to wear all *tricot* or all linen garments.[17] Soldiers were to be issued a new pair of knee breeches every year, with the old pair being kept for everyday use, and the new pair for parades. The old pair, prior to the Revolution, was allowed to be blackened for winter undress. This fashion may have been abandoned by 1799.[18]

Grande-Equipment

As well as his clothing, a soldier would be issued leather equipment. This would comprise an ammunition box (*giberne*) carried out of a shoulder belt (*porte-giberne*) to which the *bayonet* (sharp edged weapon mounted at the end of a rifle) could be affixed. Grenadiers, corporals and *sous-officiers* wore a *sabre briquet* from a shoulder belt (*baudrier*). The soldiers clothing, rations and personal property was carried in their *havresac*. Rations were carried in a sack (*sac à toile*) and every man would be issued a canteen (*petit-bidon*) – each company had a *grand-bidon* (a larger canteen), but not each man. *Sous-officiers* were allowed a different pattern *giberne* under the regulations of 1786:

> The *giberne* of *Fourriers* & Sergeants will be the same as above, except that it will be smaller & lighter; the box of the *giberne* must be only seven *pouces* long by two *pouces* six *lignes* high & two *pouces* three *lignes* thick; said box in addition will not be pierced with cartridge holes: they will be placed in two square-shaped openings which will use the entire length of the box, except for a separation of three *lignes* which will be left between them.

The *giberne* was to be stripped of all its polish using pumice stone annually. The surface of the *giberne* was to be made 'perfectly smooth' using the 'back of a brush' and polished together with the brass ornaments until 'quite brilliant'. After being inspected by the file leader they were to be lacquered (2 thin coats to prevent it cracking) ensuring that they were free from 'any particle of dust'. The regulations of 1792 tell us how it was to be cleaned:[19]

A soldier of the *Régiment de Picardie* – presumably, a grenadier – wearing full dress according to the regulations of 1786.

A fusilier of the *Régiment de Piedmont*, the future *3ᵉ de Ligne*, wearing full dress according to the regulations of 1786.

It is necessary to melt, in a vase of any material, provided that it is clean, a pound of wax (yellow or white); then put in another smaller vase, an ounce and a half of German black, on which we will pour hot wax, stirring continuously with a wooden spatula, until it is reduced to a well-diluted paste, the remaining wax remains in the larger vase; put everything on the fire, always stirring it, until the composition is boiling; it is then removed from the fire; and we pass it immediately through a sieve, or through a cloth, to pour it into the moulds we have prepared. If you cannot find a German black, which is usually made with wine lees, you could substitute ash from the vine leaves, but not ivory or smoke black; these two qualities of black are not good for this composition. The amount of black should always be proportionate to that of the wax[.] [W]ith [a] solid pumice stone, remove the hardened black layer, which would prevent the wax from entering the leather; the new wax would soon flake without this precaution. It is then necessary to wax the *giberne*, and to make the wax flame, so that it penetrates into the leather. We take the *giberne* from the fire and put on more wax, and flame the wax for a second time, so that the wax also penetrates, because the leather has to soak up the wax, so that when we wax the *giberne* from time to time, it prevents the wax from flaking off. Then it is necessary to polish the *giberne*, and to put black wax everywhere. If there are some defects in the leather, if there are small holes, then one takes some wax, and press it firmly into the holes to close them, and one continues to polish, until the *giberne* is perfectly smooth; then polish, either with a cork, which does not scratch, or with what is most suitable; and when it is hot, you wipe it only an instant later to bring out the gleam; because by wiping it off when the wax has just been heated, it loses its shine. A piece of old fine cotton handkerchief, or fine broadcloth, which is formed as a plain tampon, is suitable for this use. After the *giberne* is wiped, and there remains no stain, [use] the fingertips or the palm of the hand, which must be totally dry, [to] rub it lightly, to give it a very beautiful lustre. As for the parts that are greasy and where the wax can no longer be shiny, you have to rake the dirt with a knife, after having heated it in the fire, wax them, make them flame like the other parts, and finish them the same. You should never be afraid of flaming a *giberne*; on the contrary, the wax which penetrates the leather nourishes it and gives it body. If a *giberne* has become deformed, [you can fix it.] [I]t is when the leather is hot in this way, that one can, after giving gentle blows, [you are able] to hold it one moment with the hands of the side that we want to make it go [into place]; being cooled, it will remain there. In summer, a *giberne* worked in the shade succeeds better than in the sun, because the less heated wax acquires more shine.

One major innovation of 1786 was the change from a waistbelt to a shoulder belt to carry *sabres* for grenadiers, *sous-officiers*, drummers and musicians. The shoulder belt was called a *baudrier*.[20] The design remained unchanged until cross belts were abolished in the army. Under the *Arête* of *AnVIII* (1799 to 1800), it was 65mm wide and varied from 1m 40 to 1m 60 long. The change over to this new item of equipment took time. The regulation-

16   The Armies of the French Revolution

service period for a waistbelt (*ceinturon*) was 20 years. No colonel would 'chuck away' serviceable equipment. It is exceptionally likely that any *baudriers* were in use until losses on active service warranted the re-supply of items to the latest regulations.

Petit-Equipment

In addition, the solider was to be issued items for personal use. The regulations of 1786 state:[21]

> EACH *Sous-officiers* & Soldier will have three good shirts; two white basin neck stocks; two pairs of *culottes* [underpants]; two pairs of shoes, including a new pair; a pair of white canvas gaiters [protective covering for the upper foot and lower leg, usually of cloth, with a strap passing under the shoe and numerous small buttons to close it along the outside of the leg]; a pair of blackened canvas gaiters; a pair of gaiters of black woollen twill fabric, lined with canvas; two pairs of white canvas gaiter cuffs with black buttons; two handkerchiefs; two pairs of stockings; a black stock and buckle; a pair of shoe buckles; two pairs of garter buckles, one for the *culottes* & one pair for the gaiters; a powder bag & a powder puff; a lice comb; a cleaning comb; a brush for the coat & hat; two shoe brushes; a small brush to clean the copper; a brush to bleach the *buffleterie* [cross belts]; an awl some thread; needles; a button puller; a tamper; an *epinglette* [vent prick]; a screwdriver; pieces of old broadcloth to rub the stains of his coat; & old linen to clean his gun.[22]

Havresacs

The soldier carried all his worldly goods in his *havresac*. The 1786 decree stated:

> The knapsack will be made of calf skin, lined with a strong canvas; it will be one *pied*-[foot][23] deep, four *pouces* thick & eighteen *pouces* wide, forming a square-long; the top of the knapsack will be made so as to cover the opening well, to guarantee that the effects it will contain from the rain; he will sew, inside, a piece of canvas the length and height of the knapsack, to form a separation in the middle; & he will sew up yet another piece of canvas, from the partition to the front of the knapsack, to place the shoes, the powder bag & the tin case; the other party will turn to put the bread. This knapsack must contain, in addition to the bread for four days, the effects of the small equipment that the Soldier will have to wear in the marches, regardless of what he will have on him then; it will be closed with three small straps & their buckles, & worn with buff leather strap.
>
> Each Soldier will also have a canvas bag for distributions, in which he can wrap himself for sleeping.[24]

Clearly, the *havresac* came without the partitions, which were to be added by the solider. Was this ever acted on to a universal degree? The text certainly gave a degree of latitude

Clothing the Soldier 17

A fusilier of the *Régiment de Provence*, wearing full dress according to the regulations of 1786.

A grenadier of the *Régiment de Navarre* wearing full dress according to the regulations of 1786.

in how the compartments and dividers were to be made. The manual for the infantry (*infanterie*) of 1807 stated the following:[25]

> 47. Form of the backpack
> The backpack is divided into four compartments: that of the front and back (depth) are separated by a piece of raw linen cloth. The third compartment is situated to the side of the pack, and is designed to take the soiled linen, and finally the closing flap contains a pocket which forms the fourth compartment.
>
> 48. Employment of the compartments
> That of the rear (depth) is designed to take the principal effects; the two shirts which are assumed to have been rolled up as tightly as possible and placed one beside the other at the bottom of the compartment. They are placed in the bottom because they are not required every day and it is better to place the objects required daily above them; the shirts do not take up all the length of the sack, one places at the free side the socks rolled together with the comb, the stock, and the spare gaiters. Over the gaiters, are placed the trousers turned inside-out carefully folded along the length of the sack. Placed within the trousers are the *martinet* [a wooden wedge-shaped spatula for polishing the *giberne*], and the button stick, making sure that they do not dirty the trousers or injure the body of the soldier.
>   The black gaiters, turned inside-out and folded are placed over the trousers, one beside the other.
>   The 'bundle' [*trousse*] is placed in one of the corners of the sack.
>   The front compartment is designed to take the bread, salt, cooked meat etc.
>   The interior sack encloses the soiled linen.
>   The lining pocket of the lid contains the shoes; – the leather polisher [*polissoir*] wrapped in paper; – scraper [*curettes*]; – a small bag of wire-wool or emery; – the shoe-brush, wrapped in paper or a piece of cloth; – the box of grease; – the wax for the cartridge box; – a small bag enclosing the 'Spanish white', the pipe-clay, the rottenstone [*tripoli*]; – a sponge or piece of cloth.

Other cleaning kits and tools would comprise a *trousse garnie* (a tool kit, with various tools for various chores – in essence a sewing kit for mending the uniform), a *vergette* (clothes beater) an *alène* (an awl to pierce leather, for leather repairs), a *martinet*, the *astique* (rust scraper) for cleaning brass and a *polissoir* (polishing brush).

For personal hygiene, the soldier would have some soap, and a linen towel, a comb (*peigne*), and he would be shaved by the company barber twice a week.[26]

Sacs à Toile

We mentioned this item earlier. This was a multipurpose item: it was both the bag in which the soldier carried his bread ration and also served as a sleeping bag. It was made from a coarse heavy-weight canvas. It had several purposes, the main one was to carry any kind of distribution from the place of delivery to your tent, or room in the barracks, and you could carry not only your distribution but other ones of your mess as well, to speed handing out. On campaign it was carried in the *havresac*. This is confirmed in the regulations of 1791, which also confirmed it could be slept in. In 1801, it was regulated to be made from a double thickness of canvas and measure 157cm long by 76cm wide.[27]

Gaiters

Gaiters had been adopted in the French army by 1714. Under the regulations of 1779, soldiers wore white linen gaiters with white cloth covered buttons for parades; black linen gaiters with bone buttons for summer, ordinary and campaign dress, and in the winter black twill gaiters.[28] In 1786, in normal full dress, and on campaign for the line and light infantry long black wool gaiters closed with 20 to 24 small black leather buttons were worn, and white gaiters as before.[29] From 15 January 1792, the black linen gaiters were discontinued.

The regulations of 1799 stated that gaiters were to be cut in proportion to the height of the man, having between 20 and 24 black leather buttons. The buttonholes were to be 12mm deep, sewn from linen. The button stand was reinforced with a strip of heavy-grade linen 34mm wide, the raw edge turned under, and ran the full height of the gaiter. The top and bottom edges of the gaiter were reinforced with linen: a strip of linen 30mm wide once the raw edge had been turned under and sewn down, was at the top edge of the gaiter and around the foot. The foot strap was made from blackened leather. The total cost of the black gaiters was set at 2 francs 50 centimes.

Shoes

The issued infantry shoe had no difference between a left and a right foot. Soldiers were supposed to alternate shoes between left and right, this would avoid excessive wear. They would fasten with either a metal buckle or leather thongs. The leather soles had hobnails knocked in around the periphery. A soldier was issued 2 pairs of shoes a year.[30] Regulations stated the following:

> After the March, but before the Soup … [each file leader was to] Inspect the shoes, gaiters, socks and feet of each *Soldat*. He was to ensure that the Shoes had their nails; the soles were in good repair; the gaiters had their buttons and were well-fitted; the *Soldat* was wearing socks and they were in good repair. The Shoes were to be 'well waxed' before commencing the march [i.e. so they stayed properly waterproofed].[31]

Where possible, the men were to wash and dry their feet every day. How reality reflected practice is impossible to tell. Most soldiers by 1794 were lucky to have shoes let alone socks.

A grenadier of the *Régiment d'Armagnac* wearing full dress according to the regulations of 1786.

A grenadier of the *Régiment de Champagne* wearing full dress according to the regulations of 1786.

Officers

The regulations of 1786 also dealt with the appearance of the officers:

> Regimentals of Officers will be perfectly conformed to that of the Soldiers of their regiment, & will be differ only by the quality of the clothes which will be from Elbeuf[32] or manufacturers of identical type, as well as by the buttons which will be gilded or silvered.
>
> They will not wear, under any pretext, lining of silk to any part of their Regimentals that this may be, nor lace or buttonholes of gold or silver thread, than those which will be established for the uniform: every type of seen backing, strip piping of colour & distinctions whatsoever, other than those determined for the Regimentals of Soldiers, are & will remain prohibited.
>
> The hooks of the coat collar & the two first of the breast will be always fastened; the frill of the shirt will never be apparent.
>
> The cuffs [of the shirt] will be of muslin or Cambric,[33] of eighteen to twenty *lignes* high, edged by a flat hem, without embroidery or festoon; the practise of lace cuffs continues to be absolutely prohibited.
>
> The stock will be of white dimity;[34] of twenty to twenty-four *lignes* wide; & will be worn in the manner that it covers entirely the collar of the shirt.
>
> The Officers will be able to wear in summer *vestes* [waistcoats] & breeches of white dimity; but they will be uniform in each regiment, both for the quality as for the cut which will be similar to that of the broadcloth *vestes*; waistcoats without *basques* are prohibited.
>
> They will wear from the 1st October to the 1st April breeches of black wool fabric in *Calemande*,[35] *Prunelle*[36] or other of identical type, as well as stockings of black silk or wool; & it is expressively ordered to Commanders of regiments to take a hand that all Officers may be turned out uniformly in this respect, except when they will be on guard or parade drill[37] & consequently in the instance of wearing the breeches & white gaiters.
>
> They will have shoe buckles of silver, similar to the model which will be sent to each regiment … Officers, during peacetime, will have double-breasted uniform *redingotes* [double-breasted overcoat] … Only at times of war, will the Officers of Infantry be able to wear broadcloth cloaks of the colour as that for the coat, without any other distinctive colour, the cape of these cloaks will be bordered by a gold or silver tape one *pouce* wide, according to whether the button of the uniform shall be gilded or silvered.
>
> Officers' hair will be tied at the rear in [a] *Cadogan*,[38] which will be covered by a blackened leather; those on the face will be arranged properly & simply forming a simple curl on each side.[39]

Officers were armed with a musket, *bayonet* and carried a *giberne*. They also had an *épée* (duelling sword) as a side arm.

Orders of Dress

The regulations of 1786 gave the officers, *sous-officiers* and soldiers this guidance on appearance:

> UNIFORMITY in the arrangement of items of clothing and equipment for the Soldier, must be combined with great cleanliness; the officers and low officers will take care carefully that both of them are observed with exactitude, and that all the parts of the said clothing and equipment are maintained in the best condition; they will make responsible for the execution of all that will do hereafter prescribed on this subject, and will conform to it with the most scrupulous precision, in what can concern them personally.
>
> Only Grenadiers can wear moustaches; and they are forbidden to wax them and to put no drugs or greasy matter in them, the use being unclean.
>
> The hair will be tied in a *Cadogan*, covered with blackened leather, the use of which is known; they hair will be cut short on the head; the side beards will be brushed '*avant garde*'.
>
> The hair will be powdered on parade days & Sundays and Holidays: it is expressly forbidden to use powder and ointment to enlarge the *Cadogan*, which can only be the volume of the hair in its natural state.
>
> The hat will go down on the right eyebrow, the central horn placed above the left eyebrow, which will be exposed to the thickness of half an inch; it will be well brushed, cleaned, and always kept in the same repair, without any kind of change being made.
>
> The stock will be tight without being over tight; it will keep up as much as possible, will cover entirely the collar of the shirt.
>
> The Troops will only use soap, and as little as possible, to maintain the cleanliness of the clothing, without detracting from its solidity: the use of any other material recognized as caustic & corrosive remains prohibited.
>
> All parts of the clothing will be well beaten & brushed; all the stains will be removed, either with soap, or with stone to be detached, used with very clean water which will be left to dry naturally on the stain, and which will then be removed by lightly rubbing the fabric against itself; the buttons & loops will be perfectly lightened with diluted Spanish white, which will form a liquid paste with which we will brush the objects that need to be cleaned; & so that this interview does not spoil the clothes & the blouses, the buttons will be encased in a piece of wood made expressly, the shape of which is known in most regiments, & by means of which, the fabric being covered, the buttons can be rubbed without inconvenience.
>
> It is forbidden to wash clothes completely in any circumstances whatsoever; this method being very harmful to the preservation of fabrics.
>
> The collar of the *habit* will always be fastened, as well as the two hooks at the top of the *revers*; the sleeves of the coat will be drawn low enough so that the wrist, the shirt cannot be seen; the *retroussis* [rolled up] will be hooked back.

Clothing the Soldier 23

A gunner of the *Corps Royal d'Artillerie* wearing full dress respecting the regulations of 1786. The uniform barely changed between 1786 and 1812.

A gunner of the Coast Guard Artillery. His facings are described as sea green in the regulations of 1786.

> The jacket [*veste*] will be buttoned in its entire length, & well pulled at the bottom, so that it perfectly fits the hips.
>
> The *culottes* will be pulled up as far as possible, the belt of which will be secured above the hip by means of a copper buckle. The *culottes* will be closed at the knee by the knee buckles.
>
> The gaiters will be button up strait, ensuring that they are well pulled up and tight fitting, so that they are well fitted and uniform.
>
> The weapons will be clean without being polished; the rifle strap will be plated & hooked against the weapon, the half-loop at the height of the nasturtium; the screws & nuts will be kept in good condition; stones well placed & contained between two sinkers; they will drive out the battery well, & the corners will make them broken so as not to spoil the cannon or injure the Soldier.
>
> All the buff work will be perfectly whitened; the *giberne* will also be well waxed, even on the sides, & a boxwood polisher will be used to rub the wax well in; but this polish will be renewed as little as possible, so that the leather is not dried out.
>
> The arrangement of the different parts of the clothing in the rooms, contributing greatly to their preservation, and giving officers and *sous-officiers* the opportunity to view them with ease, we will observe the greatest order in this regard.
>
> The clothes will be arranged on shelves, the lining outside; the hat will be on the same shelf & covered. The name of each Soldier will be written on what belongs to him.
>
> All knapsacks, filled with the possession of each soldier, will be placed above their bed, as well as the *giberne* & the belt; all hung on hooks placed at the same height.
>
> The musket will be placed in its rack, the lock covered and hammer forward; each will have a card attached with the name of the soldier to which the musket belongs.[40]

Even on the march soldiers were expected to wash and shave, and clean their weapons, uniform and equipment.

Chapter 2
1791 and All That

Despite the regulations of 1786 being signed off on 1 October 1786, we find,

> Decision of the council of war, 24 November 1788
> ALL Regiments of the Army, both Infantry as well as Cavalry, Dragoons [*dragons*] & Horse *Chasseurs* (with the exception of the formation of the *Artois* Division, which will receive individual orders), will proceed with the manufacture of their regimental clothes, according to the costume prescribed by the Regulation of the 1st October 1786.[1]

How far this was acted upon is impossible to say, as barely 6 months later, on 14 July 1789, France was shattered by revolution. The small professional King's Army still basking in the success from America, which numbered only about 130,000 in 1792 would swell to a force of 600,000 by 1794 – a number that far surpassed the enemy armies arrayed against France combined – the men had to be trained, fed, clothed and equipped; officers needed appointing, and *sous-officiers* required training. By the time the French Revolutionary government declared war on Austria on 20 April 1792, most of Louis XVI's officers had fled France, leaving the army listless and barely in a cohesive state. This was an army of volunteers arrayed alongside a hard core of *sous-officiers* and men of the King's Army, the seasoned professionals that had fought in America.

Making a Republican Army

On 1 January 1791, regimental titles were abolished, and the line (*ligne*) infantry was reorganised into 104 line regiments and 12 *chasseur* battalions, which were ostensibly light infantry. Each battalion was composed of 8 companies of fusiliers and 1 of grenadiers; each comprised 1 captain, 1 lieutenant, 1 *sous-lieutenant*, 1 sergeant major, 2 sergeants, 1 *fourrier*, 4 corporals, 4 chosen men, 1 drummer and 40 grenadiers or fusiliers. A few months later, on 22 July 1791, the formation of 185 battalions of *Gardes Nationaux voluntaries* was ordered. This new army of volunteers could not be mistaken for Louis XVI's army.

During 1791 and 1792, the Revolutionary government undertook drastic steps to reform the army and, perhaps more importantly, to win its loyalty. A 'quick win' was to re-introduce promotion based on ability and end the test of nobility to become officers. Units were allowed to elect a percentage of officers; the rest being appointed by the government. It is undeniable that promotion within the army was slow: some officers had been in

An officer of the newly created *14ᵉ de Ligne circa* 1791. (*Musee de l'Armée*)

post for over 20 years. With no major conflict to thin the ranks, regimental command and control became ossified. The emigration of thousands of officers and the death of many more meant that the government needed to react to this situation. Promoting *sous-officiers* and men to officer status was a 'quick win'. However, the election of officers

A fusilier of the former *Régiment du Colonel-General* respecting the regulations of 1791.

A fusilier of the former *Régiment de Lyonnais* respecting the regulations of 1791. (*Collection KM*)

became nothing short of a popularity contest: officers and senior *sous-officiers* had to be competent to carry out their duties rather than popular. Promoting men to command companies or higher positions meant that regimental organisation and administration very quickly broke down through ignorance. The government compounded this by failing to invest in educational establishments to train officers and men – Napoléon on coming to power fixed this issue through investing in the *École Militaire* (military school) and other training institutions. He also removed the election of officers. It is unfair to say that before 1792 officers were not promoted from the ranks: it did happen. Of the units we have looked at in this study, at least one man from the ranks was promoted to officer status. The army of Louis XVI, despite many officers being in their fifties or sixties with the rank of lieutenant, was not a moribund and corrupt organisation: in many ways the training and tactics – operational ability – was superior to what came after it and would not be achieved for over a decade. The decline in operational ability was, as we said, due to a lack of competent officers and men: they learned their trade on the battlefield. The veterans of America were either dead or fled: France had to almost 'start from scratch' in building its armed forces. That France actually won some campaigns speaks more of the ardour and enthusiasm of the men, than any tactical and training transformation. It also speaks of the lack of flexibility of competing nations armed forces. Without Louis XVI's regulars, the Republic would have fallen at the battles of Valmy and Jemappes.

Despite dressing the volunteers in the new national colours of blue, white and red, the old regular regiments of Louis XVI's army kept their integrity despite experiencing a desertion crisis, which witnessed 60 per cent losses of manpower in 18 months, and clung tenaciously to their white uniforms of the regulations of 1786. The new volunteers and conscripts formed their own units after hastily being handed muskets and uniforms, when either was available. The volunteers were to wear republican blue, which only emphasised and exacerbated the differences between the new and old soldiers.

Other changes in the in the period from 1791 to 1792 included corporal punishment being replaced with blows from an old shoe. As 1793 dawned, in terms of demographics, Louis XVI's army

A fusilier of the former *Régiment Royal des Vaisseaux* respecting the regulations of 1791.

had changed in many drastic ways, but its organisation had not changed, it had no need to. The biggest and most important change came with the new regulations of 1791.

At the heart of this development were the ideas of Colonel Claude de Guibert, who in Lazare Carnot had found a champion. The regulations of 1791 advocated his doctrine of simplicity, flexibility and manoeuvre, as well as many of his technical tactical recommendations. De Guibert's warfare was light, flexible and swift, enabling the French to strike with overwhelming force before the enemy could react. His ideas provided a reformed tactical manual, operational principles, strategic maxims and an organisational substructure. The lack of logistical support, however, and calling for the men 'to live off the land', meant that in due time this support network had to be created. De Guibert called for a citizen army led by a dynamic man of personality and passion. He called for well-trained officers, which France was sorely missing, as well as *sous-officiers* – the bed rock of a company – who were proficient, in theory, and had practice of the regulations. To do so de Guibert stressed that regiments should spend 3 months out of every 12 at a training camp. He called for the professionalisation of the army – with officers taught mathematics, well-schooled in the theory of battle and the drill regulations as well as administration. Given the chaos that engulfed the French state from 1793, de Guibert's lofty aspirations, by and large, were not enacted until the Consulate was created. It is, however, undeniable that de Guibert's tactical organisation allowed a flexibility of operational method, which was evident in many contemporary armies. Thanks to the new regulations, the French army was able to deploy from column to line on the battlefield, using the simplified evolutions that de Guibert provided and stressed the offensive. The regulations of 1791 laid the ground work for the *Grande Armée*.

The soldiers for the Republic were to be more than an 'instrument of war': they were to be revolutionaries, propagandist advocates of the new Republic and model citizens. In a war of ideas between monarchy and representative democracy, soldiers were a political instrument bestowing the virtue of the Republic and republican idealism:

> The Republican Soldiers cannot be compared with those of the despots, the first act only by honour and as members of the social body, the others on the contrary obey servile to the whims of a man whose passions are usually who animate it, make it a monster in the eyes of Philosophy as well as in Society.
>
> The French Soldier, since the Revolution, has not had the time to take a close look at his condition: tired of the arduous work of the war and even more of the little intrigues of some great scoundrels who had not destroyed the tyranny only to become tyrants themselves. He could not see the dignity of his profession as a soldier. Citizen, he has not yet been able to taste the ineffable goods of the Revolution, but the time has arrived, when he can, penetrated by his obligations to the Fatherland, say to himself, by satisfying it: I am happy by exposing myself for it, since I find in reward the truth, the solid honour and the friendship of my fellow citizens that I will have defended by defending my Freedom, my property and my life.
>
> Let us establish here, as succinctly as possible, the qualities that it is essential to have to be a Soldier, and while each one will have recognized the truth of the

Principles that I lay down, that he will be well penetrated by it and that he will put them into practical. We could say to have an army made up of men made to impose on the universe by their virtues and by their value which is always inseparable.

The soldiers' obligations are no more painful than those of the Citizen; like him, he is only subject to obedience to the laws, and in the military state, as in the particular state, any person who is against the law, is a dangerous being against whom it must prevail.

The Man who is destined for the military state must therefore have obedience, more than value. He must never be reckless, because then he could compromise the lives of his comrades and the public interest. A reckless man is always dangerous, Courage and Valour are warlike virtues, just as recklessness is a vice which usually takes its source in drunkenness or vanity. Besides, the soldier accustomed to obey[ing] only his chiefs, will be able to master his passions and be only a courageous man.

So, we say that a Soldier must be obedient: no doubt yes! But it is to the laws and not as formerly to the whims of men. Nothing is so natural as obedience to the laws, first, because they are an emanation of our will, and that by obeying them, we only confirm orders made by us. Finally, it is because the laws were made for the happiness of all, and that to disobey them is to declare oneself the enemy of public happiness.[2]

Recruiting men into the armed forces was just one part of a much bigger picture. A man without a musket was not a soldier. A man with a firearm was not a soldier until he had been trained. Clearly, he could not go to war in his own clothes, so he needed a uniform and equipment. In the King's Army this was all done 'in house' in the regiment's depot (*dépôt*), but for the ever-increasing army of volunteers new means and methods were needed as we shall see. This *ad hoc* method of clothing the men created the '*sans-culottes*' of popular print and imagination.

Bonnets de Police of the revolutionary epoch. (*Musée de l'Empéri, Collections du Musée de l'armée, Anciennes collections Jean et Raoul Brunon*)

Clothing and Equipment Reforms

In an attempt to bring a new sense of nationalism to the French army, in April 1791, new regulations came into force, for what was still a royal army. This brought in new items of clothing, regimental titles were swiped away by numbers; everyone was to adopt white and new facing colours were allocated:

1791 and All That

Regimental Number							Buttons	Pockets	Revers	Cuffs	Collar and Cuff Flaps
1	13	25	37	49	67	82	Yellow	Horizontal	C	C	C
2	14	26	38	50	68	83	Yellow	Horizontal	C	C	
3	15	27	39	51	70	84	Yellow	Horizontal	C		C
4	16	28	40	52	71	90	White	Horizontal	C	C	C
5	17	29	41	54	72	91	White	Horizontal	C	C	
6	18	30	42	55	73	93	White	Horizontal	C		C
7	19	31	43	56	74	102	Yellow	Vertical	C	C	C
8	20	32	44	57	75		Yellow	Vertical	C	C	
9	21	33	45	58	78		Yellow	Vertical	C		C
10	22	34	46	59	79		White	Vertical	C	C	C
11	23	35	47	60	80		White	Vertical	C	C	
12	24	36	48	61	81		White	Vertical	C		C
Black	Violet	Rose	Bleu Celeste	Crimson	Scarlet	Dark Blue					

* C means colour.

Despite being practical, the *pokalem* was replaced by the more stylish dragoon-style *bonnet de police*. It comprised a triangular *flamme* (wing), which was often laced in the regiment's facing colour and tassel. The headband was decorated at the top edge with a strip of cloth 14mm wide. At the front, on the cloth plaque appeared the regiment's

An infantry helmet according to the regulations of 1791. (*Musée de l'Empéri, Collections du Musée de l'armée, Anciennes collections Jean et Raoul Brunon*)

number or a cut-out cloth device of a grenade or *fleur-de-lys*. This design was an *amalgame* (amalgamation) of the *pokalem* and dragoon style, as the turban could still fold down.[3]

Simultaneously, the *chapeau* was withdrawn from fusiliers in favour of a *casque* (helmet). The regulations stated that the helmet was made from leather or felt and made to the model delivered to the regiment by the Ministry of War (*Ministère de la guerre*) for contractors to copy.[4]

From examination of original items, these *casques* had a blocked felt skull, with a leather or cardboard peak and a bearskin *chenille* (horsehair crest in the form of a caterpillar). The skull was reinforced with a tangential copper strap that passed over the crown. Removed from use officially in 1799, the *casque* was technically only worn by the regulars, the volunteers under the decree of 21 February 1793 wore *chapeaux* with the formation of the *demi-brigades*. The *chapeau* was the same dimensions as before.

The decree allowed a white plume tipped with feathers of the regimental colour to be worn in the helmet on parades.[5] A woollen pompom (a decorative tuft of wool, usually smaller than a plume, affixed to the front or side of a headdress) 3 *pouces* tall and 2 *pouces* in diameter (0m 76 by 0m 50) and was worn on the left side of the *casque*. A cockade 3.5 *pouces* diameter (0m 80) was worn in the *chapeau* for the infantry, as well as for *dragons* and *cavalerie*. The cockade used on the *casque* was 2 *pouces* (0m 50) in diameter.[6]

To mark out status of grenadiers, under the regulations of 1786, grenadiers were issued with red broadcloth shoulder straps piped white – the same shape and form as the straps for fusiliers. Red fringed *epaulettes* were authorised. Fusiliers continued to wear simple shoulder straps through to the end of the *1ᵉ Empire*.

More changes followed on 15 January 1792, reflecting the increased number of regiments with the disbandment of foreign regiments:

Regimental Number					Buttons	Pockets	Revers	Collar and Cuff Flaps	Cuffs
49	61	79	93	108			C	C	C
50	62	80	94	109	Yellow		C	C	
51	67	81	96	110		Horizontal	C		C
52	68	82	98	111			C	C	C
53	70	83	99		White		C	C	
54	71	84	101				C		C
55	72	87	102				C	C	C
56	73	88	103		Yellow		C	C	
57	74	89	104			Vertical	C		C
58	75	90	105				C	C	C
59	77	91	106		White		C	C	
60	78	92	107				C		C
Crimson	Scarlet	Dark Blue	Dark Green	Light Green					

* C means colour.

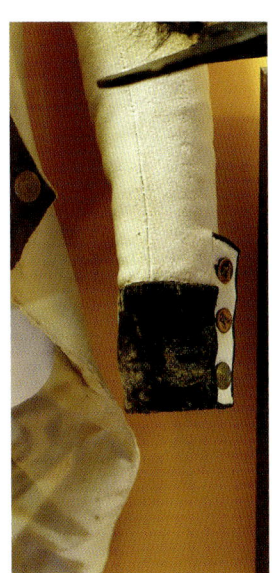

An officers' *habit* of the *8ᵉ de Ligne* respecting the regulations of 1791. (*Musée de l'Empéri, Collections du Musée de l'armée Anciennes collections Jean et Raoul Brunon*)

The facings of the *1ᵉ* to *48ᵉ de Ligne* were left unchanged. The *102ᵉ*, *103ᵉ* and *104ᵉ* were formed from the suppression of the Parisian National Guard, and now adopted white *habits*. The regulations of 1792 abolished the black linen gaiters: for route marches the soldiers now wore gaiters made from natural linen closed with horn buttons. Based on practical experience of campaign life, officers were allowed to adopt *manteaux-trois-*

quatre (cloaks with shoulder cape) made from dark sky blue broadcloth. The collar was to be in the regiment's distinctive colour, and the cape was allowed to be edged in gold or silver lace depending on the button colour of the regiment. For senior officers, the lace was 41mm wide, and for company officers 27mm. It was lined in dark sky blue *shalloon* (superfine *serge*). Officers were allowed to retain the *chapeau* rather than wear a *casque*. The decree also reminded unit commandants that grenadiers were to wear red and only red plumes in the bearskin. Commanding officers were also reminded to ensure that officers in their regiment wore *epaulettes* and *épées* all of the same model, to ensure uniformity rather than individuality.[7]

To try and bring some degree of uniformity to what was worn by officers, on 24 June 1792, a further memorandum was issued. It stated officers were to wear their hair in queue, covered in a black silk ribbon, fastened with a pin rather than tied with a bow. Officers were reminded that bearskins and *casques* were not worn on active service. Furthermore, officers were to habitually wear a white stock, unless on the march or campaign when a black stock was to be worn. The stock was to be made from silk and was to be worn to totally conceal the shirt collar, the wings of which were forbidden from protruding above the stock. When not on duty, officers were to wear buckled shoes, and on duty *bottes à la anglais* (jockey style). The regulation *épée* was to be worn from a whitened leather *baudrier*, which was to be lacquered. Only senior officers were allowed to use a waistbelt. Off duty, company officers were tolerated to use a waistbelt with gilded plate, the *sabre* knot was to be tricolour rather than silver or gold to match the buttons. In summer, *vestes* and *culottes* in nankeen were tolerated, and black silk in winter.

On 25 August 1792, drummers were ordered to remove the King's Livery from their uniforms – so too were all the cavalry trumpeters. On 21 September 1792, with the declaration of the Republic, all buttons would carry the fascines in the centre with the legend *Republique Francaise* (French Republic) around the edge.[8]

Regulations in Practice

As France was beset by civil war while fighting an initially defensive war, the ability of the state to supply cloth and other materials became deeply compromised. Due to shortages of buff leather, blackened cowhide was used to make cross belts and other items. An order given to the Army of the Rhine (*l'Armée du Rhin*), dated 18 April 1793, stated that blackened cowhide was to be used due to the scarcity of buff. General Balthazar Schauenbourg noted in an inspection of the *31ᵉ Demi-Brigade*, in Strasbourg, on *15 Pluviôse AnV* (3 February 1797), that all the musket slings, *giberne* belts and *baudriers* were made from blackened cowhide. The practice was, in theory, abolished on *11 Thermidor AnVII* (29 July 1799), yet Schauenbourg in a report on *30 Pluviôse AnX* (19 February 1802) of the *110ᵉ Demi-Brigade* stated that the majority of *giberne* belts and *baudriers* were made from blackened leather, of which a part had been bleached. Indeed, as late as *3 Nivôse AnXIV* (24 December 1805), General François-Étienne-Christophe

A grenadiers' bearskin of the National Guard of Orléans, 1789–1791. They are respecting the regulations of 1786. Those worn by the line were ostensibly identical bar the front plate. The scarlet plume is missing. (*Collection and photographs of Bertrand Malvaux*)

The National Guard of Paris, 1789–1792. (*Musée Carnavalet*)

An officer of the National Guard, 1789–1792. (*Musée Carnavalet*)

de Kellermann informed the minister for war, General Henri Clarke, that he found in the stores at Strasbourg a great quantity of *giberne* belts and *baudriers*, as well as musket slings made from blackened cowhide, which he had to issue to conscripts as they passed through the depot as no buff items existed.[9] It would not be until after the Battle of Jena that all the blackened cowhide equipment was removed from service.

Volunteers of 1791

The levy (*levée*) of national volunteers in autumn 1791 brought new stress on an exhausted and bankrupt French fiscal system. The French state had no means to rapidly clothe, arm and equip these men. These men, the French state decreed, were to arrange for the production of their own uniforms and equipment. In September 1791, the minister for war, Louis Lebègue Duportail, wrote to each department (*département*) in France, placing the emphasis on clothing and equipping these men who had no means to fund their own uniforms as problems for the department to solve and not the state: 'the departmental directors will provide without delay the equipment for those recruited to the volunteer national guards who do not have the means to provide it themselves'. Each volunteer had to provide themselves with 1 blue *habit*, 1 white *veste* (under jacket), 2 pairs of white *culottes*, a *bonnet de police*, 3 shirts, 2 white stocks, 1 black stock, 2 pairs of shoes, 1 pair of white linen gaiters, 1 pair of grey linen gaiters, 1 pair of black worsted gaiters, 2 handkerchiefs, 2 pairs of stockings, 1 *havresac* and 1 canvas bag (*sac à distribution*).[10]

In order to facilitate the production of clothing, Duportail issued to the departments detailed instructions concerning each item of clothing. Each *habit* was to cost, materials included, 28 francs 7.5 centimes. The *habit* was to be national blue with scarlet collar and cuffs, and white *revers* piped scarlet. The under jacket (*veste manche* – waistcoat with sleeves and a low collar. Cut to have a V-notch at the centre front) was to be made from white broadcloth, lined in *serge*, but where broadcloth was not available *tricot* was allowed. The garment was to cost 13 francs 4 centimes. The *culottes* were to be broadcloth, *sous-officiers* were allowed their own pattern *chapeaux* costing 4 francs 10 centimes; grenadiers' cost 3 francs 15 centimes including the plume. The *bonnet de police* had a blue wing (*flamme*) and a scarlet turban. Each man cost 115 francs 1 centime to clothe. A considerable expense.

Because of this cost, and understandably so in a country with an economy in ruins, only in the wealthiest parts of France could the volunteers afford to buy their own uniform. Perhaps reflecting the Girondin (Girondins were a political group during the French Revolution) government under Jacques Pierre Brissot, it was a mobilisation of the middle class and not the working poor: the 'possessing classes' excluded from positions of power through lack of nobility and title were the immediate beneficiaries of the Revolution. The failure of the Girondins during 1793 led to the terror and disintegration of France. We digress. As an example of the difficulties the department administration faced in forming a volunteer battalion is exemplified through the records of Normandy

The National Guard of Parthenay. (*Collection KM*)

A grenadier of the National Guard of Nanterre wearing a blue coat with yellow and red facings. (*Collection KM*)

(*Normandie*). Due to the relative poverty of the area, it was rapidly discovered that the department authorities would have to take a far more major part in clothing their battalions than had been anticipated. A report dated 15 September 1791 reveals that for the two 800-man strong volunteer battalions of the *l'Eure* (district), for immediate needs, 892 *habits*, 937 *vestes*, 944 pairs of *culottes*, 644 *chapeaux* and 457 muskets were required. More than 50 per cent of the men were unable to fund the purchase of their regulation clothing or provide a fire arm.¹¹ Even with the direct intervention of the department administration, this was not a solution to the relative poverty of the men who stood forward. The volunteers who could afford to provide their uniforms, often did so by 'cost cutting' concerning quality of work and materials. The purchase of substandard clothing – men were willing to fight but hesitant at using their own money to do so – meant that by 1 October 1791, rather than a decrease in the numbers of items needed, we see an increase in clothing needs. By the start of October 1791, for immediate use, 898 *habits* were needed, 957 *vestes*, 1,942 pairs of *culottes*, 743 *chapeaux*, 1,148 shirts, 2,750 white and black stocks, 1,599 pairs of shoes, 2,874 pairs of gaiters, 1,269 pairs of stockings, 962 *havresacs* and 966 *sacs à toile*.¹² So severe were shortages of raw materials – broadcloth, *serge* and leather – in the department that they had to be obtained from Paris and Metz. The mayor requested in November 1791 that Paris send ready-made items and materials to clothe the battalions. The mayor himself travelled to Paris to plead his case, returning in December 1791. His mission was successful, as later that month the battalion received 320 shirts, 393 pairs of stockings, 92 *chapeaux* and 386 pairs of shoes, and by March 1792 had taken delivery of 1,500 shirts and 1,000 pairs of stockings, and 2,422 *aunes*¹³ of broadcloth, *serge* and linen to make uniforms. The men clearly wore clogs (*sabots*) as the battalion only possessed 925 pairs of shoes, yet each man received 1 *habit*, 2 pairs of *culottes* and 3 pairs of gaiters.¹⁴

The shortages of shoes, cloth and above all money to pay for items was widespread. The state, by offsetting the direct cost to itself, in making the volunteers pay for the privilege of fighting for France allowed for a rapid expansion of the army, at minimal cost to the state, but it placed a huge and often crippling burden on the budgets of the department. Undeterred, however, the state sought to repeat this 'cheap and cheerful' approach. One can only begin to imagine the low standard and lack of uniformity among the volunteers. The wealthier men would no doubt have had their *habits* sewn at home or by a tailor – thus, each man would have been wearing a *habit* different to the rest: little matter, the country was in danger, what was needed was patriotic fervour and men under arms, it was only a small concern how they were dressed.

In September 1792, a third volunteer battalion in each department was to be formed, again clothed by the men themselves or at the cost of the department, and like the other 2 existing battalions, had to muster 800 men.

After the initial first equipping of the volunteers – a cost traditionally born by the state – all successive items of clothing were costed at the expense of the state. Bit by bit, the volunteers were subsumed into the regular army. Thus, we find in January 1793, the mayor of l'Eure requested to the Ministry of War in Paris to provide the funds for 400 *habits*, 450 pairs of *culottes*, 150 *chapeaux*, 200 shirts, 200 pairs of stockings, 450 pairs of gaiters and 400 pairs of shoes as replacements. Also needed, he reported to make up losses, were 530 *sacs à toile*, 530 *havresacs*, 500 musket slings, 500 musket worms (corkscrew style devices used to remove unspent charges from the barrels of muskets), 500 *gibernes*, 400 *giberne* belts, 20 *sabres* and 190 bayonets. Funds were also needed to repair 100 muskets he noted.¹⁵ Thus, from this data, 50 per cent of the men in the 3 battalions had no *habit* or

A sergeant of the National Guard of Brest. He has officers' *epaulettes* rather than the expected stripes. (*Collection KM*)

The National Guard of Chartres. (*Collection KM*)

veste, 70 per cent no *culottes*, 80 per cent no *chapeau*, 90 per cent no shirt, 70 per cent no gaiters, shoes and equipment – at least of army pattern – and 90 per cent had no musket in good condition! The picture presented here, I am sure, was repeated right across France. We must image an *ad hoc* melange of civilian and army clothing and equipment.

Yet did the regulars fare any better? We now look at the *ligne*.

3ᵉ Régiment d'Infanterie de la Ligne

The *3ᵉ Régiment d'Infanterie de la Ligne* was reviewed on 1 January 1792. The *etat-major* (regimental staff) comprised 15 officers and specialists, such as the master workmen and the 8-man regimental band. The regiment proper comprised 1,392 grenadiers, *chasseurs* and fusiliers, as well as 6 *carabiniers* (marksmen armed with rifles). The men's clothing dated from 1789 to 1791, showing that 2 regulations were in operation side by side. Of the *habits*, 382 were issued in 1789, 297 in 1790 and 836 in 1791, with 400 needing replacement during the course of 1792. All the men's *culottes* and *chapeaux* were issued in 1791, with every single pair of *culottes* being replaced in 1792, the existing pairs to be dyed black for use in the barracks in the winter. The inspector added that 200 sets of *chevrons* were needed. Of the men themselves, 69 men wore 3 service *chevrons* indicating 21 years' service, 79 had served for 14 years, 196 had served for 8 years, 290 between 4 and 8 years, and 773 for under 4 years. In terms of height, 107 were 1m 55 tall, over 700 stood between 1m 60 and 1m 70, and just 20 men stood 1m 90 tall. The grenadiers wore *chapeaux* and, presumably, had *epaulettes*.[16]

11ᵉ Régiment d'Infanterie de la Ligne

Inspected on 9 March 1792 was the *11ᵉ Régiment d'Infanterie de la Ligne*. The regiment mustered 1,114 other ranks. The unit had no band we remark. Every man was issued a *chapeau*, and the inspector ordered all the clothing issued in 1789 was to be replaced in the course of 1792, which included 7 drummers' *habits* laced in the King's Livery, as well as 54 grenadiers' *habits* and 210 fusiliers' *habits*. Every single pair of *culottes* in use were to be replaced, and again were allowed to be dyed black. The inspector ordered 347m blue worsted lace for *chevrons* to be purchased, some 12mm wide, to make 167 pairs of corporals' *chevrons*. The inspector further instructed that 106 bearskins were to be ordered, to supplement the 18 issued in the previous year and more *chapeaux* were to be ordered rather than 'helmets made in felt or varnished leather'. The repair bill to mend the men's clothing was estimated at 5,700 francs, and 55,800 francs to replace life expired clothing: a grand total of 70,400 needed to be spent during 1792 to clothe and equip the regiment.[17]

12ᵉ Régiment d'Infanterie de la Ligne

Reviewed by the *Comte* (Count) de Rochambeau, hero of America, on 26 January 1792 was the *12ᵉ Régiment d'Infanterie de la Ligne*. In his report, he notes that the grenadier company in the first battalion had a mix of headdress: for 62 men, we note 62 *chapeaux* and 32 *bonnets de police*. They carried their *sabres* from a waistbelt. In the second battalion, the grenadiers likewise had *chapeaux* and waistbelts, but were authorised to adopt 8 bearskins. Clothing wise during 1792, 515 *habits* were needed, including 9 for drummers complete with the King's Livery. Every pair of *culottes* was to be replaced,

The National Guard of Dreux. (*Collection KM*)

In scarlet, with white facings and blue tail facings, the National Guard of Anet looks more Swiss or British than French. (*Collection KM*)

1,515 examples, as well as every *chapeau*, and 515 *bonnets de police* were also authorised to be made. We also note 9 medallions for veterans were to be issued during the year. Of the men in the regiment, 1 man was from Santo Domingo, 29 men wore 3 service *chevrons*, 91 men wore 2 *chevrons* and 151 a single *chevron*. There were 577 men who had served for under 4 years, roughly 50 per cent of the regiment. In terms of height, 128 men stood 1m 55 and just 41 men stood over 1m 75. In terms of the men's professions prior to enlistment, we record 25 bakers, 38 carpenters and wagonmakers, 8 surgeons,

A grenadier of the National Guard of Paris. (*Collection KM*)

A volunteer from 1792 depicted by Hoffmann.

54 shoemakers, 398 agricultural labourers, 14 blademakers, 76 masons, 34 farriers, 37 wigmakers or hairdressers, 14 saddlers, 63 tailors, 26 tanners and 264 urban labourers: a very 'mixed bag' of skilled and non-skilled tradesmen. The inspector lamented that many of the men had chest infections at the time of the review, were weak, malnourished and unlikely to support the rigours of war. He added 'a great number of the younger men had simply disappeared', but proudly commented that the old soldiers were 'good, robust, well able to sustain the fatigues of military service'. De Rochambeau, who was made

the minister of war, stated that 'the regiment is well dressed for war. The grenadiers, however, do not precisely accord to the regulations', adding that the equipment 'was of good quality; it has been well tanned'. We note that during the course of 1791, one man was promoted to officer status.[18]

13ᵉ Régiment d'Infanterie de la Ligne

The *13ᵉ Régiment d'Infanterie de la Ligne* was reviewed on 22 December 1791. The regiment mustered 1,140 other ranks, including a 6-strong regimental band, a master tailor, master armourer and master shoemaker. In the last year, 26 men had died, 56 had deserted and 15 had been sent home due to ill health; 76 had 'been chased away' with a further 49 leaving due to old age, and 2 because they were gentlemen and would not serve an army against the church and king. We note that one man was promoted to officer. Clearly, promotion from the ranks did occur before it became official policy. In terms of clothing, we note during the course of 1792, 500 men needed a totally new uniform, which included 12 drummers needing new *habits* with the King's Livery decoration. Also needed were 1,500 pairs of *culottes*, 1,400 *chapeaux* and 150 pairs of blue worsted lace *chevrons*. To be awarded were 15 veteran medallions. The unit had 8 *sapeurs* equipped with axes – with cases and belts – and aprons. We note grenadiers and *bas-officiers* – sergeants, *fourriers* and sergeant majors – were issued 331 *ceinturons* to carry their *sabres*.

A group of national guards and volunteers of Narbonne.

In returning to the men, we note 59 men wore 3 service *chevrons*, 65 wore 2 *chevrons* and 166 a single *chevron*, and 539 had served for under 4 years, or just under 50 per cent of the total strength. We note 109 men stood at 1m 55 and 7 men stood at 1m 80. In terms of the men's trade before enlistment, we report 10 had been bakers, 23 carpenters, 5 surgeons, 48 shoemakers, 493 agricultural labourers, 9 farriers, 22 masons, 34 wood turners, 28 wigmakers or hairdressers, 5 saddlers, 23 knifemakers, 63 tailors, 4 tanners and 373 urban labourers: an almost equal number of urban to rural workingmen, with some skilled artisans volunteering to fight as regular soldiers.[19]

Chapter 3

Levée en Masse and *Demi-Brigades*

The military setbacks of 1792 reflected the growing pains of the new French Republic. As with society at large, the military was moving from its monarchical roots to something decidedly different, which was not an easy task for a nation verging on bankruptcy.

It was the professionals of Louis XVI's royal army who, ironically enough, had saved the Revolution in 1792. Viewed with some degree of scepticism about its loyalty, this was all to be swept away. The Committee of Public Safety, again acting for the military, decided to undertake the *amalgame* in 1793, which aimed to 'integrate the ranks – and make regulars, volunteers, and, later, conscripts brothers in arms' and 'break up units of the royal army, and reduce the threat of a military coup against the Republic', as well as surround the new troops with steady, experienced men. Yet nothing was done immediately.

Proposed on 21 February 1793, the army was to be re-made: regiments were to be disbanded and formed into *demi-brigades*. The decree was not put into practice until *21 Nivôse AnII* (10 January 1794).[1]

The soldiers clothing was partially made at regimental level, but also issued from state stores. A decree of 31 March 1793 allowed the *petit*-equipment – shirts, stocks, *bidons* and other essentials – to be issued from government stocks.[2] To provide uniforms and equipment, 6 workshops to make army clothing were established in Paris: it was patriotic to sew uniforms for the army. Each workshop had a number of tailors who cut out the uniforms to the 3 regulation sizes, these were then 'put out' as piece work to families in Paris who made the uniforms. The completed uniforms were sent back to the workshop, where the work was inspected and, if acceptable for use, 15 days after delivery the family was paid.[3] The same system was employed in the production of shoes and every other item of a soldier's clothing and equipment. France was divided into military districts, headed by a military governor, and each district had to produce a set quota of shoes, *havresacs* and uniforms.[4] Penalties and bonuses existed to encourage speed of production. Items were stockpiled in departmental depots, from which regiments sent a requisition order to clothe their men.[5]

As well as making a truly republican army, the Committee of Public Safety, realised that the army was crippled by desertion and battlefield attrition: to solve this the government resorted to conscription. Before the decree of the *levée en masse* on 23 August 1793, the government had enacted a smaller *levée* in February 1793, to call 300,000 troops into the French army. Each department would supply a particular percentage of the 300,000 through recruiting volunteers. Historian Alan I. Forrest holds that 'the *levée en masse* meant much more than a simple call to patriotism. It included a direct appeal to civic virtue and public responsibility.'[6]

A fabled *sans-culotte* or soldier from 1793.

A period image of the mix of uniforms seen in a *demi-brigade*, combining the blue clothed volunteers and white clad regulars.

The *levée* of August 1793 aimed to create an army a million men strong. The *levée* was carried out by municipal authorities under the close supervision of local Jacobin clubs and representatives on mission. The actual designation of men for the army was carried out by drawing straws – just like the hated militia of the Old Regime, which had been abolished in 1789 after general condemnation. But unlike the militia – and unlike the conscription system Napoléon would institute after becoming the ruler of France – the *levée en masse* granted no exemptions to specific categories of civilians (such as workers in war industries) and did not allow designees to hire replacements to serve in their stead. In addition, there was no term of service; those called to arms were expected to serve until the end of the war. Deeply resented, it is little wonder that the *levée* ultimately failed to raise a million-man strong army. Despite this, it did succeed in its principal goal, that of 'getting a large number of men into uniform in a very short time'.[7]

Demi-Brigades de Bataille

The main problem with the volunteers was their lack of training. There were no formal training institutions (outside of unit drill sergeants) for the new men to train like the regulars. As a result, the volunteers were trained literally, trial by fire. Soldiers quickly built battle experience, but putting the new units at the front that had never experienced combat risked instability among the troops and increased the chances of defeat or rout. It is notable that of the few massed training camps De Rochambeau conducted during 1792, they 'apparently proved disappointing … Much had to be done that winter, as the volunteer battalions joined the regulars.' Author John A. Lynn argues that even though 150 new battalions joined the Army of the North (*l'Armée du Nord*) in a 6-month period 'they hardly added to its strength', because 'they were so underprepared to face the enemy'.[8] The weight of the fighting was born by the regular soldiers.

To address this problem, the Committee of Public Safety, again acting for the military, decided to integrate the ranks, making regulars, volunteers – and later conscripts – brothers in arms. Thus, breaking up units of the royal army and reducing the threat of a military coup against the Republic. This also integrated the new troops with experienced men.[9]

Another goal of the *amalgame* was to decrease tensions between the career soldiers and the rambunctious, ill-disciplined volunteers who saw the professionals as unpatriotic.[10] Bringing both recalcitrant groups together, it was hoped, would improve battlefield performance. Before he 'sneezed into the basket' – a common term for being guillotined – General Adam Philippe Custine was tasked with whipping the army into shape by establishing training camps in a precursor to those at Boulogne. Custine ensured that selected men from each unit went to train at the camp for several weeks and then return to impart their newly-acquired knowledge on their peers as drill instructors.[11] This proved to be highly successful as Custine's commissaires, Varin and Celliez, reported that 'the soldiers devote themselves to drill with indefatigable zeal, and the great number of battalions manoeuvre with a precision that one does not see in troops of the line'.[12] Slowly but surely, the army of the Republic began to regain its lost professionalism.

The *amalgame* when it came on *21 Nivôse AnII* (10 January 1794), purposefully broke apart all army units and reformed them into large '*Demi-Brigades* of three battalions, with companies of forty volunteers and twenty regulars'.[13] At a stroke, regimental lineages dating back to Louis XIV were broken as a new national army was forged in the crucible of war. The volunteers of 1792 and 1793 failed in most of their battles and campaigns, not due to a lack of courage, but from a lack of training. Only after the *amalgame* of 1794 and the experiences of both defeat and victory, did the French army become a cohesive fighting force, enabling the army to outfight its enemies by 1797.

It was hoped to combine the discipline of the old regulars with the revolutionary zeal of volunteers. Each battalion comprised 8 companies, 1 of which was the elite grenadier company. A grenadier company comprised 1 captain, 1 lieutenant, 1 *sous-lieutenant*, 1 sergeant major, 2 sergeants, 1 *fourrier*, 4 corporals, 4 chosen men, 48 grenadiers and 2 drummers: a total of 65 men. Fusilier companies had an additional 1 sergeant, 2 corporals, 2 chosen men and 19 fusiliers. Grenadier companies were made the same strength as fusilier companies, each company now mustering 104 men. The rank of chosen man was removed. Attached to each *demi-brigade* was a company of artillery manning six 4-pounder field guns. The number of guns was reduced to 3 in 1795. The decree provided for the amalgamation of the 198 battalions of the line, united with 396 battalions of volunteers, to form 198 *demi-brigades* of line infantry of first formation.

Clothing the *Demi-Brigades*

Faced with a massive increase in the number of men under arms, the state had to change the way the men were provided with clothing. With an army that numbered nearly 500,000 men under arms, the constant re-supply to the men to replace lost, damaged, and worn-out clothing and equipment could not be supplied by depot-level production. The state actively began the production of stockpiles of clothing and equipment as we shall see in our second case study.

From the 15 March 1794, each battalion or squadron was to be administered by a council of administration. At battalion level, it was responsible for discipline, expenses incurred by the battalion, as well as detailing the number of men and horses on a daily basis, and noting those on leave, on detachment or in hospital. It was to comprise the battalion commander, who would act as president, an officer, a *sous-officier* (either a sergeant major, sergeant or corporal quartermaster) and 2 privates. The officer was to be nominated by their fellow officers from the battalion and then elected by drawing of lots if more than one candidate was put forward. The *sous-officier* was to be nominated in the same manner. It was the duty of the sub-officer to report those men of the battalion absent, on leave or in hospital. In the absence of the battalion commander, his duties were to be replaced by the senior captain. Each company of the battalion was to present 2 soldiers to the council. These men had to be elected to the position by a majority vote. Of the soldiers presented, the 2 most senior were to be elected to the council. All members of the council were to be elected for a period of 6 months, and could only continue to be members if returned by election. If for any length of time the battalion was detached from the regiment proper over a distance of 13.5 miles, it was to act for the council of the regiment instead.[14]

The council of the regiment was to comprise the regimental colonel, who was to act as president of the regiment, 3 officers, 3 *sous-officiers* and 6 privates. In the absence of the regimental colonel, his place was to be taken by the senior battalion commander. Election

A group of Revolutionary period soldiers, including a grenadier. The wide variety of legwear shown is documented in the archive material generated at the time.

to the regimental council was for 6 months. In the first half of the year, the members were to come from the first battalion, and in the second half of the year from the second battalion. The *sous-officiers* had to be nominated after election through majority from the members of the battalion council. In addition, the battalion commander, quartermaster treasurer, was an *ex-officio* member and carried out the function of secretary.

According to the decree of 20 July 1794, the administrative council was attached to the regimental staff. The council was responsible for authorising the purchase of clothing, equipment, horses, forage, discipline of the regiment, promotions, as well as the discharge of horses, men and the disposal of worn-out items of clothing. The council oversaw the payment of the regiment, and the docking of pay to purchase consumables when in the barracks or lodgings. This was to be overseen by a commissioner for war. Provision of rations for the men, and clothing and equipment was vested in specific officers of the regimental staff. They had to ensure that the correct quantity of feeds was purchased, according to government guidelines, and that all purchases were fully accounted for.[15]

The lieutenant clothing officer had to oversee the purchase of all items of equipment and clothing for the other ranks (*sous-officiers,* corporals, drummers and privates). Officers provided their own uniforms and equipment, and funded the regimental band. The regimental council oversaw that the items purchased on the regiment's behalf were of good quality, that they matched the regiment's specifications and that the cost of purchase was as agreed in the contract. All receipts had to be lodged in separate account books that were overseen by a commissioner for war. This was to ensure that officers did not profit from the regiment obtaining contracts. The specification for each item of uniform was recorded in a register of uniforms. The commissioner for war was to ensure that items purchased matched this register. All deliberations of the council in obtaining contracts for clothing and equipment from contractors were to be recorded so that the commissioner for war could see how and why a regiment chose a certain contractor. The clothing officer also had to ensure that all regimental property held in the regimental magazines at the depot were in good condition and all accounted for. The clothing and equipment of men in hospital was also the responsibility of the clothing officer, who had to ensure it was stored in good condition while the member of the regiment was hospitalised. Each company commander had to keep a report of the items of clothing and equipment issued to their company, and note what items needed repairing, what was beyond use and what items were new. These reports were submitted to the clothing officer who then collated the information. The magazines and regiment were to be inspected every year by a commissioner for war to ensure that the paperwork of the regiment matched reality, and to agree to the disposal of worn-out clothing and equipment.[16]

The council of administration prepared the paperwork for the total purchase of cloth, buttons, leather items etc. needed to replace worn-out items and needed to equip new entrants to a regiment. These discussion documents were classed as 'exercise' – basically an expression of obtaining formal quotes to tender for the provision of items. These items were then purchased through *marches*, which in essence were bills of sale. They listed what items were ordered, from which supplier and their address, when the order was placed, when the bill was paid and also when the items were delivered. Items were either ordered from suppliers as complete items or the material was obtained to make the items. Each regiment had up to 6 master workmen. Their workshops were located in the regimental depot. Each workman would take on at least 2 of the regiment's children as

Dressed almost in rags, these soldiers show the shambolic nature of the French army in the mid-1790s. Archive documents support this far from uniform appearance.

apprentices. The workmen included a master tailor, master armourer, master cordwainer and master gaiter-maker:

> Master tailor. He ranked as a sergeant and was responsible for manufacturing uniforms for his regiment, as well as making repairs to the uniforms. Every man that joined the regiment would be measured and have a uniform altered to fit. Uniforms came in three sizes. In addition, from 1810 it seems each company had at least one tailor, and company funds were used to pay his wages.
>
> Master armourer. He ranked as a corporal, and it was his duty to ensure weapons were kept in good repair and repaired as needed.
>
> Master cordwainer. The master shoemaker ranked as a corporal and was responsible for manufacture and repair of shoes and boots.
>
> Master gaiter-maker. The gaiters of a regiment had prior to 9 September 1799 been made by the master tailor, after that date the duties were passed to the gaiter-maker.

The system for production of clothing and equipment, back engineered from the surviving documents, operated in this manner. Under the terms of the decree of 1794, for clothing and equipment, once a regiment had been inspected by an inspector of review, he sanctioned what new items were to be made and what was to be repaired. Once this had been agreed with the council of administration, the authorised funds were to be released from state coffers to pay for the said items. The regiments had to buy cloth and other materials like lace and leather at set government prices from reputable suppliers. Items, such as shoes, were often bought in bulk from factories rather than made in house, as were metal fittings like buttons. Each regiment, it seems, kept a sealed pattern for each item of equipment, which was the established model to be copied by suppliers. The cost of the men's uniform came from stoppages in their pay. They were paid, in theory, weekly, according to rank and status. In all cases, the pay was subject to a number of deductions for communal funds (*masses*), which left very little actual pay. The purpose of the pay was actually not to give the soldier pocket money to spend on wine, women and gambling but so he could pay for fines, pay repair bills for his clothing and equipment, purchase soap and cleaning equipment, and, if needed, buy new items of clothing. All repairs were carried out under the auspices of the *caporal-fourrier*. Minor repairs were to be carried out to clothing and equipment by the soldier; for more major repairs, the *caporal-fourrier* took the solider and his damaged items to the captain clothing officer who authorised the regimental workmen to undertake the repair. If the repair was judged to be the fault or negligence of the soldier he had to pay for the work or a replacement item from his pay.[17] The costs for clothing came from the general fund (*masse générale*).

56 The Armies of the French Revolution

A grenadier of an unknown *demi-brigade* whose uniform apart from his unorthodox legwear matches the regulations fairly well, including the white metal kidney shaped canteen.

Regulations in Practice

The *amalgame* did not happen instantly. Changes of this magnitude took time. Cost and time preclude a total study of all the units created in this period. A random sample of 10 archive boxes provides the following information. It is clear that the regulations of 1786 were still not full enforced. It is also clear that the helmets in accordance with the regulations of 1791 had been a total failure: often made from felt rather than leather, these items had a lifespan of around 18 months and were hastily replaced with *chapeaux* with a decree of *2 Ventôse AnIV* (21 February 1796). The decree furthermore marked the end of the white *habit* – if any existed. The decree also repeated an instruction of 4 September 1793, removing the King's Livery from drummers' clothing. Bearskins had been abolished on campaign as early as 1792 and no mention was made for grenadiers' *epaulettes*.[18]

2ᵉ Demi-Brigade

The *2ᵉ Régiment d'Infanterie de la Ligne* had been commanded by Étienne Jacques-Joseph-Alexandre Macdonald since 12 November 1792. In spring 1795, still clinging to the old unit title, he set about resolving chronic shortages in his regiment following the *amalgame*. His regiment needed new clothing and was chronically under strength: just 828 other ranks. He had been made general of the brigade in November 1794, but, as yet, had not been replaced as colonel by the newly appointed De Marpaude who had been given the new rank of *chef du brigade*.

Drawn up on parade on *12 Ventôse AnIII* (2 March 1795), the overwhelming majority of the men's clothing was utterly 'knackered'. Out of 818 *habits* in use, 10 men had no *habit*, 121 needed repairs and 647 total replacement. Of the *vestes*, 84 needed repairs and 614 total replacement. Of the men's headdress, 698 helmets needed total replacement, so too did 212 *gibernes* and 347 *porte-gibernes*, and 72 *baudriers* were required to replace the *ceinturons*. The inspector of review ordered 901 pairs of *culottes*, 983 shirts, 1,397 pairs of shoes, as well as 786 pairs of grey gaiters, 16 pairs of black gaiters, 830 pairs of stockings and 300 linen smocks to be made by the regimental artisans or purchased from military suppliers. The helmets were to be entirely replaced with *chapeaux*.

This review marked the transition from white to blue: 426 blue *habits* were needed to replace white *habits* in addition to new blue *habits* to replace those in use, but worn out, with the same number of white *vestes* and blue *bonnets de police*. Macdonald's accounts report that scarlet broadcloth was needed for the collar and cuffs of the *habit*, for the piping to the *habit*, and also for the collar and cuff of the *veste* and the turban of the *bonnet de police*. White broadcloth was needed for the *revers* of the *habit*, and piping to the *habit* collar, for the *veste*, and to decorate the turban of the *bonnet de police*. White *tricot* was purchased to make *culottes*, as well as white *serge* to line the *habits* and *vestes*. Linen was purchased in different grades to act as an interlining to the tails of the *habits*, as well as to line the sleeves and centre back of the *habits*, and moreover, to make pocket bags. Interestingly, the fusiliers of the regiment needed 1,165 helmets and the grenadier company wore *chapeaux*.[19]

13ᵉ Demi-Brigade

Inspected on *16 Germinal AnII* (5 April 1794), the clothing of the first battalion was 'extremely tired'. For example, of 688 *habits*, 250 needed repairs and 230 immediate replacement. Again, similar numbers of *vestes* needed repair or renewal, and 622 pairs of *culottes* had to be replaced, leaving just 46 pairs in good condition. Remarkably, 51 men had no *giberne*, and of those in use 267 needed repairs and 51 replacing. No campaign equipment was issued. Every man had a *chapeau*. The inspector noted the clothing and equipment was 'entirely bad' and needed totally replacing.[20]

We know almost nothing about the dress of the *demi-brigade*s at their first formation, not how far, if at all, the various dress regulations had been enacted. Much more research is needed, which hopefully future researchers and historians will undertake.

Chapter 4

Demi-Brigades d'Infanterie de Ligne

Less than 2 years after the first *amalgame*, in order to combat the huge reduction in strength of the army through desertion, battlefield attrition and recruitment problems, a second *amalgame* was enacted. The decree of 18 *Nivôse AnIV* (8 January 1796) consolidated the 238 existing *demi-brigades* into 140 new *demi-brigades*; 110 line infantry *demi-brigades* and 30 light infantry *demi-brigades*. *Demi-brigades d'infanterie de ligne* came into being with the decree of *12 Pluviôse AnIV* (1 February 1796). Henceforward in a *demi-brigade*, each fusilier company comprised 1 captain, 1 lieutenant, 1 *sous-lieutenant*, 1 sergeant major, 5 sergeants, 1 *fourrier*, 8 corporals, 2 drummers and 104 fusiliers. A grenadier company differed by the virtue of it having 4 sergeants and just 64 grenadiers. A *demi-brigade*, in theory, mustered 96 officers and 3,300 men.

As noted earlier, this was all paid for with stoppages from pay. Government funds allowed each of the 95 *demi-brigades de bataille* and the 26 *demi-brigades légère*, 12,000 francs a year: a total budget of 1,452,000 francs. The cavalry was far costlier, each regiment of *Carabiniers à Cheval* was allowed 36,000 francs, the *cavalerie* 24,000 francs, the *hussards* (hussars), *dragons* and *chasseurs* 36,000 francs each, the foot artillery 12,000 francs, the engineers 9,600 francs, and the horse artillery 24,000 francs. A total national budget of 4,982,400 francs, or 138,400 francs every 10 days, being spent on the armed forces in issuing the men their first uniforms and paying for repairs and replacements.[1]

Major changes to the dress of the army envisioned with this decree. The new regulations allocated each soldier to have – in theory at least – a national blue coat (*habit*) with white sleeved waistcoat (*veste*), knee breeches (*culottes*) as well white, black and linen gaiters. He also had an ammunition box (*giberne*) with its belt (*banderole* – shoulder belt from which the *carbine* or *sabre* in grenadier companies was carried), as well as his backpack (*havresac*), and for corporals, grenadiers and *sous-officiers* – sergeants, *fourriers* and sergeant majors – a *sabre* and its belt (*baudrier*). He would also have his *chapeau* and off duty cap (*bonnet de police*). The *chapeau* was of a larger dimension than before. Grenadiers were allowed a bearskin and a *chapeau*, their *giberne* decorated with a copper grenade-device, fusiliers had numbers on the *giberne*. Grenadiers, as in 1791, were allowed to have scarlet fringed *epaulettes*, and drummers had their own pattern. We are totally ignorant of the difference between the two. We note also tricolour *aigrettes* (plumes made from horsehair – decorative feather ornaments worn in a *chapeau*) for use in the *chapeau* was authorised, as well as pompoms in company's colours for fusiliers and scarlet pompoms for grenadiers. Drummers were allocated 1 *pouce*-wide tricolour lace, to be placed on their *habit* in the manner of the regulations of 1786 – at the collar, cuff and 7 or 8 *chevrons* on each sleeve – and musicians 1 *pouce*-wide silver lace to decorate the

The *chapeaux* according to the regulations of 1794 was larger than its 1786 predecessor, but offered little in the way of head protection. It was cheap and quick to produce, however.

collar and cuff. Each man was issued a set of 3 buckles – a pair of knee buckles, a buckle to adjust the back of the breeches and a stock buckle – as well as a white stock, black stock, with spare *rabats* (white piping) and card liners.[2]

On *12 Nivôse AnVI* (1 January 1798), the regimental artillery was done away with until 1809, but unit organisation was left unchanged.

Bernadotte's Reforms

Overlooked by historians, re-enactors and others are the major changes that future marshal of France, General Jean-Baptiste Bernadotte, rolled out during his tenure as minister for war. Bernadotte provided Napoléon with the building blocks for the *Grande Armée* in terms of uniform equipment, supply of clothing, as well as matters organisational. His reforms changed the way in which the cavalry procured its horses, and sought to end fraud in the provision of horses, as well as uniforms and equipment. It was Bernadotte who authorised inspectors of reviews to begin annual reviews of regimental accounts: regimental colonels could not be trusted to audit their own accounts. Despite the 1794 changes to procurement, the administrative chaos of the 1794 to 1798 period prevented close attention to the oversight of regimental and governmental funds. Bernadotte sought to 'overhaul the system'.

On *14 Messidor AnVII* (2 July 1799), Bernadotte on his first day in the job as minister for war oversaw the creation of an army reserve, termed *Bataillon Auxiliaires dit Bataillon Départemental*. The project had been inherited from his predecessor and these battalions became the departmental legions from *24 Floréal AnVIII* (14 May 1800) during Louis-Alexandre Berthier's tenure as minister for war from November 1799. Each battalion was to comprise 10 companies, of which 1 was designated as grenadiers. They were to act as a reserve to the National Guard, and provide a body of troops for internal defence, much as the British Volunteer movement provided. The prefects of the departments, in theory, were supposed to be the commanders of these reserve companies, similar to a colonel. Napoléon took their designation as reserve companies literally and continually drew off men from them to reinforce his active troops. The men were dressed in the same manner as the *ligne* – and could be designated fusilier or *chasseurs* by the commandant – and were issued a *chapeau*, *habit*, *veste*, 2 pairs of *culottes* and a *bonnet de police*. They were also allowed 3 shirts, 1 black and 1 white stock, 2 pairs of shoes, 1 pair of white gaiters, as well as pairs in linen and black twill amongst other items. Equipment was the same as the *ligne*, although *sous-officiers* were allocated *ceinturons* for their *sabres*.[3]

From 1797, regular inspections of regiments had begun again by general inspectors. It was obvious that after a reporting gap of 4, 5 or 6 years, that the army was dressed in a wide array of clothing and equipment, with no single decree in place standardising what was worn. It was also clear that regiments faced acute shortages of clothing and equipment: men went to war wearing a medley of civilian and military dress. To bring some order from chaos, the Ministry of War embarked on a route and branch reform regarding how the army was dressed and how it would be dressed.

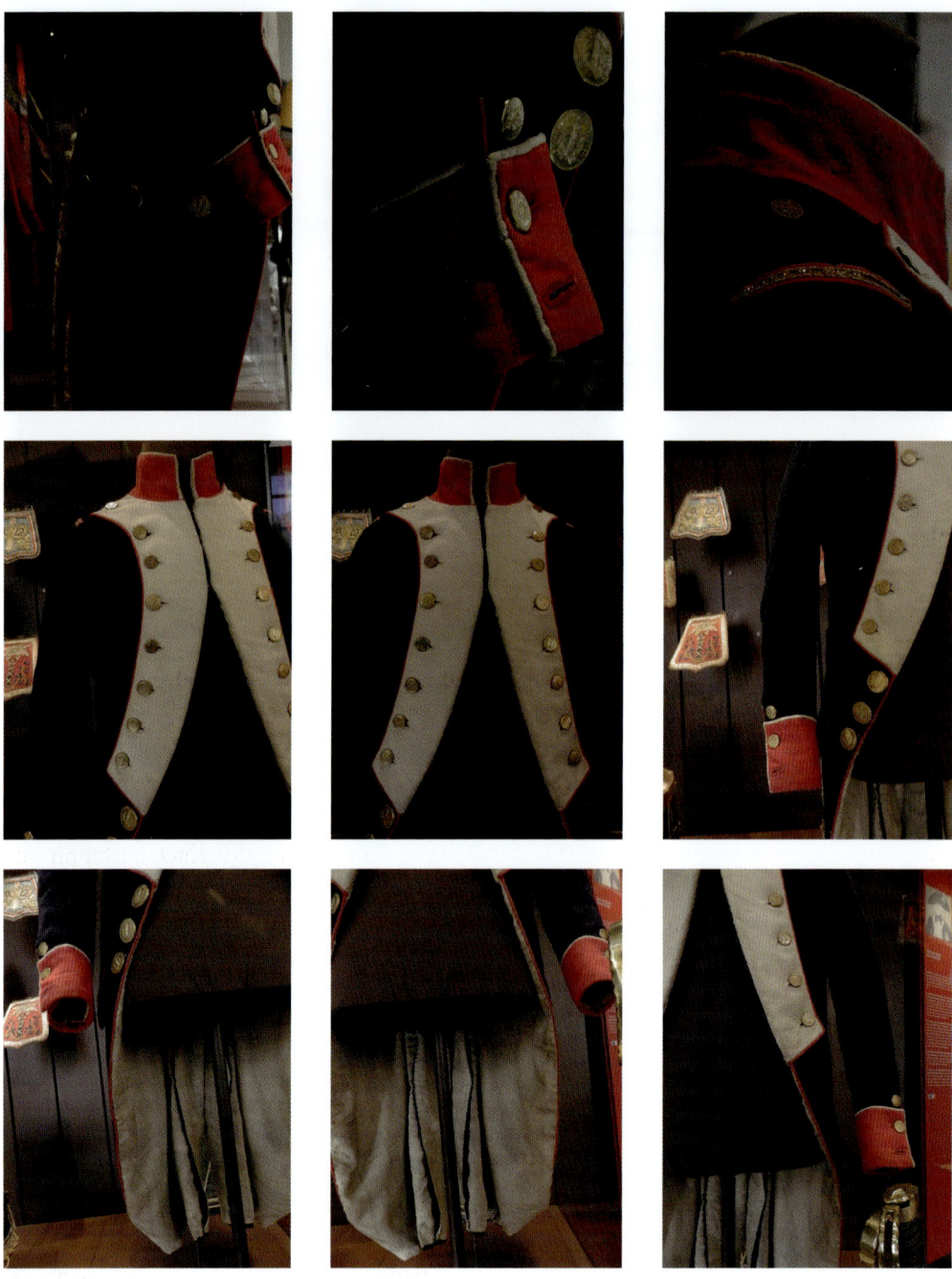

Details of an excellently preserved officer's *habit* according to the regulations of 1794. (*Musee de l'Armee*)

On *11 Thermidor AnVII* (29 July 1799), Bernadotte rolled out a new comprehensive decree affecting all aspects of the men's uniform and equipment. The decree was the brain child of engineer officer Louis Marie Antonie Destouff de Milet de Mureau, who had been minister of war since 21 February 1799. This decree, in theory, was an enabling decree for the standardisation of uniforms into 3 sizes, enabling civilian contractors to

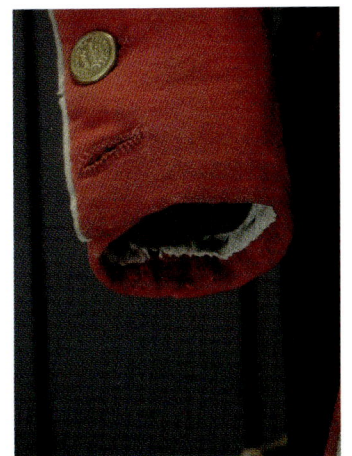

being production of clothing and equipment for the army, rather than relying on each regiment to act as the contracting agent. It allowed the state to generate reserve stockpiles of clothing, adding an additional burden to the Ministry of War.[4] The enabling measure was a new piece of legislation detailing the 3 regulation sizes of each garment of clothing, as well as the amount and type of materials required. The text informs us a *habit* required

1m 14 blue broadcloth for the body, 0m 13 scarlet broadcloth for the piping to the collar, *revers*, cuff flaps and pockets on the tails, 0m 17 white broadcloth for the piping for the *revers*, 3m white *serge* to line the *habit* of which 1m was to be deducted to allow for linen to line the sleeves, and 0m 14 linen for pockets and button stands. The *gilet* was sleeved, the front being made from broadcloth, the back and sleeves from *tricot*, and was lined in white *serge*. The sleeves were unlined. The collar and cuffs were white as no blue or scarlet cloth was allowed. We note that the *légère* (light) *habits* had blue cuffs piped red and red cuff flaps piped blue, fastened with 4 buttons. The *bonnets de police* were now authorised to be made from new materials, namely 0m 17.5 blue broadcloth, 0m 71 scarlet broadcloth, 0m 12 linen, 2m 38 scarlet round worsted cord and 0m 59 white cord. So, we must imagine a red turban, with blue *flamme*. The turban piped white and the *flamme* red. The tassel was made from strips of cloth. The earlier model was made entirely from cloth recovered from old *habits*, and was entirely blue with scarlet or white (*légère*) piping to the turban, and a tassel cut from cloth strips. This new *AnVII* (1798 to 1799) model was replaced during *AnX* (1801 and 1802). The black worsted gaiters were fastened with black leather buttons: copper or brass buttons were not regulated until Bardin.[5]

Another regulation appeared during the tenure of Bernadotte as minister for war. The decree of *26 Fructidor AnVII* (12 September 1799) for clothing to be issued during the following year. The *chapeau* for the infantry was confirmed as larger than allowed in 1786: 6 *pouces* tall in front, 6 *pouce* 5 *lignes* at the rear. Felt *schakos* were adopted for the *légère*, as well as the light cavalry: 6 *pouces* 7 *lignes* tall for *légère* and 6 *pouces* 8 *lignes* for the cavalry. The *giberne* was also changed: henceforward, 2 straps under the *giberne* appear to carry the rolled *bonnet de police*. Hereinafter, *bonnets de police* were allowed to be made from new cloth and off cuts from making clothing. The turban was to be made from scarlet cloth, decorated with a band of white cloth around the upper edge. The *flamme* was blue with scarlet worsted cord decoration. The end terminated with a tassel cut from strips of cloth. A new larger pattern *havresac* was adopted, confirming changes from a year earlier.[6]

Bernadotte was pushed from power on 14 September 1799: *Abbé* (priest) Emmanuel Joseph Sieyès and Charles-Maurice Talleyrand feared that he was using his position to grab power for himself and as part of a neo-Jacobin coup. Sieyès feared that Bernadotte would initiate his coup before he could make his own bid of power led by Napoléon. Therefore, Sieyès removed Bernadotte.[7] Despite being Napoléon's brother-in-law since 1798, along with other officers like General Jean Moreau, Bernadotte was opposed to Napoléon's power grab, and sought to restore some semblance of democracy to France with the so-called Butter Jar Conspiracy. This coup was orchestrated by his chief of staff, General Édouard François Simon, and supported by other prominent Jacobins and Girondins. Paul Barras – ousted by Napoléon as director of France – hoped that at a review, 20 generals would murder Napoléon in the manner of Julius Caesar by Marcus Junius Brutus after he had been thrown from his horse. To do so, the plotters organised that the horse was to be spooked on purpose. Barras and Bernadotte hoped to remove 'the Corsican tyrant'.[8] The plot was found out in May 1802, but as 'one of the family' Bernadotte was tolerated by Napoléon and made

Demi-Brigades d'Infanterie de Ligne

A French fusilier dressed in his regulation uniform.

marshal of France: the maxim 'keep your friends close and enemies closer' was never a truer sentiment. Bernadotte – protected by his friend Joseph Fouche, head of the secret police, from being arrested for his part in the plot – went onto be one of the most able corps commanders in the famed campaign of 1805, until Napoléon's hatred branded him a traitor from summer 1806, resulting in the marshal exiling himself to Sweden as king at the request of that nation's government.

With Napoléon firmly in place with the coup of *18 Brumaire AnVIII* (9 November 1799) as *defacto* dictator of France – his position was confirmed at the Battle of Marengo but not secured until Moreau's victory at the Battle of Hohenlinden – the Ministry of War, under the ever-loyal servant Berthier, was tasked with easing the bureaucratic burden on production of clothing. To that end, a major change to the clothing of the army came on *9 Thermidor AnVIII* (28 July 1800), with the creation of the department of clothing in the Ministry of War. It was to be overseen by 3 directors who reported to the minister of war. The directors were to be men of consequence 'in the production and procurement, production and of other necessities'. Basically, the state recruited the most able men from industry to oversee military production. The directors were to liaise with the civilian manufacturers to oversee the production of clothing, equipment and materials for the army, oversee the transportation of cloth, leather and other materials to workshops, and of the finished goods to the army. It was also the directors' responsibilities to make sure that the items of clothing and equipment

An excellently well preserved grenadier's habit respecting the regulations of 1794. It is lacking is scarlet *epaulettes*. (*Private Collection*)

each unit needed following the annual inspection were procured on the inspector's orders. Quality control was overseen by commissioners for war. In order for the supplier of goods to the military to be paid, the goods were examined by a commissioner for war, an inspector, as well as the council of administration. If the goods were to the required standard, the supplier was paid in cash within 5 days of acceptance to a nationally agreed level of charges. The funds *'masse d'habillement'*, as noted earlier, were supplied to each administrative council from the state by the director of the public treasury.[9]

Taking the lead we assume from Napoléon, Berthier ordered on *9 Fructidor An VIII* (27 August 1800) that *demi-brigades* were reduced to 2 battalions by disbanding the third and fourth – if it existed – war battalions into the first 2. At the same time, new buttons were to have regimental numbers: gone was the inscription to the Republic. The depot battalion was retained as a training establishment of one company. On *4 Brumaire An X* (26 October 1801), Berthier in an effort to standardise the dress of the

A group of soldiers around – we assume – a *vivandière* (female *sutler* – a person who sold provisions to the army) or regulated *sutler*.

army, re-issued Bernadotte's decree on clothing and equipment: there is no such thing as regulations of 1801. It sought to bring some semblance of order to the army now it was for the first time in nearly a decade on a peacetime footing, and in thorough need of a shake down in organisation. The decree of *3 Ventôse AnX* (22 February 1802) laid out the dress of the *ligne*. Again, it retained Bernadotte's reforms and those of 1792, but with minor changes: it allowed that *bonnets de police* to be made from cloth recovered from old clothing, and importantly for the *ligne* infantry and *légère* linen *vestes* and *pantalons de route* for use on the march and campaign were to be allowed.[10] This was in essence 'tinkering around the edges' while the consul, Napoléon, made up his mind about the organisation and appearance of his army. This was codified on *1 Vendémiaire AnXII* (24 September 1803) when the *demi-brigades* were re-christened as regiments, to comprise 3 battalions. For more on this decree and Napoléon's army, see the author's book *Napoléon's Army at Austerlitz* also published by Frontline Books.

Regulations in Practice

How the regulations were put into everyday use is best assessed from regimental and battalion records at the time. Word count, as well as time, cost and constraint, prevents a summary of every unit in the 1796 to 1803 period. What follows is a 'snap shot' of a random sample of units.

1ᵉ Demi-Brigade

Inspected on *24 Prairial AnVI* (12 June 1798), it mustered 2,113 men. Clothing was in moderately good condition and most men had their regulation issue: 71 men had no *habit* – but 386 needed replacing – 50 men had no *veste*, 53 no *culottes* and 70 men had no *chapeau*. The grenadier companies had 254 bearskins, but we note the unit had just 950 *bonnets de police* in use, 1,163 were needed. Equipment was in moderate condition the inspector noted, 244 *baudriers* and 661 *gibernes* were needed, and a further 1,542 new needed issuing to replace those damaged on campaign. Likewise, just 169 musket slings were in use, 394 muskets were needed, as were 397 *bayonets* and 113 *sabres*. All the equipment the inspector noted was in deplorable condition and needed replacing. Likewise, the muskets were of different models and some were of non-French calibre, and again needed replacement. The 44 men making up the regimental artillery needed totally dressing as such. Stores held no materials whatsoever, but held ready to issue, 1,543 *habits*, 2,104 pairs of *culottes* and 633 *capotes* (single- or double-breasted overcoat, worn over the *gilet manche*, a single-breasted sleeved jacket in lieu of the *habit* when on the march or active service).[11]

Inspected on *13 Prairial AnXI* (2 June 1803), the reviewing officer, General Louis Friant, remarked that the dress of the officer and *sous-officiers* was excellent, at least superficially, and accorded to the regulations. He noted that each man had 27 or 28 francs taken from their pay to cover the costs of issuing white linen *culottes*, and he reminded the company commanders of the 3 grenadier companies, that grenadiers and

An officer of fusiliers wearing the new national uniform in the colours of the tricolour, which he proudly displays.

sapeurs were to wear moustaches. Clearly, they were clean shaven. Nothing was said about *sapeurs* having beards. On closer inspection of what the men were wearing, Friant had 'choice words' when it came to the clothing of the regiment. He noted the cloth used was very low grade and the clothing was badly cut, badly sewn and fitted the men 'where it touched'. For example, of the 1,485 men on parade, 646 men had *habits* that needed repairs and 956 men had a *habit* that required immediate replacement: everything was bad and had to be replaced with new. Incredibly, 284 men had no *giberne*, and of those in use, just 212 were in serviceable condition. Likewise, the *porte-gibernes* and *baudriers* also needed replacing as they were either very old, or made from blackened cowhide. No man had a musket sling. Friant ordered that 2 of the *sapeurs*' 14 aprons needed replacing as they were damaged beyond repair. Stores held almost no materials, 42m blue broadcloth, 53m scarlet broadcloth, 31 pairs of *culottes* and little else. Friant authorised 845 *habits* and *vestes* to be made, 1,991 pairs of *culottes*, 845 *chapeaux*, 95 *gibernes* and belts, 2 *sapeurs*' aprons and 36 bearskins to compliment the 216 in use.[12]

The next inspection post-dates the unit's re-formation as the *1ᵉ de Ligne*.[13]

2ᵉ Demi-Brigade

Reviewed on *8 Germinal AnVII* (28 March 1799), the unit had 2,669 *habits* in use, needed 476 to issue 1 to every man, and of those in use, 938 needed repairs and 549 immediate replacement. Again, we note 685 men had no regulation *veste* and 1,124 needed replacement of those in use. Over 50 per cent of the regiment lacked a pair of *culottes en tricot*, and of the 1,503 pairs in use, every single pair was listed as needing replacing. Presumably, the men were wearing whatever legwear they could buy or obtain by other means. A huge amount of the unit's clothing was improvised from civilian garments: the image of the *sans-culottes* wearing a motley collection of clothing is certainly true. We note no grenadiers' bearskins existed, 1,978 *chapeaux* were in service, leaving 1,167 men without 1, and of those in use, again every single example needed immediate replacement. Equipment was in a similar appalling condition, 233 men had no *giberne* and belt, and of those in use, 500 needed immediate replacement as life expired. Just 169 musket slings were in use, so we have to imagine pieces of string or other material used to make improvised slings. Even more telling, 244 men had no musket. The inspector ordered 933 *habits* to be made, 848 *vestes* and due to a lack of *tricot*, just 24 pairs of *culottes*, 190 *gibernes* and belts and, remarkably, 18 musket slings, meaning most men had no army issue sling on their musket.[14]

5ᵉ Demi-Brigade

The oldest inspection report that we can find for the *5ᵉ Demi-Brigade* is dated *28 Floréal AnIV* (17 May 1796). We remark that the 79 grenadiers of first battalion had both bearskins and *chapeaux*: of the 70 *chapeaux*, 60 were life expired and 10 considered serviceable; 9 men lacked a *chapeau* and we note 4 men lacked a uniform *habit*. The 83 grenadiers in

Demi-Brigades d'Infanterie de Ligne 71

A period engraving of a *general en chef*, a rank that would transmute to marshal.

second battalion had both *chapeaux* and bearskins. Despite having 2 types of headdress for grenadiers, we note no one in the company had their full allocation of clothing and equipment, and what existed was 'knackered' and needed complete replacement. The inspector noted the officers were dressed well and very regular in appearance:

> the soldiers were uniform but due to the low quality of the cloth used, a great number of the uniforms are not serviceable and need repairing, which has been greatly neglected.

He continued,

> a great number of the *habits* and *vestes* require prompt replacement, the *culottes* also need entirely replacing, a ¼ of the men lack a *chapeau* and wear instead their *bonnet de police*.

About the equipment he noted,

> the buff work is all very good and is almost entirely complete with the exception of the waistbelts for the *sous-officiers* of grenadiers and there are insufficient *baudriers* for the drummers.[15]

In theory waistbelts had been abolished in 1788 – yet remembering these items had a regulation life span of 20 years, is it surprising some were still in use?

Reviewed on *8 Brumaire AnIX* (30 October 1800), the *demi-brigade* possessed the following items of clothing and equipment:[16]

Item	Total Items	Items Needed	In Good Condition	In Need of Repair	To Be Written Off	To Be Replaced	Total
Habits	402	443	269	10	123	566	845
Vestes in *Tricot*	391	454	281	1	109	563	845
Culottes	430	415	336		94	509	845
Chapeaux	441	404	409		32	436	845
Bonnets de Police	331	514	331			514	845
Baudriers	40	136	40			136	176
Gibernes	379	434	356	1	22	457	814
Porte-Gibernes	379	434	359		20	455	814
Musket Slings	286	528	286			528	814
Drums and Carriages	13	17	10		3	20	30

* Please note that the figures shown in the table are taken directly from the source, but some of the totals appear to have been calculated incorrectly.

The *demi-brigade* was in a very poor condition. Inspected on *27 Floréal AnX* (17 May 1802), it had the following clothing and equipment in use:[17]

Item	In Good Condition	In Need of Repair	To Be Written Off	Total	Total Made Since Last Inspection	To Be Replaced
Habits	687	226	610	1,523	889	610
Sleeved Waistcoats	695	329	488	1,512	1,322	488
Culottes	698		877	1,575	1,908	877
Chapeaux	944	212	323	1,479	1,476	663
Bonnets de Police	683	155	663	1,501	710	663
Gibernes	1,273	53	2	1,328	521	
Porte-Gibernes	1,299	29		1,328	1,226	
Baudriers	739	9	1	739	1,000	1
Musket Slings	1,219	29	7	1,255	2,000	7
Drum Carriages	26			26	10	
Drums	26			26	16	
Muskets	1,383	51		1,434	1,090	
Bayonets	840	19		859	1,090	
Sabres	726	12	1	739	400	1

* Please note that the figures shown in the table are taken directly from the source, but some of the totals appear to have been calculated incorrectly.

The grenadiers did not have bearskins and not a single pair of *epaulettes* existed either, unless they were counted with the *habits* to which they were physically fastened. In terms of cloth used by the regiment, and clothing and equipment issued during the course of the period 23 September 1800 to 17 May 1802 was as follows:[18]

Item	In Depot on 23 September 1800	Purchased Since 1800	Total	Amount Used	Remaining in Depot
White Broadcloth		59m 40	59m 40	20m 34	29m 60
Blue Broadcloth		854m 50	854m 50	291m 94	562m 56
Scarlet Broadcloth		74m 25	74m 25	25m 60	48m 65
White *Tricot*	1,993m 14	1,559m 25	3,552m 39	1,926m 56	1,622m 83
White *Serge*		2,914m 10	2,914m 10	1,144m 97	1,769m 13
Linen	1,681m 32	1,064m 25	2,745m 57	1,606m 15	1,140m 42

* Please note that the figures shown in the table are taken directly from the source, but some of the totals appear to have been calculated incorrectly.

The cloth had been used to make 698 *habits*, of which 62 remained at the depot, and 1,137 *vestes*, of which 84 were at the depot. A staggering 2,228 pairs of knee breeches had been made with 702 remaining unused at the depot. At the same time, the regiment had made 1,406 shirts, 1,053 black stocks, 1,170 pairs of socks, 2,467 pairs of shoes, 245 pairs of long grey gaiters, 714 pairs of long black gaiters, 95 *sacs à toile*, 404 *havresacs* and 1,201 cockades. The long grey gaiters were used for campaign dress, and black for parades.[19]

11ᵉ Demi-Brigade

On *1 Brumaire AnXII* (24 October 1803), the *11ᵉ Demi-Brigade* was amalgamated with the *104ᵉ Demi-Brigade* as part of the re-organisation of the army to recreate regiments of the *ligne*. We only have an inventory of the unit's stores from this period and no earlier inspections can be found. Stores held 411m blue broadcloth, 188m white broadcloth, 29m 16 scarlet broadcloth, as well as white *serge* linen, white *tricot*, black twill for gaiters, bleached white linen and ecru linen for gaiters. Stores held 72 *chapeaux*, 603 *gibernes*, 258 *porte-gibernes*, 9 drums and carriages, 151 *baudriers*, 11 shirts, single examples of grey and black gaiters, linen and woollen stockings. For the men under arms, 309 *habits* were needed, 214 *vestes*, 102 pairs of *culottes*, 185 *chapeaux* and 1,014 *bonnets de police*. Stores also reported, but none were held, grenadiers' bearskins, *capotes*, gold lace for musicians, drummers' lace and tricolour feather hackles to be worn in the *chapeau*, 72 *chapeaux* and 115 pairs of grenadiers' *epaulettes*. Drummers' *epaulettes* are recorded but we are ignorant as to how these differed from grenadiers' examples. Stores did hold 125 fusiliers' pompoms, 1 grenadiers' pompom, and 198 *sous-officiers* and grenadiers' sword knots. Also lodged in stores were 582 black stocks with *rabats* – the removable piping – as well as knee, stock and breeches buckles.[20]

17ᵉ Demi-Brigade

Inspected on *1 Brumaire AnXII* (24 October 1803), before being reformed as the *17ᵉ de Ligne*, regimental stores were filled with cloth and clothing. We find 3,366m black twill for gaiters, 29m 23 bleached white linen for white gaiters, 25,072 horn buttons for gaiters, 62 *capotes*, 12 copper grenades for grenadiers' *gibernes*, 601m drummers' lace, 56m white worsted lace, 279 tricolour *aigrettes*, 106 fusilier *ganses* (piece of lace that holds the cockade to the *chapeau*) for the *chapeaux* and 36 for grenadiers. Stores also held 1,616 pompoms for fusiliers, 31 grenadiers' pompoms, 38 pairs of grenadiers' *epaulettes*, 86 pairs of drummers' *epaulettes* – how were they different to grenadiers? – 37 grenadiers' sword knots and 63 for drummers. Stores also held 8 pairs of white gaiters, 20 in natural linen and 80 in black twill. Other items of note are 245 queue pins, 339 black stocks, 343 white stocks with 52 spare buckles and 64 *rabats*.[21]

By the time of the next review, all the drummers' lace seems to have been used. We note the 8-man strong band and 36 drummers were issued light cavalry *mousquetons* in *AnXI* (1802 to 1803).[22]

An engraving of a *general de division*, his rank shown by the scarlet waist sash.

21ᵉ Demi-Brigade

Drawn up for review on *26 Fructidor AnV* (12 September 1797), the regiment musted 3,097 other ranks. The men's dress was described as good, but lacked any uniformity, the clothing being considered mediocre and badly sewn, but the equipment and armament was in good condition and well maintained the inspector noted. He added, that rather than being made from broadcloth, all of the 2,969 *habits* in use were made from *tricot*. Likewise, the 33 blue broadcloth *vestes* for the regimental artillery men were made from blue *tricot*. A staggering 50 per cent of the *habits* and *vestes* needed immediate replacement as they were damaged beyond repair. Likewise, 50 per cent of the *culottes* were life expired. Of the men's headdress, 2,191 *chapeaux* out of 2,950 needed replacing, and 1,556 out of 2,710 *bonnets de police*. Despite the equipment being in good condition, 710 *gibernes* out of 2,471 needed renewal, 1,819 musket slings were missing and every single sling in use needed replacing. Stores were devoid of cloth or any clothing to issue.[23]

22ᵉ Demi-Brigade

Reviewed on *19 Prairial AnV* (7 June 1797), the unit had 2,065 *habits*, 101 men lacked a *habit*, and just 196 were considered good. We note 320 needed repairs and 1,448 needed to be replaced. The grenadiers lacked bearskins and almost every man had a *chapeau*, but no man had a *bonnet de police*. Likewise, 256 men had no *giberne*, 215 men had a *giberne*, but no regulation belt to carry it. There were 1,659 improvised musket slings in use; the 44 regimental gunners had no specific clothing allocated, but were armed with their regulation pistol. The men had adopted blue *habits* by this date.[24]

Inspected again on *1 Fructidor AnV* (18 August 1797), 1,916 *habits* were in service, 32 were needed, 1,686 needed repairs and the remainder were fit only for rags. The grenadiers had 238 bearskins and all, bar 25, men had *chapeaux*. The 45 regimental artillery men had their blue broadcloth *vestes* and *culottes*.[25] We have no inspections for the regiment for the Battle of Marengo. Alas, the next is dated *10 Ventôse AnX* (1 March 1802). The grenadiers had lost their bearskins, and of the 1,462 *habits* in service, 190 needed repairs and 359 immediate replacement, so too did all of the 1,462 *chapeaux* in service.[26]

Inspected again on *26 Prairial AnXI* (15 June 1803), of the 1,678 *habits* in use, 1,234 had been issued since the last review, yet 315 still needed repairs and 355 needed immediate replacement. As before, the grenadiers had no bearskins.[27]

28ᵉ Demi-Brigade

Reviewed on *24 Prairial AnVI* (12 June 1798), the regiment had 92 officers, 22 members of the *petit-etat-major* – which included 3 tailors, 3 shoemakers and 3 armourers – and 2,394 *sous-officiers* and men. The other ranks clothing was described as bad, many of the *habits* 'not being well sewn' and the leather equipment was of bad quality. The *gibernes* were made from low-grade leather, many were old, the stitching had rotted and needed

An engraving of a *general de brigade*, his rank in part shown by the sky blue waist sash.

to be re-made. Again, most of the unit's muskets came in for harsh critique being rusty and in bad condition: it was easier to re-arm the unit that to repair the existing weapons. Overall, of the 2,378 *habits* in service, 650 needed repairs, 428 were worn out and 326 needed total replacement, roughly 50 per cent. The men were wearing 286 felt *chapeaux* and needed 1,982 further examples to replace worn out helmets: 433 were in stores to be issued immediately. No grenadiers' bearskins existed. To provide materials, 65m blue broadcloth, 1,137m white *serge* and 325m linen were authorised to be obtained to make *habits*, and 110m white *serge* and 55m linen to produce new *vestes*. The inspector noted that old *habits* were to be cut up to make *bonnets de police*.[28]

The next inspection, made on *5 Messidor AnXI* (24 June 1803), tells us that on *1 Vendémiaire AnIX* (23 September 1800), the unit was wearing 1,139 *chapeaux* – adopted before the Battle of Marengo we assume. No *sapeurs'* equipment existed and no bearskins for the grenadiers.[29]

Reviewed again on *1 Prairial AnX* (21 May 1802), we note no bearskins or *sapeurs'* equipment.[30]

30ᵉ Demi-Brigade

Reviewed on *7 Messidor AnIV* (25 June 1796), the unit comprised 3 battalions, with 98 officers, and 3,517 men – including 24 men of the *petit-etat-major*, among which we find 8 men forming the regimental band. There were 3,493 men were under arms. A huge amount of clothing was missing: 2,964 *habits* were in use, 2,740 *vestes*, 2,683 pairs of *culottes* and 2,927 *chapeaux*. Of the *habits*, 834 needed repairs and 718 total replacement. Of the *vestes*, 1,153 needed replacing, as well as 1,245 pairs of *culottes*. Indeed, the inspector noted that, as most of the clothing was in bad condition, it would be easier to replace it all rather than 'make do and mend'. He added 'the shoes and the gaiters are all in bad condition because they are badly made'. The artillery company was issued with 43 pairs of pistols and holsters, the inspector authorised 69 *habits* and 67 *vestes* to be made for the company.

Reviewed on *27 Pluviôse AnX* (16 February 1802), roughly 50 per cent of the unit's clothing and equipment needed repairs or total replacement, and the inspector ordered 12 sets of *sapeurs'* equipment to be purchased as those in service were 'knackered'. Indeed, the inspector noted, 'absolutely everything is totally defective'. Stores held almost nothing, 5m 11 white broadcloth and 5m 69 blue broadcloth, 141m 80 white *serge* from which to make and repair uniforms. We note 75 old *habits* had been cut up to repair 64 *habits*. Likewise, 100 *gibernes* had been cannibalised to repair 100, and 164 *giberne* belts had been cut up to repair 223.[31]

Inspected once more on *28 Floréal AnXI* (18 May 1803), every man was dressed in a *chapeau*, and we note 50 per cent of every item of clothing needed replacing, bar the *culottes* where every pair needed to be replaced. Of the leatherwork, 1,732 *gibernes* and belts were in use, but 320 needed repairs and 132 replacing. Times of 'peace and plenty' did not always correlate with regiments completely solving issues over supply of uniforms.[32]

An engraving of an adjutant general. His rank must not be confused with the rank of general, such officers were, in fact, senior staff officers, acting as an aid to a general. The rank was equivalent to the *adjutant-sous-officer*, who worked with a battalion adjutant as his secretary (in essence his personal assistant).

35ᵉ Demi-Brigade

Inspected on *1 Brumaire AnXII* (24 October 1803), we note that there should have been white linen for gaiters, horn buttons for white gaiters and *culottes*, and bearskins and grenades for grenadiers' *gibernes*, but none existed at the time of the review. Again drummers' lace is reported but none was in stores. The same is true of grenadiers' *epaulettes*, pompoms and sword knots, as well as drummers' sword knots and *epaulettes*. We note 396m 88 black twill for gaiters, 19 *bonnets de police* and that a considerable about of the clothing in use needed total replacement. For example, of 1,128 *habits*, 563 were life expired, so too were 666 *vestes*, the same number of *chapeaux* and 588 *bonnets de police*. Of note, 34 men had no regulation *culottes*.[33]

40ᵉ Demi-Brigade

Reviewed on *8 Floréal AnVII* (27 April 1799), the regiment had 108 officers, 22 *sous-officiers* and specialists on the *petit-etat-major*, and 2,051 other ranks. Drill was considered good, in theory, but needed more frequent exercises to make the officers and men proficient. Clothing wise, out of 2,198 *habits* in use, 161 needed repairs and 897 immediate replacement, every man was wearing a *chapeau*, 2,199 in use and 1,226 needed to be replacement immediately. Only *sous-officiers*, corporals and drummers were issued *sabres*, 602 *baudriers* being issued, of which 377 needed immediate replacement. Of the 652 *sabres*, 355 needed replacement. Interestingly, more *sabres* existed that *baudriers*. How were the extra *sabres* carried we wonder? No bearskins for grenadiers existed, and no mention is made of any distinctions for drummers or *sapeurs*.[34]

Inspected on *18 Ventôse AnX* (9 March 1802), this tells us that on *1 Vendémiaire AnX* (23 September 1801) the regiment had no *sapeurs*' equipment and no bearskins for the grenadiers.[35]

41ᵉ Demi-Brigade

Inspected on *1 Brumaire AnXII* (24 October 1803), before being incorporation into the *17ᵉ de Ligne*, regimental stores were filled with cloth and clothing. We find 96 *habits*, 494 *vestes*, 15m 87 gold lace for *sous-officiers*' rank stripes, 75m 48 yellow lace for corporals' stripes, and 58m 64 for service *chevrons*. Of note, the regiment's *capotes* were made from green broadcloth, stores holding 128m 29 of this cloth inherited from the *41ᵉ Demi-Brigade* and also 24m 59 green *tricot*, again to make *capotes*. We assume the *17ᵉ de Ligne* had green *capotes*. We also find 2,402m linen to make smocks.[36]

43ᵉ Demi-Brigade

Inspected on *13 Nivôse AnVII* (2 January 1799), the regiment mustered 90 officers, 21 officers and specialists – 25 tailors, 3 shoemakers and 2 armourers – on the *petit-etat-major*, and 2,066 *sous-officiers* and men. Theoretical and practical training was considered

On the left is as an adjutant or staff officer, and to his right, denoted by a *brassard* (arm band), an *aide-des-camp*.

good, as was discipline, but the inspector urged the officers to ensure the newly promoted *sous-officiers* and corporals thoroughly understood their duties. It was important, the inspector noted, that the officers regularly drilled the men, especially at battalion level manoeuvres. Uniformity of dress was considered acceptable, and the regiment had taken delivery of new *habits* to clothe the recently joined conscripts, but the inspector noted they were of low quality. Many muskets needed repairs, added the inspector.

Looking in detail at the men's clothing, of 2,087 *habits* in service, 162 needed repairs and 877 total replacement. In addition, 276 garments were needed to give every man a *habit*. We also note that 877 *vestes* were needed, 2,087 pairs of *culottes en tricot*, 1,988 *chapeaux* and 877 *bonnets de police*. The inspector also noted that the grenadiers were lacking bearskins. In terms of leather equipment, of the 680 *baudriers*, 358 needed replacing, as did 288 *gibernes* and belts, 625 musket slings and 18 of the 54 drum carriages. As we noted earlier, the weaponry was in poor shape: 962 muskets and *bayonets* out of 2,012 needed total replacement, as did 280 of 680 *sabres*. Despite the huge shortfall in clothing, the inspector ordered just 162 *habits* and *vestes* making.[37] We assume the regiment looked fairly shabby at the Battle of Marengo. On *11 Ventôse AnX* (2 March 1802), the grenadiers still had no bearskins, so we can be confident that they did not exist during the Battle of Marengo.[38]

44ᵉ Demi-Brigade

Reviewed on *21 Messidor AnIV* (9 July 1796), the regiment mustered 2,845 other ranks, which included the band, and comprised 6 musicians and 1 chief musician. We note 53 men needed a *habit*, but we also note just 2,397 *vestes* were in use, 402 men needed a *veste*, 450 men had no *culottes*, and of those in service 563 pairs needed repairing and 507 replacing. The men were issued 2,029 helmets, 344 *chapeaux* and 2,647 *bonnets de police*, and 305 bearskins were to be obtained, where possible, the inspector ordered. Very few men had their full allocation of clothing and equipment, and what was in use was either in need of repair or total replacement. The 46 men in the artillery company possessed 41 blue *vestes*, no *habits* and just 8 pairs of *culottes*. They were armed with 40 pairs of pistols in leather holsters.[39]

We know nothing else until the regiment was inspected once more on *26 Pluviôse AnX* (15 February 1802). The inspector noted, 'clothing is in a very sorry state … the men have constantly been on campaign and the soldiers have been constantly obliged to sleep in their *habits* on the ground or on straw … every single one is to be replaced.' We note that the inspector ordered, over the next 8 months, all of the 1,955 *habits*, *vestes*, *culottes* and *chapeaux* were to be replaced. Equipment was also in poor condition. Of 1,335 *gibernes*, 521 needed repairs and 314 total replacement, and of 464 *baudriers*, 402 needed replacing.[40] We note that none of the bearskins ordered in 1796 ever seem to have arrived with the regiment.

Reviewed on *12 Thermidor AnXI* (31 July 1803), shortly before its transformation into a *régiment de la ligne*, the inspector noted,

Demi-Brigades d'Infanterie de Ligne 83

A *commissaire-ordonnateur* (an officer in charge of overseeing the supply process of the army with food, munitions and clothing).

the clothing is in need of repair, the tailors need to pay closer attention to the cut, many *habits* are too long or too tight in the chest and do not represent the three regulation size … the majority of the cloth used by the regiment is very poor indeed … the *chapeaux* are all in bad condition, the grenadiers have no bearskins … the equipment is almost all entirely bad … the regiment has 1,560 muskets which are not the 1777 model.

All in all, even in times of 'peace and plenty' the regiment was in very poor shape. Indeed, we note of 1,843 *habits*, 538 needed repairs and 775 was life expired, every single *veste* needed repairs or replacing, so too the *chapeaux*.[41]

59ᵉ Demi-Brigade

Reviewed on *16 Floréal AnX* (6 May 1802), the inspector commented,

the clothing of the ½ brigade is very bad. It needs totally replacing in two stages. The inspector general notes that the collars of the *habits* are too tall, the *habits* are too long and the collars do not close … the administrative council needs to be stricter … in the production of uniforms to ensure they correlate to the model sent from the ministry exactly … the gaiters are all of different cuts, they need to be of the same cut and always have black leather buttons; the shoes are of the model established by the minister, the stock buckle, for the knee and shoes are in copper and are all uniform; the men's hair is all cut and fastened in the regulation manner, but many pins for the queue are missing … the dress of the officers is very regular, as is the cut of the *habits* and *vestes*.

Looking in detail at the report, we find of 1,189 *habits* in use, just 188 were in good condition, 98 needed repairs and 901 were to be 'written off'. The inspector ordered 2,383 to be made. Likewise, 1,417 *vestes*, 818 pairs of *culottes*, 2,850 *chapeaux*, 2,200 *bonnets de police*, 450 *gibernes* and belts, and 453 *baudriers*. The unit had 24 *sapeurs*, each was issued an apron, axe with case and belt.[42]

70ᵉ Demi-Brigade

Inspected on *24 Frimaire AnVII* (14 December 1798), the *70ᵉ Demi-Brigade* mustered officers, 3 surgeons, 25 officers – *sous-officiers* and specialists on the *petit-etat-major* – and 3,209 *sous-officiers* and men. Drill – both theoretical and practical – was 'generally very mediocre'. The inspector noted that 'the instruction of the soldiers is by necessity poor because that of the officers and *sous-officiers* is mediocre'. As could be reasonably expected, discipline in the unit was 'hit and miss', the overall appearance of the unit was 'very bad' and the men's uniforms 'incomplete, very bad' with – no surprise here – the regimental administration being 'extremely bad and in great disorder'. All in all, the *70ᵉ*

Demi-Brigades d'Infanterie de Ligne

On the left a grenadier and on the right a fusilier wearing the new national uniform.

Demi-Brigade was a long way from being good soldiers. The regimental quartermaster came in for harsh critique, so too the unit's commander and clothing officer: all the regimental books were in chaos and badly kept. The drill instructors were to be sacked and new ones appointed once they were thoroughly familiar with the regulations of 1 January 1791 and 24 June 1792.

Despite the administrative chaos, the men's clothing was in fairly good shape. Of 3,234 *habits* in use, 386 needed repairs and 376 replacing, meaning almost 2/3 were in good condition. Yet, 2,224 pairs out of 3,234 pairs of *culottes* were fit only for the rag merchant, as were 2,385 *chapeaux* and every single *bonnet de police*.[43]

Inspected on *10 Ventôse AnX* (1 March 1802), of the 1,719 *habits* in service, all had to be replaced: every single item of clothing and equipment bar the *giberne*s, *bayonets* and muskets were 'knackered'. Among the few items of equipment in good condition were 18 sets of *sapeurs'* equipment, all but 1 set issued, but we note that the unit had no bearskins.[44]

Inspected again on *6 Messidor AnXI* (25 June 1803), we again note no bearskins, so we can be fairly confident none were in use at the Battle of Marengo.[45]

71ᵉ *Demi-Brigade*

Inspected on *1 Brumaire AnXII* (24 October 1803), before disbandment into the *35ᵉ de Ligne*, we note white linen for gaiters, horn buttons for white gaiters and *culottes*, bearskins and grenades for grenadiers' *gibernes* but none existed at the time of the review. Again drummers' lace is reported but none was in stores. The same is true of grenadiers' *epaulettes*, pompoms and sword knots, as well as drummers' sword knots and *epaulettes*. We do note 22 *habits*, 2 *vestes*, 12 pairs of *culottes*, 390 *chapeaux*, 2 *bonnets de police*, 254 *gibernes*, 186 shirts, 154 pairs of linen gaiters and 29 pairs of black gaiters all brand new and ready to be issued in stores. Furthermore, the report tells us stores also held 81 pairs of knee buckles, and 490 white and 364 black stocks. Of the men under arms, a lot of their clothing was missing or needed replacement. For example, of 1,265 men, 333 men had no *habits*, and of these in use 117 were life expired, so too were 280 *vestes*, 195 pairs of *culottes*, 130 *chapeaux* and 225 *bonnets de police*, and we note 869 men lacked this item. Equipment was also in desperate need of repair: 575 *gibernes* and belts, 79 *baudriers* and 123 musket slings, and 137 men had no *giberne* and belt; 1,078 men used *ad hoc* improvised musket slings.[46]

73ᵉ *Demi-Brigade*

Inspected on *11 Ventôse AnX* (2 March 1802), the unit's clothing was in fairly good shape. Of the 1,651 *habits*, 430 needed repairs and 250 replacing, also needing repairs were 306 *vestes* and 600 *chapeaux*, and needed replacement were 142 *gibernes* and belts. The unit had 7 *sapeurs'* issued aprons, axes and axe cases, but no bearskins existed. The men had both grey linen gaiters and black twill examples. The inspector noted that the cloth used

Demi-Brigades d'Infanterie de Ligne 87

A period engraving of the elaborate uniform of a *chef du brigade*, who commanded a *demi-brigade*. The title was replaced by colonel during the Consulate period.

88   The Armies of the French Revolution

to make the uniforms 'was of very low quality, but it is impossible to find better, and times dictate that therefore the uniforms must stay in use'.[47]

Inspected again on *21 Messidor AnXI* (10 July 1803), shortly before its disbandment on *1 Vendémiaire AnXI* (23 September 1802) into the *23ᵉ Régiment de Ligne*, the inspector reported of the 1,146 *habits* in use by the 2 battalions, 180 needed repairs and 848 immediate replacement; falling into the same category were 881 *vestes*, 632 pairs of *culottes*, 879 *chapeaux*, 302 *bonnets de police*, 347 *gibernes* and belts and 219 *baudriers*. About the *habits* in particular, the inspector noted that the regiment's master tailor needed to ensure that the measurement of each man was made, and the garments adjusted to fit; perhaps because the broadcloth used was low quality and had shrunk in the rain, as well as simply not fitting, many *habits* were too tight on the men's chest to allow them to drill properly. The inspector noted that the tails of the *habits* were cut too long, noting the bottom of the tails just touched the ground when a soldier knelt down on one knee. He added that for the men in the first line – the tallest – the *revers* of the *habits* were to stop 3 *pouces* 11 *lignes* – approximately 10cm – above the waist. He added the men's *chapeaux* did not match the regulation dimensions, and noted no bearskins existed for the grenadiers.[48]

74ᵉ Demi-Brigade

Formed in 1796 from elements of the *73ᵉ Demi-Brigade de Bataille* and the *185ᵉ Demi-Brigade de Bataille* (*1ᵉ Bataillon 105ᵉ Demi-Brigade de Bataille*, *1ᵉ Bataillon Les Volontaires de la Republique* and *4ᵉ Bataillon Les Volontaires de la Meurthe*), the unit was inspected on *16 Prairial AnV* (4 June 1797) and the men's clothing was in a very poor state indeed. The inspector noted 103 men needed a *habit*, 327 a *veste*, 573 men had no *culottes*, 174 no *chapeau*, 499 men had no *bonnet de police*; 488 *gibernes* were needed, as well as 204 muskets and 1,065 *bayonets* amongst other items. Regarding the clothing and equipment that existed, of the 1,360 *habits*, 496 needed repairs and 379 total replacement. The unit's clothing and equipment was either worn out or simply missing. The men under arms were described as weak and malnourished except the grenadiers and *sous-officiers*. Stores reported that 82 helmets had been issued, all being lost on campaign, as well as 200 pairs of linen *pantalons de route*, 1,275 pairs of gaiters, 648 shirts, 3,398 pairs of socks, 3,646 pairs of shoes and 398 black stocks. Then unit had 31 gunners, 27 of whom had blue *vestes* and *culottes*.[49]

Reviewed once more on *4 Pluviôse AnX* (24 January 1802), we note stores held linen for making shirts, linen for grey gaiters and woollen twill for black gaiters. The unit never seemed to have bearskins for the grenadiers.[50]

82ᵉ Demi-Brigade

The *82ᵉ Demi-Brigade* was destined for colonial service: the third battalion was based in France. During the course of 1803, the detached battalion had returned from Martinique on *6 Vendémiaire AnXII* (29 September 1803) and the regiment was re-organised.

On the left we have a regimental drummer. Tricolour lace was allowed from 1799 and may simply be confirming previous practice. On the right is a member of the artillery company attached to each *demi-brigade*.

90 The Armies of the French Revolution

The third battalion of the unit was reviewed on *1 Nivôse AnXII* (23 December 1803), to enact the decree of *1 Vendémiaire AnXII* (24 September 1803), to disbanded it into the newly formed *106ᵉ Régiment d'Infanterie de Ligne*. Stores held 1,748m white *serge*, 2m 44 white broadcloth, 31m 95 blue broadcloth, 72 *bonnets de police*, 14 *gibernes*, 2 drum carriages, 97 muskets with *bayonets*, 29 *sabres* and 178 musket worms. We also note stores held 5m 65 gold lace for sergeants' stripes, 16m 21 *aurore* (dark yellow) worsted lace for corporals' stripes, 11m 30 blue worsted lace for corporals' stripes – the white *habits* of the regulars had blue stripes for corporals – 7m 20 red worsted lace for service stripes, 953m 62 round worsted scarlet cord for *bonnets de police*, 373 scarlet tassels for *bonnets de police*, 13 pairs of grenadiers' *epaulettes* accompanied by the same number of grenadiers' pompoms and 96 for fusiliers. The battalion's clothing was incredibly incomplete. For 466 men, 321 *habits* existed, 406 *vestes*, 402 pairs of *culottes*, 72 bearskins, 225 *chapeaux*, 196 *bonnets de police* and 466 *gibernes* with belts amongst other items. Was this all the items the battalion had or just those that were still serviceable? Unit accounts tell us that since September 1802, 600 pairs of stockings had been purchased, 835 francs 86 centimes had been spent on lace, distinctions for *sous-officiers* and corporals, sword knots and pompoms for grenadiers, and 1,753 francs on grenadiers' bearskins. We also note that 600 black stocks, 1,000 white stocks and 318 *chapeaux* were in course of production at time of disbandment.[51] The 2 war battalions had clearly transitioned into blue, as battalion stores held 273m 25 blue broadcloth and 23m 85 scarlet broadcloth for piping, and needed amongst other items 36 blue *habits* and 73 grenadiers' bearskins. Clothing was grossly incomplete: 495 men had 455 *habits*, 182 *vestes*, 366 pairs of *culottes* and 496 *chapeaux*. Indeed, no man had his regulation-issue clothing and equipment. Those *habits* that did exist 'overall did not correspond with the models sent by the direct minister, nor does any of the cloth used or held in stores ... everything must be replaced', reported the inspector.[52]

92ᵉ Demi-Brigade

Inspected on *22 Brumaire AnXII* (14 November 1803), the inspection reports unit stores were almost entirely empty, but did hold 29m gold lace for *sous-officiers'* ranks stripes, and 49m 50 drummers' lace. The men's clothing was missing or life expired: for 1,312 men, 656 *habits* needed total replacing and 550 men had no *habit*. Again, we report 150 *vestes* were missing, 148 pairs of *culottes*, 590 *chapeaux* and 1,312 *bonnets de police*. Of those men in *culottes*, every singly pair was life expired. We also note 42 *sabres* were missing, and every single item of leatherwork needed replacing or was missing. For example, 206 *gibernes* were life expired and 561 men had no *giberne*.[53]

96ᵉ Demi-Brigade

Reviewed on *11 Brumaire AnVII* (1 November 1798), drill – both theoretical and practical – was considered good and 'being worked at', the inspector noted. In terms of dress, the

Demi-Brigades d'Infanterie de Ligne

Three grenadiers wearing full dress in the mid-1790s. Archive documents tell us very few units ever had grenadiers with bearskins.

officers were well dressed 'military, well turned out, uniform', but 'their dress is bad'. The inspector added that the clothing 'is badly made and incomplete'. Equipment was well maintained but the muskets and other weapons were 'in extremely bad condition'. Regimental finances were badly maintained and administered, and the officers 'had to pay better attention to the regulations of 1 January 1792.' All in all, the regiment was failing in a number of key areas, but at least the bread ration was 'good and regular'.

Looking in detail at the men's clothing, we note of the 2,116 *habits* in service, 662 needed repairs and 1,136 needed replacement. Even so, 235 men had no *habit*, 1,298 men had no *veste*, 1,669 men no *culottes en tricot*, 637 men no *chapeau* and 1,806 men no *bonnet de police*. The regiment's clothing was either completely worn out or non-existent. For immediate needs, stores held 163 pairs of *culottes*, as well as 2,137m blue broadcloth, 148m white broadcloth, 185m scarlet broadcloth, 2,785m white *tricot*, 6,036m white *serge*, 1,472m linen, 13,772 large uniform buttons and 36,784 small uniform buttons. Clearly, materials existed to make and repair clothing, but perhaps due to administrative chaos, no one had actioned production. Indeed, the officer in charge of clothing noted that due to financial difficulties, *bonnets de police* were cut from old *habits* and it was impossible to fund buying bearskins. The inspector also noted that 106 shirts were needed, the men had no socks, 1,447 pairs of black gaiters and 1,385 pairs of linen gaiters were missing, and he added 2,353 pairs of shoes were needed. Furthermore, the men had no regulation stocks or cockades for their *chapeaux*. We can only assume the men wore shoes, *sabots* and civilian legwear, often made from stripped ticking.[54] The 96ᵉ *Demi-Brigade* lived up the stereotypical image we have of how Revolutionary soldiers dressed.

Moving on to *4 Germinal AnX* (25 March 1802), we note that no bearskins for grenadiers existed, nor had they on *5 Vendémiaire AnIX* (27 September 1800), so we can be very confident the regiment did not have these at the Battle of Marengo. Again, no *sapeurs*' equipment is officially recorded.[55]

98ᵉ *Demi-Brigade*

Inspected on *22 Brumaire AnXII* (14 November 1803), prior to amalgamation into the newly formed *92ᵉ de Ligne*, the inspection report is hugely informative. It reports 304m black twill was in stores along with 3,780 small copper buttons for gaiters, as well as 43m 50 drummers' lace. The report lists tricolour *aigrettes* for *chapeaux*, but none existed. Likewise, musicians' lace. Stores also held 149 pairs of grey gaiters, 445 pairs of black gaiters, 346 pairs of shoe buckles, 477 pairs of knee buckles and 776 stock buckles. Listed but none existed were pins for the queue, as well as spare *rabats* (the white piping that slotting into the black stock) of which 145 black examples were in stores and 615 white. Cloth in stores included 150m 40 green broadcloth, and 1,024m 5 fine linen for shirts. Listed, but again none existed, were *epaulettes* for grenadiers and drummers, as well as sword knots and pompoms for grenadiers, and drummers' sword knots, copper grenades for grenadiers' *gibernes*, and *sapeurs*' aprons, axes and axe cases.[56]

101ᵉ *Demi-Brigade*

Inspected on *1 Messidor AnIX* (20 June 1801), the reviewing officer noted, 'the dress of the officers under arms is almost perfect, however … many are too negligent to conserve

Battalion artillery of the *33ᵉ Demi-Brigade*, unusually with sky blue facings.

their good turnout.' He added, 'the dress of the *sous-officiers* is good, that of the soldiers is acceptable. Many of the men from the new levy have been mostly dressed.' The officer did comment that 'the majority of the clothing is made from substandard materials and is badly made; the broadcloth supplied to the corps over the previous year is of extremely low quality.'

This probably accounts for comments made just over 7 months later about the poor condition of the uniforms. Of note, the officer observed, the *habits* did not accord to the regulations and the majority of the *chapeaux*, including newly issued examples, had to be replaced as the felt used to make them was incredibly bad quality. It seems, due to economic stress, that regardless of what the regulations said, as long as the cloth was blue, white or some shade of red, regiments had no choice but to use it. The inspecting officer further noted that the grenadiers and *sapeurs* wore their hair in a pony tail without any plaits contrary to the regulations of 1792. Remarkably, no bearskins or *sapeurs*' equipment are recorded – at least officially.[57]

Reviewed on *28 Pluviôse AnX* (17 February 1802), the clothing of the 3 battalions was in disarray. Of 1,653 *habits*, 200 needed repairs, 508 were life expired and the inspector ordered, rather than 'make do and mend', 1,308 new *habits*. Remarkably, stores had issued since 20 June 1801, 945 *habits*, and repaired 226. Clearly, the men were 'wearing them to death'. Every single *chapeau* had to be replaced. Grenadiers' bearskins are listed, but none existed. We also note 18 *sapeurs'* aprons exists, but only 16 axes with cases and belts.[58]

104ᵉ Demi-Brigade

On *1 Brumaire An XII* (24 October 1803), regimental stores held 431m 60 blue broadcloth, as well as white *serge* and *tricot*, 125 fusiliers' pompoms, 1 grenadiers' pompom, 115 pairs of grenadiers' *epaulettes*, and 198 grenadiers and *sous-officiers'* sword knots. Stores also reported, but none were held, grenadiers' bearskins, *capotes*, gold lace for musicians, drummers' lace, and tricolour feather hackles to be worn in the *chapeaux*. Drummers' *epaulettes* are recorded, but we are ignorant as to how these differed from grenadiers' examples. Also lodged in stores were 582 black stocks with *rabats* – the removable piping – as well as knee, stock and breeches buckles.[59]

Case Study: Armies of the Rhine and Danube

As well as producing clothing 'in house' the state employed contractors, who delivered clothing and other items to large warehouses. These were established in each military division or army. Each army corps would provide a list of its needs, and the items would be issued to the regiment from the central depot. To enable this to function huge stock piles of clothing and equipment were held in the depots all across France.

The Army of the Rhine was formed in November 1799 from the previous Army of the Rhine and also from the Army of the Danube (*l'Armée du Danube*). On 22 November 1799, the stores for the Army of the Rhine held the following items at the depot in Belfort:[60] 1,852 infantry *habits*, 1,832 light infantry *habits*, 99 artillery *habits*, 6 surtrouts, 5 *pelisses* (short, braided jackets trimmed with fur), 6 *dolmans* (short, braided shell jackets), 25 *redingotes*, 1,084 infantry *gilets*, 293 light infantry *gilets*, 4 *chasseurs' gilets*, 1,025 infantry *culottes*, 292 *culottes de peau*, 2 Hungarian breeches (*culottes hongroise*), 3 broadcloth overalls, 1,056 infantry *chapeaux*, 222 infantry *casques*, 421 schakos, 26 *bonnets de police*, 4,102 infantry *gibernes*, 2,474 *giberne* belts, 599 *baudriers*, 2,547 *cavalerie* waistbelt, 4,007 light cavalry waistbelts, 33 pairs of *hussards'* boots and 1,154 pairs of dragoon boots. Furthermore, Belfort held 569 shirts, 62 pairs of stockings, 33 pairs of shoes, 263 pairs of grey linen gaiters, 415 pairs of black twill gaiters, 396 *sacs à distribution* and 1,958 stocks. Other items included, 416 heavy cavalry saddles, 62 *hussards'* saddles, 147 saddle blankets, 819 sheepskin light cavalry *schabraques* (saddle blankets), 1,613 *cavalerie housses* (square, decorated saddle *schabraque* – either broadcloth or sheepskin covers used to improve the rider's comfort), 110 dragoon *housses*, 9 *hussards'* bridles, 2,778 curb bits, 547 pairs of *chaperons* (holster caps) and 196 curry combs.

At the depot in Besançon on the same date were:[61] 30 veterans' *habits*, 5 *dolmans*, 31 infantry *culottes*, 493 linen overalls, 4,956 infantry *chapeaux*, 1,903 infantry *gibernes*, 1,836 *giberne* belts, 236 *baudriers*, 3,426 musket slings and 143 drum carriages.

Wearing something approaching regulation uniform is this grenadier. (*Collection KM*)

Dressed almost exactly in regulation uniform, this grenadier has lost his *havresac* and instead carries his belongings in a blanket.

The linen overalls are unexpected at this date. Also, at the depot were 99 *cavalerie* sheepskin *schabraques*, 49 *cavalerie housses* and 6 pairs of *cavalerie chaperons*. The army reserve held 500 *porte-manteaux* (cases carried behind the saddles), 770 infantry *gibernes*, 15 *schakos*, 67 pairs of linen overalls – proof these were worn long before the regulations of *AnX* (1801 to 1802), and these regulations were reactionary to what was then standard practice, and gave official blessing to changes once they had occurred – 294 pairs of shoes, and 144 *havresacs*.[62] Of note, not a single pair of *epaulettes* or grenadiers' bearskins are listed. Presumably, these did not exist in the Army of the Rhine, but infantry *casques* and *redingotes* did!

Belfort also held a huge stock pile of campaign equipment, most notably 30 officers' tents, 1,022 eight-man tents and 289 sixteen-man tents, along with 727 blankets, 3,624 *grand-bidons*, 3,129 *petit-bidons* (personal water canteens) made from white metal, 386 *marmites* and bags, 13 *fanions d'alignement* – presumably, battalion (or company?) flags or markers – and 11 company ropes. Tools with covers included 1,340 shovels, 1,600 mattocks, 1,680 hatchets and 1,650 bill hooks. The depot in Besançon held 1,340 cavalry

96 The Armies of the French Revolution

During the Revolutionary Wars, hundreds of thousands of greatcoats were made and issued, yet they would not be formally regulated until March 1806. Very much a case of regulations reacting to the then standard practice a decade or more late. (*Collection KM*)

Dressed in his greatcoat, with thick woollen mittens and using an Austrian knapsack, this fusiliers appearance was no doubt typical for the vast majority of soldiers at the time. (*Collection KM*)

picket pins, 41 *capottes de sentinalles* (overcoats with hoods worn by sentries), 17 *grand-bidons*, 364 *petit-bidons*, 3,148 shovels, 8,420 mattocks, 1,167 hatchets, 8,594 bill hooks, 135 *fanions d'alignement* and 693 mallets.[63]

The list confirms that 1,791 *casques* were still in use by some *demi-brigade*s as late as 1799, and no doubt were not fully replaced by *chapeaux* until 1800. In theory, they had gone out of use in September 1799, but undoubtedly it took time for decisions in Paris to be actioned by units in in the field.

The Army of the Danube was formed on 2 March 1799 and commanded by General Jean-Baptiste Jourdan. The army was a training ground for future marshals, including the commander-in-chief: François Joseph Lefebvre, Jean-Baptiste Drouet, *Comte* d'Erlon, Laurent de Gouvion Saint-Cyr and Édouard Adolphe Casmir Joseph Mortier, Duke of Treviso. After the defeat at the Battle of Ostrach, the army was reorganised and command shifted to another future marshal, André Masséna.

The correspondence of General Jean Moreau between 1797 and 1800 tells us that, due to shortages of greatcoats, he 'requisitioned' tens of thousands of civilian overcoats, no doubt similar to that shown here worn by this fusilier. (*Collection KM*)

Using a civilian overcoat was commonplace for the armies of the Rhine and Danube from 1798 to 1800. (*Collection KM*)

General Louis Marie Turreau at the head of the Army of the Danube shortly after its *amalgame* with the Army of the Rhine on 24 November 1799, reported that his *demi-brigade*s of infantry were desperately short of clothing on 27 November 1799. The army needed thousands of items of clothing and equipment as replacements amongst other items were: 438,770 pairs of shoes, 106,932 pairs grey gaiters, 112,453 pairs black twill gaiters, 17,822 *havresacs*, 11,814 pairs of *hussards*' boots, 1,840 pairs dragoon boots, 58,731 infantry *habits*, 58,731 infantry *gilets*, 176,193 pairs of *tricot* infantry *culottes*, 58,731 *bonnets de police*, 71,287 infantry *chapeaux*, 440 *cavalerie chapeaux*, 828 dragoon helmets, 3,902 *schakos* for light troops, 106,932 infantry *redingotes*, 10,609 infantry *gibernes*, 55 *cavalerie gibernes* and 1,588 light cavalry *gibernes*.

Available for issue in the first quarter of 1800 would be 14,682 infantry *habits* and *vestes*, 44,048 infantry *culottes*, 2,070 pairs of *culottes de peau* for *dragons* and *cavalerie*, 14,682 infantry *bonnets de police*, 17,821 infantry *chapeaux*, 210 *cavalerie chapeaux*, 207 dragoon

This grenadier is dressed in something approaching the regulation *capote*. No regulation existed for its colour or appearance, but we know from archive documents they were single breasted and made from beige or grey broadcloth or *tricot*. (*Collection KM*)

Blackened cowhide was officially sanctioned to replace buff leather. The last of the black items of equipment were taken out of use in the period of peace between the battles of Austerlitz and Jena. (*Collection KM*)

helmets, 975 *schakos*, 26,733 *redingotes* for the infantry, as well as 26,733 infantry *gibernes* with 2,652 belts, 13 *cavalerie gibernes*, 397 light cavalry *gibernes*, 387 *porte-carabines*, 740 *baudriers*, 2,953 pairs of boots for the *hussards* and *chasseurs*, 460 pairs of dragoon boots, 62,683 shirts, 109,692 pairs of shoes, 26,773 pairs of grey gaiters, 28,113 pairs of black twill gaiters, 26,734 *sacs à distribution* and 2,953 pairs of underwear amongst other items. It is interesting that *casques* were still in use by the end of 1799 for the infantry, stores holding 578 of them.

To make the new *habits*, the army needed 903m scarlet broadcloth, 53,329m white *serge* and 8,569m linen. The central magazine for the army held 10,932m 50 blue broadcloth, 546m 60 white broadcloth, 340m 40 scarlet broadcloth, 16,397m blue *tricot*, 23,233m 80 white *serge*, 14,381m 8 blue *serge* and 13,448m linen. Of the required materials, just 2,733m blue broadcloth, 136m 60 white broadcloth, 85m 10 scarlet broadcloth, 4,099m blue *tricot*, 5,808m 7 white *serge*, 3,597m 90 blue *serge* and 3,362m linen had been obtained.

This grenadier, for some reason, has picked up a *cavalerie sabre* rather than his infantry-style weapon. The image nicely captures the shabby and idiosyncratic appearance of the army in the 1790s. (*Collection KM*)

An officer wearing a close approximation of the uniform according to the regulations of 1794. (*Collection KM*)

The Army of the Rhine was commanded by General Moreau by the start of January 1800. Moreau noted that, as a minimum, his army needed 82,653 infantry *habits*, 41,378 as replacements and 41,275 for conscripts joining the *demi-brigades*. Of the garments needed, 45,022 were in the depot and 19,300 were being made leaving a shortfall of 18,331 *habits*. His army, for immediate use, needed 16,598 *vestes*, 81,416 pairs of *tricot culottes*, 1,519 *bonnets de police*, 27,632 *chapeaux*, as well as 6,560 *gibernes*, 8,073 *giberne* belts and 81 *baudriers*. The depot held 44,271 *redingotes* to be issued.[64] From this, we learn that huge numbers of double-breasted greatcoats were in use long before their official sanction in 1804 or March 1806. Again, regulations were reactionary to confirm the current practice.

The depot in Belfort, which supplied the Army of the Danube, held 26 infantry *habits*, 55 artillery *habits*, 6 *chasseur surtrouts*, 5 *pelisses* (short fur-lined or fur-trimmed jackets), 6 *dolmans*, 489 *redingotes*, 713 infantry *vestes*, 293 blue light infantry *vestes*, 36 artillery *vestes*, 1,025 pairs of infantry *culottes*, 295 pairs of light infantry *pantalons* made from blue *tricot*, 2 pairs of *culottes hongroise* (tight-fitting, ankle length riding breeches, frequently decorated with cloth tape on the side seam and fall-front opening), 3 pairs of *pantalons*

This fusilier has both a regulation *capote* and blackened cowhide equipment. He could be marching to the Battle of Marengo or even the Battle of Austerlitz dressed in such a manner. (*Collection KM*)

Dressed in his greatcoat and hands stuffed into a lady's muff, this grenadier is clearly keeping himself warm in winter 1798/1799.

An officer of an unknown *demi-brigade circa* 1800. (*Musée de l'Empéri, collections du Musée de l'armée, Anciennes collections Jean et Raoul Brunon*)

in blue broadcloth, 1,056 infantry *chapeaux*, 222 infantry *casques*, 421 *schakos* and 26 *bonnets de police*. Materials in the depot included 18m 76 blue broadcloth, 32m 08 white broadcloth, 439m 32 blue *serge*, 105m 01 scarlet *serge* and 62m 13 crimson *serge* amongst other items. Not a single bearskin, plume or pair of *epaulettes* are listed.[65]

Led by Moreau, the army won a stunning victory at the Battle of Hohenlinden on 3 December 1800. The battle secured peace with Austria and Great Britain. It also cemented Napoléon in power and led Moreau to his exile in opposition to Napoléon rolling back democratic gains of the Revolution as he changed from elected head of state to military dictator.

Drawn from life in 1800 by German artist Wilhelm Kolbe is this group of French infantry wearing a motley collection of civilian and army-issue clothing.

Moreau has been branded a traitor, but he genuinely believed in a different vision of society to that of Napoléon. Napoléon silenced his critiques through exile, hardly the hallmark of an enlightened ruler. Moreau, like Bernadotte, was no traitor for voicing political opinion in opposition to Napoléon, yet this pernicious slander remains. Serving under Moreau, 2 future marshals were in action, General Michel Ney and General Emmanuel de Grouchy. Another in Moreau's sphere was General Charles-Pierre Augereau, again a future marshal, who reported on 4 December 1800 that they had requisitioned from Augsburg 3,365 *redingotes* and from Munich 2,500 *redingotes*, some 5,865 examples. Of these, 500 were issued to the *103ᵉ*, 500 to the *51ᵉ* and 500 to the *23ᵉ*, and 500 to the *15ᵉ Demi-Brigade*. The *10ᵉ* and *36ᵉ* were also issued 500 *redingotes* and 2,600m cloth that had been requisitioned and passed to the workshops to produce more *redingotes* to clothe the army.[66]

An unknown officer of a *demi-brigade* wearing the undress *surtout*. This image captures perfectly the period hairstyle: cropped short on the top of the head and worn long at the nape of the neck as a mullet tied into a queue.

The Army of the Rhine was reviewed on *1 Ventôse AnIX* (20 February 1801), Moreau lambasted Berthier in the Ministry of War for failing to support his operations on the river Rhine and reported that his army had received no new clothing since *1 Vendémiaire AnVIII* (23 September 1799). He added that he had recourse to clothe his men from the reserves of the Army of the Danube where they existed. Moreau further added that he had been forced to requisition cloth and materials from Württemberg and Strasburg (in Germany) and distributed to the corps commanders to make replacement clothing as needed. Due to Berthiers reluctance to send clothing Moreau reported that he had been forced to requisition several thousand *redingotes*.[67] Such harsh criticisms of Napoléon's beloved Berthier won him no friends in Paris. Napoléon – and his supporters ever since – have blackened Moreau's name. The facts are that oppositional politics is not treason and without Moreau, the Battle of Marengo could very easily have been reversed and Napoléon removed from power.

Demi-Brigades d'Infanterie de Ligne 103

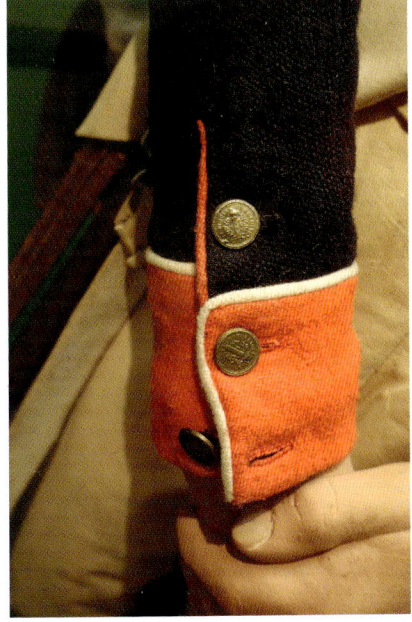

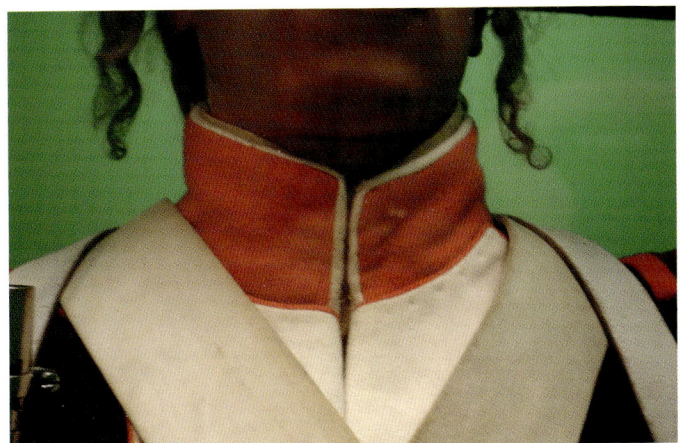

This mannequin, created from original items and recreated uniform *habits*, gives an excellent impression of a soldier at the end of the 1790s. (*Musée de l'Empéri, collections du Musée de l'armée, Anciennes collections Jean et Raoul Brunon*)

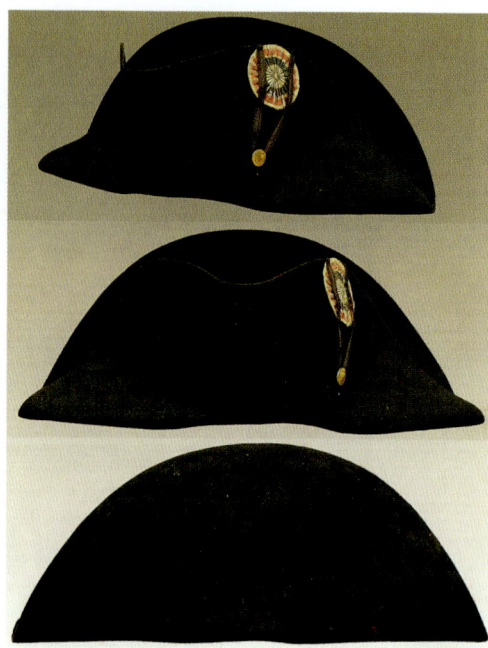

An excellently preserved *chapeau* respecting the 1799 reforms of General Jean-Baptiste Bernadotte. It is larger than the earlier models. It was cheap to make, outweighing its lack of head protection.

It is undeniable that thanks to Bernadotte's reforms of *AnVIII* (1799 to 1800), which enabled the mass production of clothing, along with requisitioning i.e. theft, the army was kept clothed on campaign. Away from their regimental depots, regiments had no means of production other than spending the clothing fund locally to buy materials and pay local tradesmen, often at highly inflated prices. To offset these issues, the army became reliant on the centralised depot system and the requisitioning of materials, and captured enemy stores in order to keep the army clothed and fed. Napoléon inherited what was in many senses, Bernadotte's military machine.

Chapter 5

Chasseurs à Pied

The French army had no light infantry elements officially until 8 August 1784 when 6 battalions of *Chasseurs à Pied* were created, each battalion comprising 4 companies, each of 104 rank and file and 1 drummer, commanded by a captain aided by 4 *sous-lieutenants*. The uniform was as outlined to be the same as the line infantry with the regulations of 1779: the *habit* was green, lined in white *serge*. The *vestes* and *culottes* – actually cut to be ankle length *pantalons* – were likewise *chamois*. They wore a Corsican-style hat with a turned-up brim on one side. Drummers wore a blue *habit* with the King's Livery adornment, with battalion facing colour distinctives for the *revers*, collar and cuffs. Each of the 6 battalions had distinctive facings piped in green: 1e *Bataillon Chasseurs des Alpes* – scarlet, 2e *Bataillon Chasseurs des Pyrénées* – crimson, 3e *Bataillon Chasseurs des Vosges* – yellow, 4e *Bataillon Chasseurs des Cévennes* – *chamois* (buff), 5e *Bataillon Chasseurs du Gévaudan* – aurore and 6e *Bataillon Chasseurs des Ardennes* – white.

The *Chasseurs à Pied* were to serve alongside *Chasseurs à Cheval* as a mixed corps of light troops. Both mounted and dismounted men had a white stock, a pair of white linen parade gaiters, a pair in black linen and a third pair in black twill, a *ceinturon baudrier* for the *sabre* to be worn over the shoulder or at the waist, and a goatskin *havresac*, as well as a *giberne* and belt.[1]

However, the 2 elements were separated into distinctive arms on 1 October 1786. The regulations stated the following:

> THE Uniform clothing suit of *sous-officiers*, Foot *Chasseurs* & Horse *Chasseurs*, will be composed of a *habit* of dark green broadcloth, lined with *serge* or cadis of the distinctive colour laid down for each regiment; of a *veste* of dark green broadcloth, lined in white *serge* or cadis; & of breeches of similar green broadcloth, lined in linen.
>
> The *habit* and *veste* will be, with the exception that the *habit* will not have figured pockets to the tails, absolutely identical, as to the design & positions of the buttons, to those of the Infantry. The turnbacks [decorated portion of the tails of a coat] of the *habits* of Foot & Horse *Chasseurs* will be trimmed with a hunting horn in green broadcloth; & the *epaulettes*, which will have between upper & the lining by a plate of flat sheet iron, will be in white wool, ornamented with lozenges with the distinctive colour.
>
> Breeches of Foot *Chasseurs*, will be made as *pantalons* form, descending to four *pouces* above the ankle; the side will be open, to start from the spot where the garterstrap is usually, & will close by six small buttons.

The breeches of Horse *Chasseurs* will be made in Hungarian style; the openings, vents & side seams will be trimmed by a flat woollen tape, four *lignes* wide, & of the colour of the breeches ... Apart from the parts of regimental clothes above, each *sous-officier* & Horse *Chasseur*, will be provided with a *surtrout* & waistcoat of broadcloth, such as they are established for the Cavalry & Dragoons, by the 1st. article of chapter IV, of this Regulation.

The *manteaux* [cloak] for the mounted *Chasseurs*, will be of green broadcloth dyed in piece, fabricated & prepared with two wrong sides; the front will not be faced at all.[2]

An officer of *Chasseurs de Lorraine* wearing a uniform according to the regulations of 1788. This is one of the few images we have of French light infantry before 1794.

The iron plate in the *epaulettes* provided, perhaps, a modicum of protection to the shoulder from sword cuts. Headdress was to be the infantry *chapeaux*, but of slightly smaller proportions. They carried infantry equipment and weapons. The *Chasseurs à Cheval* were armed with a *fusil de dragon* (short musket used by dragoons), and carried a dragoon-model *sabre*. They carried the *sabre* from a dragoon waistbelt and used *hussards*'-style *gibernes*. Headdress was a dragoon-style cooper helmet. Rather than white stocks, *chasseurs* in both arms had black stocks, the *Chasseurs à Pied* only had black twill and blackened line gaiters to 'come up only to the middle of the calf, by which they will resemble the Hussar[-]style boots in cut & the upper design; they will be opened on the side in the usual way, will close by ten small buttons.'[3] The men were to wear their hair in a queue rather than the *cadogan* (clubbed and queued). How far this regulation was implemented is not known, given officially, it was not sanctioned until November 1788. Despite this, we note that on 17 March 1788, a further 6 battalions were created:

Chasseurs à Pied 107

An officer and men of the *Chasseurs de Lorraine* wearing a uniform according to the regulations of 1788, modified with the addition of the 1791 helmet. It is very likely that this uniform was worn until the creation of *demi-brigades* in February 1793 dressed in blue rather than green. The *surtout* was confirmed with the decree of 1 November 1789, to be phased in over three years, the last new garment being made in 1792.

1ᵉ Bataillon Chasseurs Royaux du Dauphiné
2ᵉ Bataillon Chasseurs Royaux de Provence
3ᵉ Bataillon Chasseurs Royaux de Corse
4ᵉ Bataillon Chasseurs Corse
5ᵉ Bataillon Chasseurs Cantabres
6ᵉ Bataillon Chasseurs Bretons
7ᵉ Bataillon Chasseurs d'Auvergne
8ᵉ Bataillon Chasseurs des Vosges
9ᵉ Bataillon Chasseurs des Cévennes
10ᵉ Bataillon Chasseurs du Gévaudan
11ᵉ Bataillon Chasseurs des Ardennes
12ᵉ Bataillon Chasseurs de Roussillon

Each battalion had 4 companies, each comprising 6 officers and 102 men; namely, 1 sergeant major, 1 *fourrier*, 4 sergeants, 8 corporals, 8 chosen men, 2 drummers, 12 *carabiniers* and 66 *chasseurs*. The uniform became green, piped in *chamois*, with green facings and lining the *veste* and *culottes* became *chamois*. The men adopted the same *chapeaux* as the line. Mythos suggests the *chasseurs* were recruited from 'mountain men', but as noted Napoléonic author Terry Crowdy states,

> The battalion inspection reports of 1788 provide some interesting information on the first formation of independent battalions. The idea they were somehow formed of mountain men from the wilder provinces really has taken hold over the centuries. In fact, of the five battalions which were permitted flexibility of recruitment, their composition was quite diverse. The *Chasseurs* of [*des*] *Cévennes* did have their largest number of men from the Languedoc, but Ardennes had many men from Provence. The *Chasseurs* of [*de*] *Roussillon* had just four natives from that region. We should not therefore think of these battalions are having a regional composition. The majority (56%) described themselves as having a skilled trade or as townsfolk (including manufacturers of luxury goods). While agricultural labourers make up the largest single worker represented, they were as a group statistically in the minority. It is interesting to note the number of cordwainers (manufacturers of shoes) and tailors in the battalions (11%); these skilled soldiers may have found additional work manufacturing uniforms and would have been prized recruits.[4]

Each battalion was allowed a band of 4 musicians to play trumpets or horns, to be augmented by *enfants de troupe* (children of soldiers in the regiment) aged at least 14, who would play the fife (*fifre*). Likewise, each company was to have 12 marksmen – *carabiniers* – chosen from the tallest men in the company, and were to be trained to be 'crack shots'.[5]

Regulations in Practice

How the regulations were put into reality differed from regiment to regiment. The ordinance of 17 March 1788, creating the *Chasseurs de Roussillon*, mentions they will be armed, equipped and uniformed like the other light infantry battalions, but with several differences 'relative to the national costume of the inhabitants of the mountains and valleys of Roussillon'. Likewise, the *Bataillon Chasseurs des Cantabres* were to wear national costume of the *Cantabrians* and other inhabitants of the *Chasseurs des Pyrenees*.[6] Alas, the precise nature of these regional variations is not recorded. What follows is a review of the extant data.

1ᵉ Bataillon

The first inspection of the *Bataillon de Chasseurs Royaux du Dauphiné* (future *1ᵉ Légère*) was on 18 August 1788. Of the 365 men under arms, 10 had served for over 21 years, 12 for over 14 years, 38 for over 8 years and 72 for over 4 years, leaving 233 men with under 4 years' service. The majority of the men all had professional trades prior to enlistment:

The left-hand figure is wearing a green habit with white facings, as regulated for the *Chasseurs des Ardennes* in 1786. We know many regiments used a mix and match of different regulations, so seeing a light infantry soldier in green alongside another in the nationalised blue uniform with infantry helmet accurately reflects the archive documents. The *Chasseurs des Ardennes* has white *culottes* – again regulation wear from 1 November 1789.

15 were rural agricultural labourers, 29 had been shoemakers, 18 had been tailors, 5 had been wheelwrights and 4 bakers for example. In terms of demographics, 26 were from Alsace, 7 from Spain, 19 originated in Lombardy, 20 from Naples, 48 from Nice, 140 from Piedmont, 12 from Rome, 47 from Tuscany and 9 from Venice. Just 14 men came from the Dauphiné. Over 50 per cent of the regiment's clothing was made to the regulations of 1786 with 213 uniforms in accordance with the regulations of 1786 – with green *vestes* and *pantalons* – and 208 uniforms with *chamois vestes* and *pantalons*. The inspector ordered 135 new *habits*, 135 *chamois vestes*, 415 pairs of *chamois pantalons* and

A group of senior officers from *circa* 1795 to 1800. The officer in the background wears a waist sash into which he has tucked a pistol.

The rear view of a *Chasseusr à Cheval* soldier in green and to his right, dressed in blue, presumably a trumpeter of the *Chasseurs à Cheval*.

An *aide-de-camp* to the *general en chef* signified by the white over red *brassard*, which matches the waist sash of an officer of this rank.

209 *chapeaux* made in the course of 1789. Despite the regiment being a matter of months old in August 1788, given that it was equipped with old items from government stores, it is no surprise to note that 3 *bas-officers'* (sergeants, *fourriers* or sergeant majors) *gibernes* needed repairs and 8 needed replacing. Likewise, 42 *gibernes* and 22 *ceinturons* needed to be replaced.[7]

2ᵉ *Bataillon*

On the morning of 20 October 1788, the *Chasseurs Royaux de Provence* (future 2ᵉ *Légère*) were drawn up for inspection. The inspection records that 212 complete uniforms were made to the regulations of 1786 and dated from 1787, and 213 complete uniforms had been made in 1788. Needed as replacements in the course of 1789 were 213 *habits*, 213 *chamois vestes*, 425 pairs of *chamois pantalons* and 213 *chapeaux*. Seemingly, all of the 398 men on parade carried a *sabre*: 83 *ceinturons* were in good condition and 334 needed replacing.[8]

Inspected again on 6 October 1790, the inspector noted that the men who joined the regiment were of 'a bad sort, a great number are deserters or bad subjects'. He added, 'the recently received recruits are generally of a bad sort, 68 have disappeared since the last review, there are just 38 who are very distinguished'. Looking at the 299 men under arms, 9 men had served for 21 years, 14 had served over 14 years, 37 had served for over 8 years, 109 had served for 4 years, the remainder – 130 men – less than 4 years. The majority of the men previously had professional trades before enlisted: 98 men with trades and 87 labourers, of which 27 were urban workers. Of those with trades, we note 25 shoemakers, 16 masons, 10 wigmakers or hairdressers, 9 bakers, 9 tailors, 8 tanners and 5 farriers amongst other trades. The men's clothing was 'in bad condition' reported the inspector. We observe 54 *habits* dated from 1788, 100 from 1789 and 145 had been made during 1790, with 141 needed to be made during 1791, along with 141 *vestes*, 425 pairs of *pantalons* and 212 *chapeaux*. Again, we find *ceinturons* in use rather than *baudriers*.[9]

3ᵉ *Bataillon*

No archive records can be found at the time of writing.

4ᵉ *Bataillon*

The *Bataillon de Chasseurs Corse* (the future 4ᵉ *Légère*) was inspected on 6 September 1789. The inspection reports, 27 *habits* dated from 1787 with a further 230 *habits* issued between 1788 and 1789, and 144 green examples issued in 1789 to the regulations of 1788. The inspector ordered all the 1786-model *habits* – 297 – to be replaced in the course of 1790. He ordered 213 *chamois vestes* to be produced and 441 pairs of green *culottes* to be replaced with *chamois pantalons*. He also ordered the production of 223 new *chapeaux*. We note *carabiniers* and *bas-officiers* carried their *sabres* from *ceinturons*. The

Seated are two light infantry soldiers wearing the blue national uniform. The standing figures are enigmatic.

8 drummers' *habits* were to be renewed and 2 new drums and carriages purchased. As the regiment was recruited from Corsica, it is no surprise to find 383 Corsicans in the regiment, but we do note 4 Germans, 1 Flemmings/Flemish (Dutch), 10 Italians and 1 Austrian. For a regiment less than a year old, it had a proportion of veteran soldiers: 1 man had served for over 21 years, 27 for 14 years or more, 74 for 8 years, 143 had served between 4 and 8 years, and 172 for under 4 years. Before joining up, we note 374 men had been agricultural labourers, 2 had been bakers, 12 shoemakers, 6 knifemakers, 3 wigmakers, 10 tailors, 3 wood turners and just one man was an urban labourer.[10]

Lucien Rousselot's reconstruction of a *Chasseurs des Ardennes* soldier based on documentation in the Bibliotheque Nationales de France. (*Musée de l'Armée*)

A pair of light infantry soldiers drawn by Lucien Rousselot based on notes in the Bibliotheque Nationales de France. (*Musée de l'Armée*)

5ᵉ Bataillon

Inspected for the first time on 8 September 1788, the *Bataillon Chasseurs des Cantabres* (future 5ᵉ *Légère*). The inspector was incredulous, 'For an inexplicable reason the newly made clothing for the regiment has been produced not from green cloth, but from blue. I have ordered the prefecture to charge the merchant to exchange the blue broadcloth with green.' We note, 100 blue *habits*, 100 blue *vestes* and 309 pairs of blue *pantalons* were in use. We also note, 88 *habits* and 74 *vestes* had been made as far back as 1785 and had lingered in stores. Indeed, 92 *habits* and 836 *vestes* dated from 1786, and 94 *habits* and 100 *vestes* dated from 1787. Presumably, drawn from a stockpile of unissued uniforms. During the course of 1789, the inspector ordered 217 green *habits* to be made with 217 *chamois vestes* and 425 pairs of *chamois pantalons* and 100 *chapeaux*. Contrary to regulations, the unit had 4 *sapeur*-issued axes, axe cases and belts, as well as aprons. Again, we find 162 *ceinturons* in use rather than the expected *baudriers*. Of the 309 men under arms, 3 had served previously for over 21 years, 8 for over 14 years, 36 for over 8 years and 125 for over 4 years. In terms of their background, 137 were agricultural labourers and 90 were urban labourers. Of those who had trades prior to enlistment we report 7 bakers, 8 carpenters, 18 shoemakers, 4 farriers, 8 masons, 6 wood turners, 10 wigmakers or hairdressers, 1 saddler, 2 knifemakers, 16 tailors and 2 tanners.[11] On 11 August 1789, the unit was still waiting for its replacement green and *chamois* clothing: 131 *habits* were needed, 123 *chamois vestes*, 425 pairs of *chamois pantalons* and 335 *chapeaux*. Clearly, supply was slow and difficult.[12]

6ᵉ *Bataillon*

The *Bataillon des Chasseurs Bretons* (future *6ᵉ Légère*) was inspected 4 October 1788. Dressed entirely in blue with what surely were stock piled line infantry uniforms: 90 had been made in 1786, 100 in 1787 and 124 during the course of 1788. Some 201 new *habits* were needed in the course of 1789, along with 425 *chamois gilets* and 266 pairs of *chamois culottes*. Furthermore, it was noted that 266 new *chapeaux* were also needed. The regiment was formed around a cadre of veterans: 4 had served for over 21 years, 27 for over 14 years, 44 for over 8 years and 31 for 4 to 8 years. Prior to enlistment, 165 of the 319 men had been agricultural labourers, 5 had been bakers, 17 shoemakers, 4 farriers, 7 masons, 6 wood turners, 8 wigmakers and hairdressers, 8 knifemakers, 23 tailors and 1 surgeon amongst other trades. Some 69 men were urban labourers.[13]

Reviewed again on 24 September 1789, the inspector noted 137 *habits* needed replacing – we note 65 *habits* and 100 *vestes* had been made in 1787, and 118 *habits* and 180 *vestes* in 1788 prior to adoption of *chamois vestes* and *culottes*. The unit must have looked very mixed indeed. Again, despite the regulations of 1786 abolishing the *ceinturons* in favour of the *baudriers*, clearly the army had a stockpile of thousands of *ceinturons* – the *Bataillon des Chasseurs Bretons* had 404 *ceinturons* in use and needed 21 replacing as damaged beyond repair.[14]

7ᵉ *Battalion*

On 3 October 1788, the newly formed *Chasseurs d'Auvergne* (future *7ᵉ Légère*) was inspected. As with the other battalions, a lot of the clothing was new from stockpiles: 107 *habits* had been made in 1786, 106 in 1787 and 122 since the formation of the battalion. We note 213 *habits* were scheduled to be replaced during 1789. Also to be replaced were 213 green *vestes* in favour of *chamois* examples, and 425 pairs of *chamois pantalons* were to be issued, along with 266 *chapeaux*. We note 276 *ceinturons* were in use, 26 needed repairs and 16 replacing. Concerning the 316 men under arms, 11 had served previously for over 21 years, 37 for over 14 years, 43 for over 8 years and 40 for over 4 years. The men

Drawn from life by Wilhelm Kolbe in 1800 is this pair of light infantry, both sporting non-regulation *mirlitons*.

were drawn almost exclusively from unskilled labourers: 121 from agricultural trades and 108 from urban workers. Some men before enlistment previously had trades, we note 4 bakers, 10 carpenters or wheelwrights, 14 shoemakers, 6 farriers, 14 masons, 11 wood turners, 4 wigmakers or hairdressers, 8 knifemakers, 12 tailors and 4 tanners.[15]

Inspected again on 25 July 1789, 141 green *vestes* remained in service, the requested 425 pairs of *chamois pantalons* had still to arrive and 425 *chapeaux* were needed.[16]

Reported to be the *17ᵉ Demi-Brigade Légère* observed somewhere in Germany, we see a mix of buff leather and blackened cowhide equipment. The bandsman in the background has sky blue facings.

8ᵉ *Bataillon*

The *Chasseurs des Vosges* was reviewed on 23 September 1788. The battalion mustered 318 men, of which 2 men had served for over 21 years, 27 for 14 years or more, 49 had served for over 8 years and 25 for at least 4 years. In terms of background, 146 were unemployed urban labourers and 102 unemployed agricultural labourers. The remainder were artisans, who had enlisted again to escape unemployment. We note 15 shoemakers, 11 tailors, 7 bakers and 8 wigmakers or hairdressers all of whom would have found beneficial employment in their unit utilising these trades. The men's *habits* and *vestes* had been issued in 3 lots of 106 from 1786. The *pantalons* and *chapeaux* were issued in 2 batches of 159 dating to 1787 and 1788. The review authorised 213 *habits* and *vestes* to replace those of the regulations of 1786, and 266 pairs of *chamois pantalons* and 266 *chapeaux*, as well as 100 *gibernes* and belts, 133 musket slings, 129 *ceinturons*, and 4 drums and carriages to replace those in bad condition.[17]

9ᵉ Battalion

Inspected on 26 September 1788, the *9ᵉ Bataillon Chasseurs des Cévennes* (future *9ᵉ Légère*), mustered 300 men. Just 3 men had served for over 21 years, 35, however, had served for over 14 years, 27 had served for over 8 years and 40 for at least 4 years. In terms of demographics, the majority were unemployed agricultural labourers, some 127 men. Of the others, they all previously had a professional trade, except 7 urban labourers. We find among the different artisans who joined, 10 shoemakers, 9 masons, 14 knifemakers, 14 tailors, 5 hairdressers, 5 bakers, 4 carpenters, as well as 1 farrier and 1 surgeon. In terms of area of recruitment, the battalion counted 32 men from Alsace, 36 from the Franche-Comté, 71 from the Languedoc, 14 Normans and 12 Parisians. In terms of clothing, 187 *habits* were made to the regulations of 1786, and 131 to that of 1788, with 87 *habits* needed for 1789. Likewise, 207 *vestes* were of the regulations of 1786, but only 126 were to be renewed in 1789. The men's *culottes* and *chapeaux* were entirely of the regulations of 1786, with 50 per cent to be replaced, along with 94 *gibernes* and belts, 88 musket slings, 109 *ceinturons* and 4 drums and carriages.[18] Rather more than 159 pairs of *pantalons* were issued in 1789, 333 pairs were made and issued, with all of the 415 pairs in use to be replaced in the course of 1790, along with 195 *habits* and 175 *vestes*, a further 95 *gibernes* and belts, 98 musket slings and 114 *ceinturons*.[19]

10ᵉ Bataillon

The *Chasseurs du Gévaudan* were inspected on 30 September 1788. The overall appearance of the men was considered 'very military' but the uniforms themselves were 'mediocre, the equipment is in passable condition'. Of the 337 men under arms, we note 4 had served for over 21 years, 12 had served for over 14 years and 44 for over 8 years. Looking at the demographics of the men, the majority were former agricultural labourers – 173. The remainder were all artisans and 80 urban labourers. Of those with trades we note 15 shoemakers, 9 masons, 11 wood turners, 8 wigmakers or hairdressers, 5 saddlers, 4 knifemakers, 13 tailors and 4 tanners amongst others. In terms of background, 25 were Alsatian, 57 from Bourgogne, 14 from Champagne, 27 from Flanders, 44 from the Franche-Comté, 51 the Languedoc, 25 from Picardie, 13 Normans and 6 were Parisians. Interestingly for us, the unit was not wearing the felt *chapeaux*, but a *Chasseur à Cheval* headdress taken from stores, as had a lot of the clothing issued to the men: a green *habit* with *chamois* facings.[20] The *Chasseur à Cheval* helmet had been replaced by 20 September 1789 with 425 regulation *chapeaux*, although some old *Chasseur à Cheval habits* remained in service to be replaced during 1790.[21]

Two members of an unknown light infantry unit with blackened-cowhide cross belts.

A drum major and drummers of an unknown light infantry unit. Of interest is the simplicity of the uniforms. Drummer boys were tolerated in the army as long as they were over the age of 14.

11ᵉ Bataillon

Inspected on 25 October 1788, the *Bataillon de Chasseurs des Ardennes* mustered 28 officers, 9 officers and men on the *etat-major* – including 4 bandsmen and 337 other ranks. Since the unit had been formed, 7 men had died and 54 had deserted. Notably, 2 *sous-officiers* had been promoted to officers – yes promotion from the ranks existed before the Revolution as we observed with the *ligne*. We note, 24 men has passed to the *Chasseurs à Cheval*. For a unit named Ardennes, 49 men came from Provence, 44 from the Franche-Comté, 7 from Alsace, 27 the Languedoc, 3 were Parisian and 20 Normans. We note 5 were from Flanders. The battalion was formed around a nucleus of veterans: 4 men had served for over 21 years, 20 over 14 years, 40 for over 8 years and 22 for over 4 years. In terms of background, 124 men were agricultural workers and the same number urban workers and labourers. Of men with trades, we note 13 shoemakers, 11 tailors, 18 masons, 7 surgeons, 14 wigmakers or hairdressers, 9 wood turners, 7 knifemakers, 6 carpenters, 5 bakers, 6 tanners and a solitary farrier and saddler. Their clothing was from 3 issues dates: 104 uniforms from 1786, 108 from 1787 and 106 from 1788. During the course of 1789, 212 *habits*, 212 *vestes*, 266 pairs of *pantalons* and 266 *chapeaux* were needed, as well as 105 *gibernes* and belts, 129 *ceinturons*, and 4 drums and carriages.[22] A document from 23 June 1788 reports that 'there exists a great variety in the *vestes* and *culottes*, the difference needs to be resolved'. Repairing clothing in use was estimated at 546 francs 9 centimes, and to repair equipment some 202 francs.[23] On 21 July 1789, the unit's clothing was described as being in good condition, but the unit's drill and manoeuvres were noted as being poor. Of the 107 new entrants, 68 were considered 'very good' and the others as 'exceptionally mediocre' in stature and aptitude. It is remarkable that even before the wars of Napoléon, France was already lacking in a pool of intelligent and healthy men to take up arms. The recruits were all urban poor, unemployed labourers. During 1790, 106 *habits* and *vestes* were needed, as well as 425 pairs of *chamois pantalons*, 159 *chapeaux*, 16 *ceinturons*, and 4 *gibernes* and belts.[24]

12ᵉ Bataillon

The *Chasseurs de Roussillon* were reviewed on 11 June 1788. We note at the time of the review, 139 of their 232 men (60 per cent) were foreign nationals. The next most represented French provinces are Franche-Comté at 8.8 per cent and Burgundy at 6.7 per cent. In terms of experience, 4 men had served for over 21 years, 11 for over 14 years, 22 for over 8 years, and 89 for 4 to 8 years. In terms of background, of the French nationals, 45 were unemployed agricultural

Dressed in a uniform according to the regulations of 1801 is this *chasseur* of light infantry.

Drawn from life by Geissler is this group of light infantry somewhere in Germany.

labourers, 20 had been shoemakers, 14 tailors, 6 had been masons, 3 had been wood turners, and the same number wigmakers and knifemakers. The uniforms were described as in 'extremely bad condition, the items of clothing and equipment recovered from magazines are old, every item needs some form of repairs'. Indeed, during 1789, every piece of clothing was scheduled to be repaired.[25] This clothing was, indeed, issued during

This sergeant's *habit* is of the type used by the light infantry from 1794, albeit with slight changes to the cut, until the adoption of Bardin Regulation from summer 1814. (*Musée de l'Empéri, collections du Musée de l'armée, Anciennes collections Jean et Raoul Brunon*)

1789, but it still left 161 *habits*, 132 *vestes*, 425 pairs of *pantalons*, 167 *chapeaux* and 92 *ceinturons* needed as replacements.[26]

Regulations of 1791

The regulations of April 1791 state unit names were to be abolished in favour of numbers. The decree also outlined that the battalions were to wear a green *habit* with piping in distinctive colour, along with the piping to the pockets on the tails, collar and cuffs: *1ᵉ–3ᵉ* – scarlet, *4ᵉ–6ᵉ* – yellow, *7ᵉ– 9ᵉ* – rose and *10ᵉ–12ᵉ* – crimson.

The cuffs were fastened by flaps, with 3 or 4 buttons. The *chasseurs* wore the infantry helmet. The *chasseurs* wore a white sleeved *veste*, the *carabiniers* had green. The legwear comprised green *culottes*, black twill gaiters and natural linen. One major change was the abandonment of *ceinturons* in favour of *baudriers*. Drummers wore blue *habits* adorned with the Royalist Livery. Livery was abolished in September 1792.

Change took time, especially given the political and economic turbulence France was experiencing. Word count prevents a complete review of all the battalions, so we offer a 'snap shot' of the various units.

5ᵉ Battalion

Inspected on 24 May 1792, the battalion mustered 418 men: incredibly the unit had just 2 drummers. In terms of background, 3 men had served for over 21 years and 8 men for over 14 years. The vast majority, 336 men had served for under 4 years and were overwhelmingly unemployed agricultural labourers, though we do find 35 shoemakers, 24 bakers, 18 wheelwrights, 18 wood turners, 13 wigmakers or hairdressers, 16 tailors and 6 tanners. The inspector noted that immediate needs of clothing and equipment were 143 *habits*, 143 *vestes*, 693 pairs of *pantalons* and 125 *chapeaux*. All the *ceinturons* were to be replaced with *baudriers* and added that unit stores held 300 *chapeaux* for immediate issue. The requested clothing arrived on 24 February 1793 along with 268 helmets. Clearly, *chapeaux* and helmets were in use side by side.[27]

6ᵉ Bataillon

Drawn up for review on 31 December 1791, regimental needs for 1792 comprised 143 new *habits*, including new garments for the drummers, the same number of *vestes*, 693 pairs of *pantalons*, 693 helmets, 21 *gibernes* and belts and 21 *ceinturons*. No man had yet received the new regulation *habit* with yellow distinctives.[28]

7ᵉ Bataillon

Inspected on 26 December 1791, the unit mustered 429 other ranks, and the inspector noted during the course of 1792, 143 *habits*, 143 *vestes*, 693 pairs of *culottes*, 1 *sous-officiers' giberne*, and 20 other ranks *gibernes* and belts were needed. The unit still used *ceinturons* and had not adopted the helmet or other provisions in accordance with the regulations of April 1791.[29]

8ᵉ Bataillon

Reviewed on 13 February 1792, every man on parade was wearing a *chapeau* and carried their *sabre* from a *ceinturon*. No man had received a new regulation uniform, the unit needed 438 *habits* with rose distinctives, 371 *vestes*, 787 pairs of *culottes* and 386 *chapeaux*. Also needed were 7 *sous-officier gibernes* with belts, 283 other ranks examples with belts and 546 *ceinturons*.[30]

Chapter 6

The *Légère* is Born

The *amalgame* of *21 Nivôse AnII* (10 January 1794) witnessed the incorporation of the 15 battalions of light infantry united with free corps, to form 15 *demi-brigades légère*. Not long after the *carabiniers* were taken from each company and formed into their own elite company per battalion under the decree of *9 Pluviôse AnII* (28 January 1794). Rather than green, the men were to wear national uniform: blue clothing and brass buttons, the same as the infantry *demi-brigades*. The *habits* were to have short tails and pointed *revers*, the collar and cuff flaps were scarlet, the latter piped blue, the *revers* were blue piped white as were the pockets to the tails. The *habit* was lined in blue *serge*. Distinctive facing colours were abolished in favour of regimental numbers on the buttons. *Carabiniers* were allowed a bearskin and a *chapeau*, as well as scarlet fringed *epaulettes*. The goal was to make each soldier the same: to create a corporate identity for the armed forces, and foster a sense of nation and belonging to the nation rather than regimental title and tradition. The helmet was replaced by a felt *chapeau*, which was the same as the line units.[1]

The decree of *11 Thermidor AnVII* (29 July 1799) confirmed the use of the short-tailed *habit* and the infantry *chapeau* as headdress.

One of the last acts of the directory was to consolidate the light infantry regiments. The decree of *23 Fructidor AnVII* (9 September 1799) consolidated the existing formations into 26 *demi-brigades* of 4 battalions, all this changed again with the decree of *9 Fructidor AnVIII* (27 August 1800), when 4 new *demi-brigades* were created by dissolving the third battalions in the 3e, 5e, 8e, 16e, 18e, 20e, 25e, 26e, 28e and 29e, and the manpower spread between the various *demi-brigades* to bring them up to strength.[2] This decree, however, seems to have taken some time for this to come into force as the third battalion of the 18e *Légère* was not wound up until over 18 months later.[3] The decree of *4 Brumaire AnX* (26 October 1801) introduced the *schako* to *légère* regiments. Made from card covered in felt, it measured 178mm in diameter and 217mm tall, with the cockade, and plume socket on the left side. Adopting the *schako* took time as our next section shows.

Regulations in Practice

Change of regulations took time, especially when the nation was in chaos. We now look at the various *légère demi-brigades* to assess the adaption of the regulations. Again, due to word count, time and cost, we present a 'snap shot' of randomly chosen units.

4ᵉ Légère

Reviewed on *19 Thermidor AnII* (6 August 1794), the unit mustered 2,243 other ranks, rather short of the theoretical strength of 3,025 men. Clothing was in very poor condition the inspector noted, 608 *habits* were worn out and 806 needed repairs. Likewise, 617 *gibernes* and belts needed replacing, 322 *gibernes* and belts needed repairs, 908 *sabres* were damaged beyond repair and 70 needed attention to make them serviceable as did 240 muskets.

6ᵉ Légère

Reviewed on *3 Frimaire AnVII* (23 November 1798), of the 2,231 *habits* in service, 534 needed repairs, 844 were life expired and needed replacing and 1,915 needed immediate replacement as fit only for rags. Of the 3,335 *vestes* in use, 2,462 needed replacing. Likewise, there was the same number of *culottes* in use and 2,428 pairs needed replacing. Every man – 3,335 – had a *chapeau*, but again huge numbers needed replacing: 3,259. The unit was in very poor shape indeed in terms of clothing, and over 50 per cent of the leather equipment needed total replacement, so too did the muskets and *sabres*.[4]

7ᵉ Légère

Reviewed on *7 Germinal AnII* (27 March 1794), the unit's clothing was 'in shreds'. For example, of the 1,165 men on parade, 475 men lacked a blue light infantry style *habit*, and of those in use 579 were worn out beyond repair – very likely the old *chasseur* green *habits* – 46 needed repairs and just 65 were considered serviceable. We also note, 275 men had no *veste*, 275 no *culottes*, 337 no *giberne* and belt, and 661 lacked a musket sling: the unit clearly had a lot of improvised clothing and equipment in use. Stores held a considerable amount of cloth and materials: 646 *aunes* half green broadcloth, 505 *aunes* blue broadcloth, 110 *aunes* rose broadcloth, 215 *aunes* white serge, 181 *aunes* white tricot, 308 *gibernes*, 325 *porte-gibernes*, 203 whitened buff leather *baudriers*, 272 blackened cowhide *baudriers*, 151 musket slings and 398 helmets.

Clearly, the unit had begun the process to swap to blue, but still held considerable quantities of materials to produce clothing in accordance with the regulations of 1791. White metal *chasseur* buttons were also used alongside copper *demi-brigade* items, and the inspector ordered the non-regulation items to be exchanged at the arsenal of Strasbourg.[5]

9ᵉ Légère

Inspected on *9 Prairial AnVII* (28 May 1799), the inspector noted that the *sous-officiers* were very conversant with the theory and application of the regulations concerning the internal administration of their company, the registers were well kept and the men were well trained and proficient in their manoeuvres. All in all, the *9ᵉ Légère* was one of the best regiments in the army. The men were well dressed. The inspector noted, the overall appearance was 'spectacular and brilliant', the men being 'all a good sort with good physique'. However – there is always a but in praise – the cloth used to make the uniforms was considered poor quality and the firearms in use were of different models.

Looking in detail, we note of 3,169 *habits* in service, 429 needed repairs and 1,559 total replacement: despite being old the *habits* were well kept. Likewise, 1,559 *vestes* were needed, 1,554 pairs of *pantalons*, 1,592 *chapeaux* and 2,866 *bonnets de police*. Everything was either new or worn out. A similar story is repeated with the equipment: of 3,169 *baudriers*, 1,988 needed replacement. Likewise, of 3,095 *gibernes*, 1,698 needed replacing along with their belts, as did 1,685 muskets and *bayonets*, and 1,989 *sabres*. The inspector ordered 429 *habits*, 429 *gilet*s and 1,615 pairs of *pantalons* to be made. No bearskins existed for the *carabinier* company.[6]

Inspected again on *18 Nivôse AnX* (8 January 1802), the inspector, Édouard Adolphe Casmir Joseph Mortier, noted that the officers were wearing their *chapeaux* at odd angles, and need to ensure that they were well placed on the eyebrows, adding the officers' boots were of different patterns/styles and further adding that many officers wore the belt plate under the flap of their *pantalons*, which was a habit 'to be stopped'. About the other ranks, the inspector remarked that the corporals used red rank stripes rather than the regulation yellow and the men's hair was not cut in the same manner, which had to be fastened into a queue, tied with a ribbon and held with a regimental pin as described in the regulations. Again, the inspector noted that the men were not wearing regulation black stocks, and that the *epaulettes* of the *carabiniers* and *chasseurs* were worn 'too far to the back of the shoulder'. Furthermore, he noted, the *habits* and *vestes* were badly kept and infrequently brushed – the regulations stated a *habit* had to be brushed each day – noting that for campaign use *pantalons* à *cheval* as used by the *hussards* were in service. Another fault found by the inspector was that many *giberne* belts were too long. How many of these 'issues' existed during the Battle of Marengo we cannot say. At the time of the *1 Vendémiaire AnIX* (23 September 1800) inspection, no sets of *sapeurs*' equipment existed, but 14 sets of axes with cases, and belt and aprons did by *AnX* (1801 to 1802). The *carabiniers* – and we assume the *sapeurs* also – had no bearskins and it is unlikely they had them at the Battle of Marengo.[7]

13ᵉ *Légère*

Reviewed on *6 Thermidor AnV* (24 July 1797), the unit had 93 officers, 3 surgeons, 36 men on *petit-etat-major* and 3,853 other ranks filling out 3 battalions. A huge amount of clothing and equipment needed replacing. Of the *habits*, 2,076 were in use and 1,813 men had no *habit*. Of the *habits* in use, 274 needed repairs and 1,116 were life expired, again 2,231 men had no regulation *veste*, 2,560 men had no regulation *culottes en tricot*, for headdress 216 helmets and 400 *chapeaux* were in use, alongside 603 *bonnets de police*: not enough existed for every man to have an item of headdress. The same was true of the equipment, 658 *baudriers* or waistbelts were needed, 1,901 *gibernes* and belts, 3,364 musket slings and 9 drums. Of the items in use, it either needed repairing or total replacement. The unit's weapons were also in a poor condition: 267 men had no musket, and of the 3,482 muskets in use, 158 needed repairs and 60 replacement, 782 men had no *bayonet*, and just 64 *sabres* were in use for drummers, some 1,589 *sabres* being needed. We do note the men were now dressed in blue rather than green.[8]

We know nothing else until *17 Thermidor AnX* (5 August 1802), when we are told clothing was acceptable for all ranks.[9]

Reviewed again on *8 Prairial AnXI* (28 May 1803), the inspector noted,

> the dress of the men is good ... however the broadcloth used in the production of the soldiers clothing is very bad indeed, and the majority of the soldiers need new *habits* and *pantalons* within the next 6 months.

He added,

> The *tricot* used by the regiment should never have been accepted for us by the Inspector of Review, it is of very bad quality and it's forbidden for the corps to accept any more cloth from this supplier. All the cloth provided since 1802 is entirely substandard in quality, the *habits* that have been delivered made from this cloth have to be replaced after only six months, it is impossible for the *habits* to remain in use for the required two years; there is also a great variety in colour.

Clearly, the *13ᵉ Légère* could only obtain badly made local cloth and that was of so low quality that the new clothing simply fell to bits. Whatever the regulations may have stated about cloth quality, the regulations simply did not reflect army practice. Regiments bought whatever cloth they could afford to buy. This is perfectly understandable and reasonable: with hundreds of regiments, as well as the state buying up blue cloth and other woollens, it was obvious supply and demand could simply not be met, even in times of peace. We do note by this date, the unit had 1,474 *schakos* in use, 443 needed repairs and 579 total replacement. In addition, 250 bearskins had been made for the *carabinier* company, 210 being issued and 40 left in stores. Also in service were 12 *chapeaux*.[10]

14ᵉ Légère

Inspected on *1 Ventôse AnX* (20 February 1802), every man was wearing a *chapeau*, 2,291 being in service rather than the expected *schako*. The regiment had 4 *sapeurs* with aprons, but apparently, they had no axes. The men had 1 pair of shoes each, 2,893 being issued, and we assume some *sous-officiers* had 2 pairs. The inspector ordered 1,308 *habits* and *vestes* to be made, 3,922 pairs of *pantalons*, 308 *chapeaux*, 1,961 *bonnets de police* and 676 *gibernes* with belts to be produced.[11]

18ᵉ *Légère*

When the third battalion of the *18ᵉ Légère* was disbanded remarkably its manpower was split almost 50/50 between wearing white *habits*. The battalion mustered 288 other ranks and 3 *enfants de troupe*. A total of 283 white *habits* were in use, which needed replacing within 12 months, the other 5 men had blue *habits*. The men had just been issued 283 new blue *habits* with a lifespan of 24 months. In use were 283 pairs of blue *tricot pantalons*, accompanied by 283 *gilets* and 280 *schakos*. A total of 263 *gibernes* and *porte-gibernes* were in good condition and 27 needed total replacement, and we note 124 *baudriers* were in use. The depot held 26m 38 blue broadcloth, 4m 80 scarlet broadcloth, 12 pieces of superfine white cloth, 17m 90 linen, 3 pairs of *carabiniers' epaulettes*, 5 pairs of *chasseurs' epaulettes*, 4 *carabiniers'* sword knots, 19 *chasseurs'* sword knots, 4 *carabiniers'* plumes, 20 old *baudriers* and 124 *sabres*.[12]

19ᵉ *Légère*

Reviewed on *28 Ventôse AnX* (19 March 1802), the inspected noted the men were dressed, despite the newest clothing being over 18 months old and stated that 'everything is absolutely bad, materials, cut and sewing … the headdress is good … the leatherwork is neither in good condition or [sic] of the model sent by the minister.' Looking at the details we note of the 926 *habits*, 285 needed repairs and 526 total replacement, every single *veste* needed to be replaced, so too did every pair of *culottes*. Likewise, of 868 *gibernes* and belts, 447 needed repairs and 211 replacing. It is interesting to note the unit was wearing *chapeaux*, obtained from the arsenal at Turin, along with the majority of the regiment's leatherwork.[13] The inspector requested the minister of war supplied the unit with *schakos*, new clothing was to be drawn from the magazines of the Republic he noted in 1800 and due to bad administration nothing new had been produced, and requested that models of each item of uniform were to be sent to the regiment, which were to be copied exactly in 3 regulation sizes.[14]

20ᵉ *Légère*

The only inspection report we have of the unit from 1796 to 1803 is dated *28 Floréal AnXI* (18 May 1803), 'many of the conscripts are not clothed' reported the inspector to the minister of war 'the cut of the *habits* is good and conforms to the model sent by the minister for war'. We note that the unit had 883 *schakos* in service, but every single *habit* and *veste* needed totally replacing and all bar 52 pairs of *pantalons*. Needing repair were 773 *gibernes* and belts – all of them – 532 out of 1,032 *baudriers*. In fact, the regiment had very little in terms of clothing and equipment in good condition. The inspector ordered 698 *habits* and *vestes*, 1,312 pairs of *pantalons* and 428 additional *schakos*.[15]

Chapter 7

Cavalerie, Carabiniers and *Dragons*

From the late seventeen century, the heavy cavalry had comprised regiments of *cavalerie*, 2 units of *carabiniers* – originally mounted marksmen armed with rifles – and dragoons (mounted infantry, at least when the regiments were created by Louis XIV). The first two category of soldier, in theory, were big men, on for the time, big horses, armed with a straight *sabre* for thrusting. The clothing of the *carabiniers* and *dragons* was ostensibly the same bar colour and was dealt with by the regulations along with the *cavalerie* regiments.

Their clothing and equipment was specified by the regulations of 1786:

> The uniform clothing of the *Bas-Officers, Cavaliers* & *Dragons*, will consist of a *habit* lined with *serge* or cadis of the colours of distinction which will be adjusted for each regiment; a *veste* made in broadcloth, lined with *serge* or white cadis, & hide breeches: the *habit* & the *veste* will look absolutely similar, as for the shape, & the quantity & position of the buttons, to those of the Infantry; except that the *veste* will have neither cuffs nor collar of the colour of distinctive colour. The duration of each will be six years, by means of which these two parts of clothing will be replaced in the sixth year.[1]

Furthermore,

> There will also be given to each of the *Bas-Officiers, Cavaliers* & *Dragons*, a *surtrout* made from broadcloth which they will wear with a vest which will be made of *tricot* recovered from the old *surtrouts*.
>
> This *surtrout* will be made in the manner of a *frac* [single-breasted tail coat] & garnished with eight large uniform buttons, including six at the front, placed one at the top, two in the middle, three at the bottom & two at the hips; the *epaulettes* & the counter *epaulettes*, will be attached to the *surtrout* with a small button: the duration of the *surtrouts* will be three years, by means of which a third will be replaced each year.
>
> All parts of the clothing will be well proportioned to the size of the men, so that they are well fitted, without being hindered in any of their movements; & the tails will be kept long enough, so that, fastened and buttoned throughout their length, the tails will reach three and a half *pouces* from the floor, the man being on bended knee and straight backed. Those of the Cavalry will be cut large enough to be able to fasten the *revers* with the hooks and eyes and also to button them over the *cuirasse* [breastplate] which will be worn over the *veste*.

Cavalerie, Carabiniers and *Dragons* 131

The *1ᵉ Cavalerie du Colonel-General* wearing the uniform according to the regulations of 1786. It retained this number after the changes of January 1791.

> The *manteaux* will be of *gris-blanc picque de bleu* [woollen broadcloth woven from 1 blue thread for every 7 grey i.e. natural fleece]; it will be garnished with three brandings on each side, made with the stripes of the same lace as used on the *housse* [decorative cloth cover to the saddle blanket] of each regiment, & facing on the front, in *serge* or cadis of the colour of the regiment's distinctions: here will be added to the *manteaux* of *Dragons*, a shoulder cape; the duration of the *manteaux* will be twelve years.²

The reference to the *cuirass* was clearly in regard to what would become the *8ᵉ Cuirassiers*, which had retained the *cuirass*. The regulations ascribed a *chapeau* to the *cavalerie* and *carabiniers*, and a brass helmet with a seal skin turban to the *dragons*. Unlike the infantry they wore dragoon-style *bonnets de police*:

> The *Bas-Officiers*, *Cavaliers* or *Dragons*, will wear a police cap cut *à la dragon*; which will be made with the off cuts of cloth from making the new clothing & the best pieces of debris from old clothing: & the amount of broadcloth allowed will be increased consequently, by the quote below; this hat will be lined with canvas; its width will be proportional to the size of the head, & it will be twenty-one *pouces* high from the bottom to the tip, the turban being raised; the turban will be four *pouces* high behind & four *pouces* nine *lignes* on the front, and the front seam will be indented fifteen *lignes* wide & nine *lignes* deep: this same turban will be bordered strip of broadcloth in the distinctive colour, ten *lignes* wide. The *flamme* will be trimmed with a tassel made from cloth, half the colour of the *habit*, & half that of the distinctive colour; at six inches below this fringe, on the left side, he will sew a hook, & at fourteen *pouces* below an eyelet to hold the *flamme* in place.³

As we noted earlier, the regulation only came into force in November 1788. The cavalry, resplendent with regimental lace, following in many cases the colonels' coat of arms colouring, was perhaps the most conspicuously royalist element of the army. *Cavalerie* troopers, like all mounted troops, worn for stable duties a cheap garment that could easily get soiled and damaged whilst mucking out and grooming their horse without damaging the full-dress *habit* or hideously hard to clean white *veste*. The Royal Order of 24 November 1788 stated that the cold weather *gilet* was to be worn for stable duties and a linen smock was likewise introduced for service in stables.⁴ The *cavalerie*, *carabiniers* and *dragons* were issued with various types of legwear. The trademark feature of the heavy cavalry was their deer hide or sheepskin hide leather riding *culottes*. They closed at the knee, and the knees were covered by *manchettes du botte* – literally gaiters – that covered the junction of stockings on the lower legs and the bottom of the *culottes*. This protected the knee of the *culottes* from rubbing against the knee guard of the boots. Under the terms of the Bardin Regulation, they became *pantalons* i.e. closed at the ankle and the *manchettes* (knee guards) were done away with. Rather than a *capote*, the cavalry used a large cloak. At first this was a cape with a standing collar, introduced in 1791.

The *2ᵉ Cavalerie dit Mestre de Camp*, which became the *24ᵉ Cavalerie* in January 1791.

The cloak for the *dragons* was made from cloth called *blanc piqué de bleu*, whereby every eighth thread was blue, the remainder being natural undyed fleece. This gave the cloth a very light blue fleck. The collar, lining to the shoulder cape and the front opening of the body of the cloak was lined in the regiment's distinctive colour. All the linings were made from *serge*.[5] By 1800, the garment had developed a short shoulder cape. The front of the cape was closed by a row of 6 hooks and eyes.[6] In full dress *cavalerie* and *carabiniers* wore knee-length boots with a knee cuff known as *bottes forte*. They were made from stiff rigid leather – a modern equivalent being the boots worn by the British Army Household Cavalry regiments. Likewise, *dragons* wore knee-length boots with a knee cuff known as *bottes écuyer*. Unlike the heavy cavalry boots, one can easily walk in these boots as they were made from much softer leather. Because of the soft nature of the leather, each boot had a tab on outside leg that buttoned to the *culottes*, to stop the boot falling down around the ankle.

A cavalry trooper was also issued a pair of shoes for dismounted duties. Under his *culottes* he wore his *caleçons* (underpants) and a pair of linen or wool over the knee stockings. Rather than a *havresac*, cavalry troopers had a *porte-manteau* (travel bag). Under the decree of 1791, this was round and made from *tricot*. It measured 0m 21 diameter, 0m 70 long and the edges were decorated with 0m 20-wide white lace with the regimental number in the middle. The regulations stated that it was lined in herringbone weave hemp canvas (*treillis*) and that the pocket in the lid of the *porte-manteau* was to contain the trooper's grooming kit and bread ration.[7] It became rectangular in 1801, measured 0m 70 long, the ends measuring 0m 23 wide by 0m 12 tall. The ends were laced with 0m 27-wide white lace.[8] A *porte-manteau* was to last 8 years according to the decree of 1791. Therefore, the last of this model would have been taken out of service in 1810! The cavalry regulations of 1805 list the contents of the *porte-manteau* as being 2 shirts placed along the bottom of the *porte-manteau*, with the breeches and sock placed over these, along with a bag of pistol powder and spare stocks, the night cap, handkerchiefs, brushes for cleaning the *habit*, spare knee guards, then the *surtout* (single-breasted coat with the long tails, worn on campaign), and stable bag. The ration bag was to envelop the watering bit and spread out at the top of the *porte-manteau*. Under the cover of the *porte-manteau* were to be placed the *bonnet de police*, a pair of shoes and the soldier's small equipment. Under the *porte-manteau* was to be the horse's nose bag and rations, on top the rolled cloak.[9] As well as carrying their own equipment, the cavalry trooper had to also carry necessary items to look after their horse. The trooper's *gamelles* (bowls) and other eating equipment would also have needed to have been stowed as well.

Regulations of 1791

As France edged towards a representative democracy with a figure head monarch, the regulations of 1791 sought to 'nationalise' the dress of the cavalry and remove regimental lace and other unique aspects of the uniform, many originating at the end of the seventeenth century. The regulations stated the following:

The *3ᵉ Cavalerie dit Commissaire General*, which retained its unit number in 1791.

The first regiment of *carabiniers* will continue to wear the blue *habit* with *revers*, cuffs and cuff flaps in scarlet and lined in scarlet. The silver bastion loops on the *revers*, cuffs, collar and rear of the *habit* will be discontinued; the buttons will continue to carry the *fleur-de-lys*. The second regiment will wear the same *habit* with the exception that the cuff flap will be blue. In this and the other regiment the collar is to be the same colour as the body of the *habit*.

The clothing of the *Cavalerie* and *dragons* will continue to comprise a *habit* and *veste* that will be renewed every four years. The *habit* will be cut the same form as the infantry; the *veste* will not have simulated pockets and the *basques* [tails] rather than being 3 *pouces* deep from the bottom button will instead descend to the middle button of the *culottes*.

The cavalrymen and dragoons will wear *culottes de peau*, their price will not exceed 6 *livres* a year, and to pay for these the men will have stopped from their pay 10 *sous* a month.[10]

All lace was to be stripped off the *habits* and saddlery and replaced with white. Polish-style *habits* were to be replaced with the French cut. Thus, a dragoon was issued a helmet and *bonnet de police*, a double-breasted stable coat with a stand and fall collar, a *surtrout*, a pair of knee breeches (*culottes de peau*) with 2 pairs of knee guards (*manchettes du botte*), a pair of black gaiters, a pair of shoes, *sabre* belt, *giberne* and belt, as well as his large *manteau* (cloak). The list of clothing and its service life was not affected by any further regulations until 1802 in

A trooper of the *3ᵉ Cavalerie* wearing the uniform according to the regulations of April 1791, which they would continue to wear until 1804.

the mid-years of the Consulate period; it was the first major uniform reform of the era. A *cavalerie* trooper had the same kit, bar he had a *chapeau* and not helmet. The *chapeau* was reinforced with an iron crown to defend the head from *sabre* blows. A *carabinier* had a bearskin and *chapeau* rather than the helmet. The regulation also abolished regimental titles in favour of numbers. As elite troops, from 24 June 1792, men of the *carabiniers* and *cavalerie* regiments were to wear moustaches and allowed red feather plumes. The regulation also went on to note that that the men would wear habitually their *surtrout* or stable coat, the *habit* been put aside for parade. For parades both mounted and dismounted, the men were to wear their *culottes de peau*, all other times they were to wear broadcloth *culottes* with black twill or linen gaiters with shoes. At their own expense men were allowed white linen *vestes* and *culottes* for summer use. On foot the *sabre* belt was to be worn across the shoulder, mounted worn at the waist over the *veste*.[11]

The *surtrout*, for campaign and undress, was described in the regulation of 1779, as being cut from *tricot*, the front being closed by 8 large buttons, 2 at the small of the back. The regulations say nothing about the form of the collar or cuffs. It had no pockets on the tails. The old *surtrouts* were seemingly re-made into *gilets*.[12] The regulations of 1791 state this about the *surtrouts*: 'Independent of the clothing for the *sous-officiers*, cavalrymen, dragoons, hussars and *chasseurs*, they will have a *surtrout* cut from broadcloth, it will be renewed every three years, and also a stable coat, made from *tricot*, which will last for four years.'[13]

An innovation of 1791 was the stable coat. In previous years, this was the function of the *surtrout*. The stable coat, was cut from we assume *tricot*, and was to be double breasted, closed with 2 rows of 10 small uniform buttons. The colour of the stable coat was to be the same as the *habit* body. At the front of the stable coat were 2 small pockets with flaps. The cuffs were cut round. The collar was stand and fall. It was to be cut so that the bottom edge descended 1.5 *pouce* below the top button of the *culottes*.[14] On 13 January 1792, the collars of the stable coat was changed to be standing, and closed by 3 hooks and eyes, as the stand and fall collar made it impossible to wear under the *surtrout*.[15]

The regulations also broke as under traditional numbers and affiliations:

1ᵉ Régiment du Colonel-General became *1ᵉ Cavalerie*
2ᵉ Régiment du Mestre de Camp General became *24ᵉ Cavalerie*
3ᵉ Régiment du Commissaire General became *3ᵉ Cavalerie*
4ᵉ Régiment du Royal Cavalerie became *2ᵉ Cavalerie*
5ᵉ Régiment du Roi became *6ᵉ Cavalerie*
6ᵉ Régiment Royale Etranger became *7ᵉ Cavalerie*
7ᵉ Régiment de Cuirassiers du Roi became *8ᵉ Cavalerie-Cuirassiers*
8ᵉ Régiment Royal Cravatte became *10ᵉ Cavalerie*
9ᵉ Régiment Royal Roussillon became *11ᵉ Cavalerie*
10ᵉ Régiment Royal Piémont became *14ᵉ Cavalerie*
11ᵉ Régiment Royal Allemand became *15ᵉ Cavalerie*
12ᵉ Régiment Royal Pologne became *5ᵉ Cavalerie*

The *4ᵉ Cavalerie dit Royale*, which became the *2ᵉ Cavalerie* in 1791.

The 5ᵉ *Cavalerie dit Roi*, which became the 6ᵉ *Cavalerie* in 1791.

13ᵉ Régiment Royal Lorraine became *16ᵉ Cavalerie*
14ᵉ Régiment Royal Picardie became *21ᵉ Cavalerie*
15ᵉ Régiment Royal Champagne became *20ᵉ Cavalerie*
16ᵉ Régiment Royal Navarre became *22ᵉ Cavalerie*
17ᵉ Régiment Royal Normandie became *19ᵉ Cavalerie*
18ᵉ Régiment de la Reine became *4ᵉ Cavalerie*
19ᵉ Régiment du Dauphiné became *12ᵉ Cavalerie*
20ᵉ Régiment de Bourgogne became *17ᵉ Cavalerie*
21ᵉ Régiment de Berri became *18ᵉ Cavalerie*
22ᵉ Regiment de Cavalerie became *1ᵉ and 2ᵉ Carabiniers*
23ᵉ Régiment d'Artois became *9ᵉ Cavalerie*
24ᵉ Régiment Orléans became *13ᵉ Cavalerie*
25ᵉ Régiment de Nassau Saarbruck emigrated
26ᵉ Régiment de Royale Guyenne emigrated, new *24ᵉ Cavalerie* raised

On 21 February 1793, new regiments numbered *25ᵉ*, *26ᵉ*, *27ᵉ*, *28ᵉ* and *29ᵉ* were raised with *aurore* as the distinctive colour. With the loss of regimental lace and distinctive uniforms, the new corps was, like their counterparts in the line, nationalised:

Regimental Number					Pockets	Revers	Collar and Cuff Flaps	Cuffs
1	7	13	19	25	Horizontal	C	C	C
2	8	14	20	26		C	C	
3	9	15	21	27		C		C
4	10	16	23	28	Vertical	C	C	C
5	11	17	23	29		C	C	
6	12	18	24			C		C
Scarlet	Crimson	Rose	Yellow	Aurore				

* Please note that the figures shown in the table are taken directly from the source, but some of the totals appear to have been calculated incorrectly.
** C means colour.

The original 24 regiments of *cavalerie* were increased to 29 on 21 February 1793, the number dropping to 28 with the *15ᵉ* emigrating *en masse* on the 4 June 1793. Henceforward, the *16ᵉ* became the *15ᵉ* etc. King's Livery for trumpeters was abolished in favour of white lace and the *fleur-de-lys* emblem was to be removed. Trumpeters retained blue for their clothing.[16]

We now turn to look at the dress of the *cavalerie* regiments.

The *6ᵉ Cavalerie dit Royal Etranger*, which became the *7ᵉ Cavalerie* in January 1791.

Regulations in Practice

Dressed in a cut away *habits*, with felt *chapeau*, their appearance was markedly similar to their infantry counterparts, with differing lace and facing colour combinations marking out each regiment. These regiments with over 100 years of tradition behind them, would be swept away in a whirlwind of army reforms. The men had both a *habit* and *surtout*, worn over a white *veste*. They wore heavy and cumbersome *culottes de peau* both on the march and in battle. For stable duties they had a double-breasted stable coat and hemp canvas overalls, which opened on the aide with bone buttons. Footwear in the stables were wooden clogs or shoes. In terms of equipment, they carried a *giberne* and belt, which are ostensibly the same as the infantry but smaller, and a straight-bladed *sabre* from a waistbelt.

1ᵉ Cavalerie

Before 1791, the unit was the *Régiment du Colonel-General*, becoming the *1ᵉʳ Régiment de Cavalerie* on 1 December 1791. We know a great deal about the men: for example, of the 497 men, the shortest stood 5ft tall, and the tallest 5ft 11, the average height being 4ft 6 – 172 men – next being 5ft 7 – 148 men. We imagine the *cavalerie* being tall and imposing, but this was clearly not the case. We remark 118 men had served from 4 to 8 years and 245 men had served from 1 to 4 years. Before service, 12 men had been bakers, 22 shoemakers, 4 saddlers, 181 agricultural labourers, 16 masons, 15 shopkeepers and 195 town labourers. The men's uniforms ranged in issue date from 1786 – 72 *habits* – through to 1791 – 192 *habits* – with 128 needed for the coming year. Many *habits* were still as for the previous regimental denomination, as were the *porte-manteaux* and *housses*, which, in theory, were all to be changed during 1792. No *surtrouts* were issued, but *vestes* and *gilets d'ecurie* (short single-breasted coats worn for stable duties) were, along with smocks. These smocks were used for fatigue duties: loose fitting they were worn over the shirt or *veste*, along with the stable trousers for sweeping the stable yard. Made from linen, they could be easily boil washed to keep them clean. The men's saddlery comprised a *housse* and white sheepskin *schabraque*, of which 410 out if 490 examples needed replacing. We can say nothing of the dress of the trumpeters, except their clothing was issued in 1789, and may still have been of the Royalist Livery pattern.[17]

We know nothing else until *21 Fructidor AnIV* (7 September 1796). What clothing existed was either missing, or needed repair and replacement. For example, 400 *habits* were in use, leaving 107 without such a garment, 133 needed repairs, 128 were life expired and 179 needed replacing. Of the *surtrouts*, 271 were needed to give every man 1, and again the majority were in need of repair of replacement. We note 119 *gilets* were needed, 56 pairs of *culottes de peau du mouton*, 96 stable coats, 60 *chapeaux*, 78 *bonnets de police* and 125 pairs of stable trousers. Equipment and saddlery were also in poor shape or missing entirely: 82 *gibernes* were needed, 113 *sabre* belts, 113 pairs of boots, 106 *sabres*, 347 pistols, 179 saddles, 186 *schabraques* and 190 *housses*. Is it little wonder the inspector

An officer of the *7ᵉ Cavalerie des Cuirassiers du Roi*, which became the *8ᵉ Cavalerie-Cuirassier* in January 1791.

A trooper of the *7ᵉ Cavalerie des Cuirassiers du Roi*, which became the *8ᵉ Cavalerie-Cuirassier* in January 1791.

A trooper of the *8ᵉ Cavalerie dit Royale Cravate*, which became the *10ᵉ Cavalerie* in January 1791.

noted 'the dress is terrible, the clothing is in very poor condition, the men's equipment is appalling, so too the horse tack'.[18] We are ignorant of the dress of the trumpeters.

Reviewed again on *23 Floréal AnVI* (12 May 1798), the unit's clothing and equipment was still in deplorable condition. What clothing that existed was 'knackered'. For example of 311 *habits* for 334 men, 148 needed repairs, 165 were life expired and 185 had to be replaced with all urgency. No man had a *surtrout* or pair of *culottes de peau*, so what was the unit's legwear? Insufficient pairs of stable trousers (285 pairs for 334 men) were in use for every man to have a pair. Equipment and saddlery was also missing or needed repair and replacement.[19]

Our next document is dated *7 Germinal AnX* (28 March 1802) as the *1er Régiment de Cavalerie-Cuirassiers*. With the change in unit designation to *cuirassiers*, as well as period of peace, on *18 Vendémiaire AnX* (10 October 1801), the clothing of the unit was in much better shape: 181 *habits* had been made over the previous year, making 450 in service, 422 being in good condition. Many men still lacked clothing, and we note 495 *surtrouts* were in use, 33 needing repairs and 273 complete replacement. The regiment was changing over from sheepskin *schabraques* – 171 examples – to cloth *chaperons* – 284 examples – but had as of yet not received any armour of helmets.[20]

2e Cavalerie

Inspected by General François-Étienne-Christophe de Kellermann on 1 December 1791, he noted the trumpeters clothing had been issued in 1787 and needed to be stripped of Royalist Livery lace. He further noted that the bulk of the clothing had been issued during 1791 and a further 130 *habits*, *vestes* and stable coats were needed for 1792, along with 173 *surtrouts*.[21]

Reviewed on *1 Germinal AnV* (21 March 1797) as we observed with the *1e Cavalerie*, the clothing and equipment of the regiment was either missing or 'knackered'. For the 506 men under arms, 40 men had no *habit* or *veste* and just 155 of both garments were in good condition, only 20 men had a pair of *culottes de peau* and 151 men had a *surtrout*. We also note 155 stable coats were needed, 40 *chapeaux*, 65 *bonnets de police* and 322 pairs of stable trousers. So, what legwear did the regiment use? Equipment was also missing or needed replacing: 80 men lacked a *sabre* belt, and of the 426 in use, 50 per cent needed replacing. Again, 102 men had no *giberne* and belt, with 50 per cent of those that existed needing to be replaced or repaired. Armament was in the same condition, no man had a *mousqueton* (short musket), 151 *sabres* were needed and 366 pairs of pistols. We remark, every man had a sheepskin *schabraque*, but every single example needed replacing. What is notable is that since *1 Vendémiaire AnIII* (22 September 1794), stores had made 558 *habits*, 556 *vestes*, 424 *bonnets de police*, 373 *housses* and 529 pairs of stable trousers, which shows how quickly clothing broke down on campaign. Interestingly, the *surtrouts* were entirely blue, whilst the *habits* had the expected scarlet facing and lining. It also means trumpeters did not have reversed colour *surtrouts* as none were made or issued.[22]

A document of *8 Vendémiaire AnVI* (29 September 1797) states the following:

Cavalerie, Carabiniers and Dragons 147

A trooper of the *10ᵉ Cavalerie dit Royal Piémont*, which became the *14ᵉ Cavalerie* in January 1791.

the dress of the men is mediocre at best … insufficient *habits* and *surtrouts* exists to give the men one of each, and those that exist are in urgent need of repairs. It is therefore a matter of urgency that the men are supplied with a complete set of clothes … the men's equipment is mostly good but needs repairs, like that of horses, the regiment has no *mousqueton*, and 78 pairs of pistols need repairs. The *sabres* are all of different models and all need repairs.[23]

Little seems to have been done, however, as when inspected on *22 Ventôse AnVII* (12 March 1799), of the 507 men under arms, 275 *habits* existed, 63 of which needed replacing, the 189 *surtrouts* in service went someway to making up the deficiency in *habits*, the shortfall, the inspector noted being the use of stable coats in all orders of dress for many men. Indeed, 294 men had no *veste*, so their stable coat was their only upper body garment. Furthermore, 246 *manteaux* were needed and 181 pairs of stable trousers, as well as 53 pairs of *culottes de peau*.[24]

Reviewed on *1 Vendémiaire AnVIII* (23 September 1799), almost every man in the regiment had a pair of *culottes de peau*, but 297 *surtrouts* were still needed to give each man 1. Clothing was overall in good condition: 104 out of 479 *habits* needed repairs for example, 102 *manteaux* out of 501, the same story being true of the equipment and saddlery. Officially, each regiment of *cavalerie* was issued with a *mousqueton* carried from a shoulder belt (*banderole-porte-mousqueton*). The inspection shows that despite whatever officialdom said, the unit still had no *mousqueton*.[25]

3ᵉ *Cavalerie*

Reviewed on 5 December 1791, by one of the greatest French soldiers of the epoch, *Comte* De Rochambeau, he noted the regiment had almost been entirely re-dressed according to the regulations of April 1791, and that the clothing issued during 1788 would be replaced entirely during 1792. We do note that no man had a *surtrout*, every man having a *veste*, stable coat, and smock, and during the course of 1792 every man would receive a new pair of *culottes de peau*, none being in service.[26] What the unit was wearing as legwear, we are at a loss to say. Clearly, the men had legwear, we just do not know what they looked like. Presumably, civilian garments.

Inspected again on *28 Germinal AnVII* (17 April 1799), the regiment's clothing was in appalling condition: no man had a *habit*, and all bar 15 men were instead wearing *surtrouts*. Of these 303 garments, 101 needed repairs and the remainder needed immediate replacement. Just one man had a pair of stable trousers. Everything was worn out and needed replacing the inspector noted, clothing, equipment and saddlery.[27]

The review on *15 Ventôse AnX* (6 March 1802) noted that many items were missing: for 507 men, 327 *habits* were in use, but every man had a *surtrout*. Horse equipment included 260 *housses* and 260 pairs of *chaperons*, all needing to be replaced.[28]

The regiment became *cuirassiers* on *20 Vendémiaire AnXI* (12 October 1802).

A trooper of the *12ᵉ Cavalerie dit Royal Pologne*, which became the *5ᵉ Cavalerie* in 1791.

A trooper of the *Cavalerie de Lorraine*, which became the *16ᵉ Cavalerie* in 1791.

Inspected on *10 Fructidor AnXI* (28 August 1803), the general reported that the clothing of the regiment was 'good but still not all of the new model'. Every man had their *cavalerie habit* and *surtout* the inspector noted, who ordered the regiment was to receive 625 new *habits*, *surtouts* and *gilets*, 601 stable coats and stable trousers, 625 pairs of *culottes de peau*, *chapeaux*, helmets, *bonnets de police*, *ceinturons* of the new model with slings, new-model *porte-manteaux* and pairs of boots. In essence, the regiment was to

Cavalerie, Carabiniers and Dragons 151

A trooper of the *14ᵉ Cavalerie dit Royal Picardie* with *aurore* facings. It became the *21ᵉ Cavalerie* in 1791.

receive its '*cuirassier* start up kit' by the time of the next inspection in batches of 625. In addition, 9 *caissons* of new-model *sabres* were at Compiègne awaiting delivery. Not a single *giberne* or *porte-giberne* was in use, nor had the regiment received a single *cuirass*.[29]

4ᵉ Cavalerie

Reviewed on *3 Messidor AnVI* (21 June 1798), the inspector commented, 'the dress of the men is exactly to the regulation, however many items of clothing are needed to be repaired or to be totally replaced as a matter of urgency. Again, needed replacing as a matter urgency are the *culottes de peau*.' Looking in detail, for the 464 men, just 257 *habits* existed, 265 *vestes*, 205 *surtrouts* and 459 stable coats. Clearly, not enough of each existed to give each man one of everything, it was a case of either or. Indeed, a good number of men only had their stable coat for upper bodywear. No regulation legwear of any sort existed, so we are left wondering as to what was worn, and 247 men had no *chapeau*, almost every man having a *bonnet de police*. For 464 men, just 247 saddles were in use – the regiment was desperately short of horses – no snaffle bridles existed, 3 curb bridles were needed, as were 190 saddle blankets and 3 *schabraques*, but every man had a *housse*. No man had a *mousqueton*, 270 pairs of pistols were needed as were 12 *sabres* and a further 38 needed replacing.[30]

Inspected again on *2 Brumaire AnVII* (23 October 1798), clothing had started to improve: just 104 *surtrouts*, 295 *habits* and 335 *vestes* were in use, as were 585 pairs of *culottes de peau* and 101 pairs of stable trousers.[31]

8ᵉ Cavalerie

The regiment had worn *cuirasses* since the late seventeenth century, hence its title the *Régiment de Cuirassiers*. It became the *8ᵉ Cavalerie* on 1 January 1791. The decree of *23 Fructidor AnVII* (9 September 1799) tells us that the *8ᵉ Régiment de Cavalerie* had the denomination *8ᵉ Régiment* Cavalerie-*Cuirassiers*. A second regiment of *cuirassiers* was created when the *1ᵉ Régiment de Cavalerie* became the *1ᵉ Régiment de Cavalerie-Cuirassiers* by a decree of *18 Vendémiaire AnX* (10 October 1801). Colonel Jean-Baptiste-Gabriel Merlin of the *8ᵉ* bitterly complained to the minister of war that his regiment should be the *1ᵉ* as they had been wearing armour far longer. He argued that his regiment had been formed in 1665 as *cuirassiers* and although the *1ᵉ Cavalerie* had been raised in 1635, if another regiment was to become *cuirassiers*, then the *8ᵉ* should become the *1ᵉ Régiment* of the new arm. The minister of war refused Merlin's request.[32] We know the regiment wore armour during the Revolutionary era, as on *1 Vendémiaire AnVI* (22 September 1797), 288 *cuirasses* were in use. The regiments clothing needed totally replacing: of 487 *habits*, 181 needed repairs and 306 replacing. Almost nothing was in serviceable condition, merely 15 pairs of *culottes de peau*. The leather equipment was, however, almost entirely new, just 5 *sabre* belts needed replacing.[33]

The *15ᵉ Cavalerie dit Royal Champagne*, which became the *20ᵉ Cavalerie* in 1791.

On *13 Pluviôse An VII* (1 February 1799), some 289 *cuirasses* were in service. Of these, 255 were in good condition and 34 needed repairs. An additional 203 were needed as only front-rank men were armoured. Cloth was either missing or 'knackered'. For 507 men, 392 *habits* existed, meaning 115 men had no *habit*, and of those in use 202 needed repairs and 98 replacing. No man had a *surtrout*, and many men only had their stable coat (381 of these in use, 258 needing repairs and 82 needing replacement) as an upper body garment. We also note 389 white *vestes* were in use, 385 *chapeaux*, and 412 pairs of *culottes de peau*. No stable trousers existed, so the heavy, sweaty and smelly *culottes de peau* were the only legwear the men had. Interestingly – or not – the stable coats were made from blue *tricot* lined with blue *serge*.[34]

The regiment by spring 1803 had received 500 helmets and *cuirasses*.[35] The inspection returns of *14 Vendémiaire An XIV* (6 October 1805) reveal that the regiment had in the depot 259 old *cuirasses* in bad condition, and further 65 to be replaced, both types the inspector noted had been 'used since the formation of the regiment in 1666'.[36] Clearly, until 1804 the men had been wearing armour dating from the mid-sixteenth century. It is probably these *cuirasses* that were refurbished and became the so called 1804 pattern for officers. On examining these *cuirasses*, they have a very distinctive and archaic look, straight from the English Civil War.

9ᵉ *Cavalerie*

Reviewed on *30 Vendémiaire An VI* (21 October 1797), the inspector noted that 'the dress of the regiment is mediocre' and added, 'the regiment needs many *habits*. The *surtrouts* and *gilets* worn under them, as well as the *culottes de peau* are very regular, most of the *chapeaux* are in a bad way.'[37]

Reviewed on *7 Fructidor An VII* (24 August 1799), stores reported it had made 371 *habits* and issued 260 and the same number of *vestes*, as well as 204 *surtrouts*. We also note stores had issued 4 pairs of *pantalons*, 111 waistbelts with plates and held 140 *calottes de fer* (the iron crown worn on the *chapeau* to protect the head). We know from accounts that the stable coats were made from blue *tricot* with yellow collars and were lined in white *serge* with sleeves and pockets lined in linen. We also note that calf, cow and pig leather was used for making shoes and boots.[38]

Inspected on *10 Nivôse An X* (31 December 1801), the inspector remarked that 'the regiment is well dressed, but it lacks many items to clothe and equip every man'. He added, 'the clothing in use is very regular, well sewn, cut well and uniform in appearance, has not yet begun to replace its *chaperons* as ordered on 4 November last, I have passed orders to ensure this happens'.[39]

Reviewed for the last time as a *cavalerie* regiment on *28 Prairial An XI* (17 June 1803), we note 424 *habits* were in use, 504 *surtrouts*, 478 *gilets* and 497 pairs of *culottes de peau*. Despite being created in 1801, the elite company did not exist at this date and had no bearskins.[40]

Cavalerie, Carabiniers and Dragons

The *16ᵉ Cavalerie dit Royal Navarre*, which became the *22ᵉ Cavalerie* in January 1791.

11ᵉ *Cavalerie*

The *Régiment Royal Roussillon* became the *11ᵉ Cavalerie* on 1 January 1791, formerly having been the *9ᵉ Régiment* of the cavalry in seniority. Sadly, no archive documents concerning the dress of the unit between 1789 and 1802 can be found.

Inspected on *25 Pluviôse AnX* (14 February 1802), the regiment's clothing according to the inspector was in terrible condition 'the worst condition imaginable' and the regiment needed 'a capable chief with much zeal'. Of the unit's clothing, 380 *habits* were in use of which 229 were in good condition, 88 needed repairs and 63 total replacement, and of the 379 *surtrouts*, 127 were in good condition, 186 needed repairs and 66 total replacement. Of the 373 *chapeaux*, 321 needed immediate replacement, 45 needed repairs and just 7 were in good condition. The bulk of 375 *gilets* were in good condition, some 189 examples, with 101 needing repairs and 85 total replacement. We also note 50 per cent of the 355 stable coats needed repairs or total replacement. We further note that 24 *mousquetons* were in the depot but not a single *banderole-porte-mousqueton* from which to carry them! Furthermore, the regiment had 351 *sabres*, of which 75 needed repairs and 27 total replacement. The depot held stocks of cloth and materials, notably 654m 85 blue broadcloth, 15m 70 white broadcloth, 9m 54 yellow broadcloth and 0m 75 scarlet broadcloth, 234m 77 white *serge*, 214m 75 yellow *serge* and 346m 87 linen. The use of the scarlet broadcloth is we assume for making the shoulder boards for the elite company *epaulettes*, yet no bearskins existed at this point in time.

The regiment was reviewed again on *22 Vendémiaire AnXII* (15 October 1803), when the inspector noted the *habits* were overall in good condition, the *surtrouts* were passable and the stable coats were all in terrible condition. The inspector commented that the men's equipment was in passable condition except the *porte-manteaux*, which were all in bad condition. The saddles were also in bad condition. The elite company now had 59 brand new bearskins in use. Cloth in the depot comprised:[41] 673m 90 blue broadcloth, 140m 21 white broadcloth, 6m 50 yellow broadcloth, 405m 62 *blanc piqué de bleu*, 12m 86 rose broadcloth, 93m 15 blue *tricot*, 1m 25 yellow *tricot*, 474m 55 white *serge*, 166m 21 linen and 786m 93 *treillis*. The rose i.e. hot pink broadcloth is a total mystery – but we do acknowledge under the decree of *1 Vendémiaire AnXII* (24 September 1803), the facings were to be rose. Therefore, had the regiment bought cloth to change the facings? Perhaps, or equally it could have been destined for trumpeters.

12ᵉ *Cavalerie*

Reviewed on 8 December 1791, the inspector noted that during the course of the year, 283 *sous-officiers* and men had been re-clothed. This left 108 men wearing uniforms issued in 1786, 76 men in 1787 and 77 men in 1788. The trumpeters clothing had been taken out of use and they were dressed as rank and file: no doubt to remove offending iconography and lace. Interestingly, 454 pairs of cloth *chaperons* were in use, and the trumpeters and some *sous-officiers* had 128 sheepskin *schabraques*, of which just 36 were in serviceable condition.[42]

The *17e Cavalerie dit Royale Normandie*, which became the *19e Cavalerie* in 1791.

With *gris-argentin* facings, the *19ᵉ Cavalerie dit du Dauphiné*, which became the *12ᵉ Cavalerie* in January 1791.

Cavalerie, Carabiniers and Dragons 159

A trooper of the *Cavalerie de Bourgogne*. Its distinctive colour was *gris-argentin* the colour shown here, being a very close match indeed to a cloth sample of this fabric found as part of a clothing specification of the regiment.

Inspected on *20 Frimaire AnVI* (10 December 1797), the inspector noted that 'the regiment is missing many *habits*, and many of the *surtrouts*, *vestes* and *culottes* are in poor condition. The *manteaux* will all need renewing in the next 6 month.' He added that the *sabres* were in good condition, most men lacked a pistol and no man was issued a *mousqueton*.[43]

Inspected on *12 Pluviôse AnX* (1 February 1802) by General Michel Ney, who remarked that 'the headdress of the regiment is very bad, the helmet is to be adopted by this arm'. Yet it would not be until the decree of *1 Vendémiaire AnXII* (24 September 1803) that the regiment was to become *cuirassiers*. Presumably, the concept of mass conversion of the *cavalerie* to *cuirassier* had already been agreed, or perhaps more correctly, that the due to the *chapeau* offering little in the way of head protection, the Ministry of War had agreed in a now lost order, had authorised the *cavalerie* to be issued helmets. The report detailed that just 19 *habits* existed for the trumpeters and senior *sous-officiers*, everyone else was wearing 416 *surtrouts*, and despite earlier critique, 408 *chapeaux* were in use, just 96 needed minor repairs, the majority being serviceable for another 18 months. Trumpeters' lace is listed but none existed. Likewise, no *epaulettes* or *contre-epaulettes*.[44]

Reviewed on *15 Prairial AnXI* (4 June 1803), the inspector noted that the 'dress is very good, especially the parade dress, however the *surtrouts* are very gold and the stable coats could be advantageously replaced'. About the unit's weapons, he noted they were well kept, but old, many of the *sabres* had very short blades, adding only a few pistols existed, in poor condition and of different calibres. We note the elite company – created in 1801 – had 59 bearskins and stores listed trumpeters' lace, pairs of *epaulettes* and *contre-epaulettes* but none existed. Presumably, the latter for trumpeters? Stores did hold 10m silver lace for *sous-officiers* rank stripes, 41m lace for corporals' stripes, 11m 97 lace for *bonnets de police*, 11m 83 lace for the *porte-manteaux*, 225m 24 lace for the *housses*, and 40m narrow lace for figuring numbers on the *housses*. We also note stores held 167 pairs of shoes, 119 black stocks, 26 stock buckles, 167 shirts and 117 pairs of black twill gaiters. Also in stores were 11 pompoms for *chapeaux*, of which 561 were in use, and 3 scarlet plumes.[45]

The *24 Vendémiaire AnXIII* (16 October 1804) inspection report stated, upon conversion to *cuirassier*, the regiment had simply modernised its old *cavalerie habits* by shortening and re-cutting the tails. However, elsewhere the inspector noted that 'the clothing entirely conformed to the models and instructions sent by his excellency the Minister of War'. We note 486 *habits* had been made since the 1803 review, bringing the total in use up to 498 and 589 *surtout* were in use by the 594 men under arms. One oddity shown up in this inspection was that the regiment used 18m chestnut brown broadcloth and 21m 10 grey broadcloth in the production of clothing. Regimental archives note the presence of 231 pairs of gaiters. Were they made from grey broadcloth? Possibly. The chestnut brown may have been destined for legwear. In addition, the report stated the trumpeters were wearing 14 bearskins and 531 helmets were in service.[46] Presumably, these had been authorised by Ney some years earlier? The regiment received on *21 Brumaire AnXIII* (12 November 1804) 625 *cuirasses*.[47]

Cavalerie, Carabiniers and Dragons 161

A trooper of *21ᵉ Cavalerie dit du Berri* with white facings, which became the *18ᵉ Cavalerie* in January 1791.

A trooper of *21ᵉ Cavalerie dit d'Artois*, which became the *9ᵉ Cavalerie* in January 1791.

A trooper of *24ᵉ Cavalerie dit d'Orléans* with *bleu celeste* facings, which became the *13ᵉ Cavalerie* in January 1791. A cloth sample for this regiment shows that *bleu celeste* was a dyed fabric, whereas the almost identical *gris-argentin* was a melange fabric mixed to generate the same hue.

164   The Armies of the French Revolution

13ᵉ Cavalerie

Raised in Piedmont in 1635 as *dragons* it became the *13ᵉ Cavalerie* in 1791 and then became the *22ᵉ Régiment de Dragons* on *1 Vendémiaire AnXII* (24 September 1803).

Inspected on 12 May 1793, we note that the regiment lacked a lot of clothing and equipment. Tellingly, 249 *sabres* and 274 pairs of pistols were needed, 289 *habits* and *vestes*, 629 *chapeaux*, 269 *bonnets de police*, *surtrouts* and *gilets*, and 309 *manteaux*. Also needed were 250 *gibernes*, 164 *porte-manteaux*, 284 *besacs* (linen *porte-manteaux*) 184 *housses*, 274 *schabraques*, 202 saddles, 254 bridles and 320 pairs of boots.[48]

Reviewed again on *1 Prairial AnVII* (20 May 1799), the unit mustered 507 rank and file. Most of the clothing and equipment was new: just 2 *habits* out of 496 in use needed repairs and 11 replacing. Of the *culottes de peau*, 32 pairs needed repairs, and 28 pairs replacing, of the *surtrouts* – 436 in use – 26 needed repairs and 144 replacing. Stable coats were used by just 341 men, of these 65 needed repairs, and 276 replacing. Equipment wise, 5 *sabre* belts were needed, 98 men need a *giberne* and 63 men had a *giberne* but no belt for it. In terms of armament, 7 *sabres* were missing and 245 pairs of pistols.[49]

Inspected again on *23 Pluviôse AnX* (12 February 1802), we find a document that lists the *habits* were lined in white *serge*, and the *manteaux* had white *serge* lining to the shoulder cape and front opening: a massive 779m *serge* being needed for this purpose. We note the men's *vestes* and *manteaux* were made from white broadcloth. Just 31 *carabine*s were in service with no *bayonets* and 290 pairs of pistols. For stable duties natural linen gaiters were issued, and just 12 regulation stocks, the overwhelming majority of the men wearing black linen cravats.[50]

Reviewed once more on *22 Floréal AnXI* (12 May 1803), we note – rather incredulously – that the regiment had used 403m 92 *chamois* broadcloth – all that existed – 515m 25 blue, 6m white and 25m 65 crimson. At the same time, 25 *habits* and 57 *surtrouts* had been made, 170 *habits* and 164 *surtrouts* being issued since the previous inspection. We have no solutions to the quandary: either the unit adopted *chamois* as a distinctive colour or the adjutant made a mistake. Alas, we cannot say which it is.[51]

The *13ᵉ Cavalerie* was reviewed in Strasbourg for the last time on *1 Vendémiaire AnXII* (24 September 1803). The regiment had 333 *habits* in service, of which 119 had been delivered just prior to the review, some 294 *chapeaux* were in use and the elite company had 59 bearskins. The depot held stocks of cloth and materials:[52] 507m 33 blue broadcloth, 35m 18 crimson broadcloth, 294m 31 white broadcloth for *vestes*, 0m blue *tricot*, 905m 38 white *serge*, 583m 68 crimson *serge*, 24m 07 linen, 232m 66 *treillis*, 0m silver lace for *sous-officiers*, 0m white worsted lace for *bonnets de police*, 0m scarlet fringing, 105m 69 lace for *housses*, 0m *ganse* for *chapeaux* and 38 leather hides for breeches. The depot held clothing, notably 82 *habits* to be written off accompanied by 6 *vestes*, 68 *surtrouts* and 54 stable coats in the same worn-out state. New items included 5 *surtrouts*, 96 stable coats and 71 pairs of *culottes de peau*. Some 333 *manteaux* were in use and a further 49 worn-out *manteaux* were in the depot. The depot also lists *pantalons* and knee breeches made from broadcloth, 64 pairs of stable trousers, 134 *chapeaux* and 5 bearskins: all brand new. Also

Cavalerie, Carabiniers and Dragons 165

A trooper of *25ᵉ Cavalerie dit Nassau-Saarbücken* wearing the regulation polish *habit*. The unit left France at the start of the Revolution.

An officer of the *Cavalerie Royale Allemande*, which became the *15ᵉ Cavalerie* before leaving for Austria as a complete regiment to fight the Republic during spring 1793.

The *26ᵉ Cavalerie dit d'Orléanais*, which became the *Régiment Royale Guyenne* in 1788, then the *23ᵉ Cavalerie* in January 1791.

lodged in the depot were 38 *housses* to be disposed of, 16 new pairs of *chaperons*, 26 brand new *schabraques* and 189 needing repairs, 114 black stocks, 58 white stocks, 60 stock buckles, 42 pairs of shoe buckles, 42 pairs knee buckles, 372 pairs of stockings, 14 pairs of shoes, 131 pairs of linen gaiters, 127 red plumes and 302 *chapeau* cockades. Of the men under arms, 333 sheepskin *schabraques* and *housses* were in use. Clearly, the regiment had just started to adopt cloth *chaperons* as per the decree of 1801. The regiment was armed with 'old pattern' *sabres*, 63 pairs of pistols were in the depot accompanied by 29 *carabines*, none were in service.[53] Quite clearly, the regiment had formed its elite company, who wore bearskins and had fringed *epaulettes*, which we assume were scarlet.

15ᵉ *Cavalerie*

The *Royal Allemand* was one of the most distinctive of the old *cavalerie* regiments. Dressed in *habits à la polonaise*, the garment was equivalent to a *surtrout* with a stand and fall collar: each side of the centre front was 10 white lace *brandenburgs* 38mm wide and 115mm long, the stand and fall collar, cuffs and lining were crimson. They wore sheep hide leather *vestes* with white lace detail, and wore a bearskin as a headdress. The unit became the *15ᵉ Cavalerie* on 1 January 1791, having occupied the *11ᵉ* position in seniority. Potentially, the decree of 1 April 1791 gave the unit the pattern of the *habit* and *revers* according to the regulations of 1786. It left France on 4 June 1791 as a complete regiment and passed to the royalist forces fighting the Republic. In consequence, the former *Cavalerie de Lorraine*, the *16ᵉ*, became the new *15ᵉ*.

The review on *1 Germinal AnV* (21 March 1797) shows that the unit had lost its bearskins by this date and also very likely the *habits à la polonaise*. We do note that the unit's clothing was almost entirely 'knackered' or missing. For 400 men, 113 *habits* existed, of which 106 needed totally replacing, no broadcloth *gilets* existed, nor any *culottes de peau*. Just 239 *surtrouts* were in use and 349 *chapeaux*. We note 221 pairs of boots were in use, just 68 pairs were fit to wear. In place of boots men wore shoes, most of which were too small for the men to wear, and most pairs had fallen to pieces in the rain as the stitching had rotted. All the leather equipment needed to be replaced. Officially, the only legwear in use was 180 pairs of stable trousers. The inspector noted,

> The clothing of the regiment is very bad ... the items made and have been received into the magazine or from those of the republic are in general too small for the men, are of bad quality and no uniform. The *culottes* are particularly so, they are made from *tricot* or velvet and are not able to be in service for the regulation period of time. It is therefore necessary for the commandant of the cavalry to obtain *culottes* made from deer or sheep hide.

Velvet breeches! We suppose acute shortages and an attitude of 'make do and mend' to ensure men had legwear meant that 'anything goes' was inventible: soldiers needed clothing, so as long they had legwear, a hat and coat, no one really cared. The *15ᵉ* must

Cavalerie, Carabiniers and Dragons 169

The *27ᵉ Cavalerie*, disbanded in March 1788.

The *28e Cavalerie*, disbanded in March 1788.

The *29ᵉ Cavalerie*, disbanded in March 1788.

have looked bizarre even by the chaotic standards of the era. Between *1 Vendémiaire AnIII* (22 September 1794) and *1 Germinal AnV* (21 March 1797), no cloth had been used to make clothing and equipment, and the only cloth in stores was 65 *aunes* white broadcloth and 532 *aunes* white *serge*. In the same period the unit had taken into stores 120 white *vestes*, 298 *surtrouts*, 208 stable coats, 220 *bonnets de police*, 184 pairs of stable trousers and 700 pairs of velvet knee breeches. Also obtained were 862 shirts, 831 black stocks, 1,154 pairs of linen stockings, 356 pairs woollen stockings, 1,056 pairs of shoes and 346 pairs of black twill gaiters.

Issued from stores on *1 Vendémiaire AnIII* (22 September 1794) were 120 *habits*, 210 *surtrouts*, 120 pairs of *culottes de peau*, 224 pairs of *gauntlets* (gloves) and 120 sword knots. The unit was 'shambolic' in both its dress, discipline, equitation and drill.[54]

Reviewed on *1 Prairial AnVII* (20 May 1799), the unit had been recently re-clothed. Of the 507 men, 481 had a *habit* in good condition, but 26 needing immediate replacement. The concern for the inspector was to renew the stable clothing (292 stable coats were life expired, as were 120 pairs of stable trousers) to ensure every man had a *chapeau* in good condition (81 needed repairs and 172 total replacement) and to provide each man with a new pair of *culottes de peau*. He ordered the life expired sheepskin half *schabraques* to be replaced with *chaperons*.[55] The last of the *schabraques* were not phased out until *1 Germinal AnX* (22 March 1802), when 358 pairs of *chaperons* were ordered.[56]

With the decree of *1 Vendémiaire AnXII* (24 September 1803), the unit became the *23ᵉ Dragons*. Inspected on *15 Vendémiaire AnXIV* (7 October 1805), 296 *habits* were in use, all being dark green, and made to the dragoon pattern. They were used alongside 460 blue *surtrouts*, which the inspector ordered were to be re-cut as stable coats. The elite company had 72 bearskins. Stores reported that 1,052m 55 blue broadcloth had been used since 1803 and 1,349m 53 green broadcloth. Interestingly, some 7m 85 yellow broadcloth had been used – sufficient for just 34 garments, which given 296 *habits* were made suggests these garments were without *revers*, and, therefore, *surtrouts*. Stores also reports 547m 60 yellow *serge* had been used in comparison to 154m 77 crimson broadcloth and 1,342m 45 crimson *serge*. This seems a huge amount of crimson for simply repairing clothing, and suggests blue clothing was still being made.[57] By the close of 1805, the last vestiges of the *15ᵉ Cavalerie* ceased to exist.[58]

25ᵉ Cavalerie

Levied on 21 February 1793, as the *26ᵉ Cavalerie*, it became the *15ᵉ* on 4 June 1793. Inspected on *18 Frimaire AnVI* (8 December 1797), the inspection records that clothing was either missing or in need of repair and replacement. For 461 men, 352 *habits* were in use, 156 were in good condition, the remainder needed repairs or replacement. Similarly, 378 *gilet*s were in use, 339 *manteaux*, 394 *surtrouts*, 457 *chapeaux* and we note just 98 *bonnets de police*. For stable duties, 428 pairs of stable trousers existed, and just 53 stable coats. Very few men had a complete allocation of clothing and no man had a pair of *culottes de peau*, the stable trousers and non-regulation legwear being in use side by side.

Cavalerie, Carabiniers and Dragons 173

The *30ᵉ Cavalerie*, disbanded in March 1788.

The *31ᵉ Cavalerie*, disbanded in March 1788.

The *Cavalerie Royale Roussillon*, which became the *11ᵉ Cavalerie* in 1791.

We note 31 *gibernes* and belts were in use, only 283 horses were with the regiment, yet 282 saddles existed, and just 187 sheepskin *schabraques*. For 404 *sabre* belts, 380 *sabres* were in use, 307 pistols and no *mousqueton*.[59]

Reviewed on *27 Ventôse AnX* (18 March 1802), the regiment was in shambolic state. For the 441 men under arms, not a single *habit* existed, 339 *surtrouts*, all bar 70 needing repair, were in use, 282 pairs of stable trousers, 269 *chapeaux*, 311 pairs of boots, 338 *manteaux* and 300 pairs of *culottes en drap*. Regimental stores were almost totally empty, housing no clothing or equipment but it did have 156m 80 blue broadcloth, 71m orange broadcloth, 108m white *serge* and 798m orange *serge*.[60]

The *Carabiniers*

The 2 regiments of *carabiniers* were formed in the mid-sixteenth century. They were cavalry armed with rifles – French *carabines* – and at the Battle of Neerwinden in 1693 the corps was commanded by Prince de Conti. The men were drawn from each regiment of cavalry into a provisional formation. Formed into an independent regiment in 1693, the 13 May 1758 witnessed the regiment renamed *Royal Carabiniers de Monsieur le Comte de Provence*. In 1762, the *Corps des Carabiniers* was some 30 squadrons strong, formed in 5 brigades, which was reduced to a single a regiment of 8 companies in 1776. Each company comprised 145 troopers and 5 officers. In 1779, the regiment was reorganised into 2 brigades, each of 5 squadrons. In 1788, the corps was renamed the *Carabiniers de Monsieur*, comprising 2 regiments, each of 4 squadrons. From then on both regiments would serve side by side as a single cohesive brigade, confusingly called the *22ᵉ Cavalerie*!

With the outbreak of the Revolution, the privileged Royal Corps and regiments were abolished; yet with Louis XVI still nominally monarch, the *carabiniers* were retained. On 18 August 1790, the National Assembly voted to retain the 2 regiments and their traditions, and were renamed the *Grenadiers des Troupes à Cheval* – literally the grenadiers of the mounted troops – and were fitted out with scarlet fringed *epaulettes* and bearskin caps. The 2 regiments had seniority over the rest of the cavalry. Always a hotbed of royalists, the officers of the corps owed more allegiance to the crown than the state or emperor. In the wars of the revolution, the *carabiniers* fought mostly in the Army of Germany. In 1804, Louis Bonaparte (Napoléon's brother) was named colonel general of the *carabiniers*; the 2 regiments led the coronation procession from the Tuileries to Notre Dame, much to the chagrin of the *Grenadiers à Cheval* of the Imperial Guard.

1ᵉ Carabiniers

We know almost nothing about the dress of the *carabiniers* between 1788 and 1802. The *1ᵉ Carabiniers* were reviewed on *4 Nivôse AnV* (24 December 1796). For the 889 men, 112 *habits* were in use, just 4 being in good condition. Just 85 good *vestes* out of 294 were in use, 389 *surtrouts* were in service, with 36 being considered to be in good condition. For a supposed elite unit, it was in shocking condition: no man had a pair of *culottes de*

A trooper of the *1ᵉ Cavalerie* wearing a uniform according to the regulations of April 1791, which, bar a few changes to the horse furniture, was worn until 1803.

Standard bearer of the *1ᵉ Cavalerie* wearing a uniform according to the regulations of 1791. The light cavalry-style *schabraque* was regulation for parade use.

peau, no stable trousers existed, 77 wore *cavalerie chapeaux* and 229 men had a bearskin. No *mousquetons* were issued and only 80 *gibernes* and belts, and 78 pairs of pistols – issued to the men with *gibernes* we assume – and 512 *sabres* were missing.⁶¹

The *1ᵉ Carabiniers* were inspected again on *1 Vendémiaire AnVII* (22 September 1798). Clothing and equipment in use comprised:⁶²

Item	Total Items	Items Missing	In Good Condition	In Need of Repair	To Be Written Off	To Be Replaced	Total
Habits	529	144	518		11	11	673
Vestes	537	136	520		17	17	673
Culottes de Peau		673					673
Manteaux	418	250	321	44	57	57	668
Surtrouts	497	176	446	15	36	36	673
Stable Coats	15	617	12		3	3	632
Chapeaux	142	531	107		35	35	673
Bearskins	400	273	400				673
Bonnets de Police	510	163	478	10	22	22	673
Stable Trousers	9	664			9	9	673
Waistbelts	496	177	395	9	92	92	673
Gibernes	254	370	250		4	4	624
Porte-Gibernes	254	370	254				624
Pair of Boots	385	283	334	38	13	13	661
Saddles Complete	375	293	350	23	2	2	668
Bridles Complete	376	293	363	1			668
Schabraques	374	294	324	19	31	31	668
Saddle Blankets	306	362	274	4	31	31	668

* Please note that the figures shown in the table are taken directly from the source, but some of the totals appear to have been calculated incorrectly.

The depot held 80 *habits* needing to be repaired, along with 320 *manteaux* and 75 *porte-manteaux*. We know nothing more about the dress of the regiment until 1802.

Reviewed on *30 Germinal AnX* (20 April 1802), the regiment mustered 461 men under arms. We note just 185 *habits* were in good condition out of 554, 200 needed repairs and 169 replacing, despite 525 being made over the course of the previous year. Just 296 *surtrouts* were considered in good repair, 189 *manteaux*, 238 *gilets*, 532 pairs of *culottes de peau* and 284 bearskins. Every man had his allocated issue of clothing, but the overwhelming majority needed repairs or replacement. Interestingly, 551 pairs of *epaulettes* were issued and 448 pairs of *gauntlets*: nothing is said about plumes, we assume these were counted with the bearskins. Over 1,000 *cavalerie chapeaux* were in service – 1,049 examples to precise – and 8 pairs of *culottes en tricot*. We also note 600 black leather *sabre* knots were issued. The inspector authorised the purchase of 250 pairs of grenadiers' *epaulettes* and the same number of *houpettes* (felted pompom with worsted tuft at the top, worn in *chapeaux*) for 250 francs, 416 pompoms for *sous-officiers* and *carabiniers' chapeaux* costing 312 francs and 625 cockades for *chapeaux*. For the trumpet major and 8 sergeant majors, 74cm 12 *ligne*-wide silver lace was ordered, 37m of the same lace for 20 sergeants and master workmen, and again 37m for 20 *fourriers*. White worsted lace 10 *lignes* wide was ordered for 416 *bonnets de police*, 74m 12 *ligne*-wide worsted lace was ordered for corporals rank stripes, 68m 18 *ligne*-wide white worsted lace was ordered for 105 *porte-manteaux* and 68m 18 *ligne*-wide white worsted lace was needed to make 140 *housses* and pairs of *chaperons*.[63]

The regiment was inspected on *5 Messidor AnXI* (24 June 1803) when the regiments clothing was as follows:[64]

Item	In Good Condition	In Need of Repair	To Be Written Off	Total	Number Made Since 20 April 1802
Standards	4				
Habits	456	64	94	608	
Surtrouts	267	87	227	588	94
Manteaux	453	85	88	556	47
Gilets en Drap Blanc	567	49	222	608	102
Gilets d'Ecurie	196	83	446	584	8
Culottes de Peau	608		8	616	606
Pantalons d'Ecurie	563		6	569	569
Chapeaux	354		230	584	569
Bonnets à Poil	463	32	96	584	64
Bonnets de Police	209	10	383	576	48

* Please note that the figures shown in the table are taken directly from the source, but some of the totals appear to have been calculated incorrectly.

In the same period 48 *habits* were made, 139 *surtrouts*, 48 *manteaux*, 574 *gilets*, 378 stable coats, 624 pairs of *culottes de peau de mouton*, 475 pairs of stable trousers, 625 *chapeaux*, 222 bearskins and 319 *bonnets de police*. As in previous inspection returns, we have no clue as to the dress of trumpeters. The total lack of blue milled *serge* and the small amount of scarlet broadcloth used is proof positive that reverse colours were not used by both regiments. We can only assume they wore the same uniform as rank and file, but perhaps with lace to the collar and cuff of the *habit*. The lack of any period iconography is also a hinderance in making any comments about the uniform beyond it was not reversed colours.

Cavalerie, Carabiniers and Dragons   181

Senior officers of the *1ᵉ Carabiniers*. Their uniforms are adorned with silver embroidery, removed in April 1791, but based on this image created in 1803 and was restored in the Consulate period.

A *carabinier* trooper wearing something like the uniform according to the regulations of 1791. He wears an adapted line infantry coat (white tail facings rather than scarlet) – due to acute shortages attested to in the regiments archive – and wears a bearskin with front plate, again likely the standard model for infantry grenadiers. Of interest he has a long queue in the German manner, likewise his moustache.

Potentially, the trumpet major of the *1ᵉ Carabiniers* circa 1800.

In April 1791, the *carabiniers* were designated the grenadiers of the cavalry, and were allocated scarlet fringed *epaulettes* and bearskin caps. This image from 1803 captures in minute detail the uniform according to the regulations of 1791.

Before 1791, the *carabiniers* wore elaborate silver lace to their uniforms as well as a *chapeau*. (*Collection KM*)

A *carabinier* officer wearing the uniform according to the regulations of April 1791.

Chapter 8

Dragons

Dragoons historically were soldiers who rode into battle on horseback and fought on foot. Armed with a musket, the first regiment raised in France was in 1635 – the ancestors of what became the *2ᵉ* Dragons, the *1ᵉ Régiment* was not formed until 1656, the *3ᵉ* was formed in 1649 by the Duke of Enghien, the *4ᵉ* was formed in 1667 and the *5ᵉ* in 1668. The last of the *Ancien Régime* regiments was formed in Metz in 1744, the *18ᵉ Dragons*.

Whole sale change occurred on 1 January 1791 as regimental numbers replaced old titles and numbers, and new facing colours were allocated severing unit traditions dating back almost 150 years to Louis XIV:

1ᵉ Régiment du Colonel-General became *5ᵉ Dragons*
2ᵉ Régiment du Mestre de Camp General became *10ᵉ Dragons*
3ᵉ Régiment Royale became *1ᵉ Dragons*
4ᵉ Régiment du Roi became *18ᵉ Dragons*
5ᵉ Régiment de la Reine became *6ᵉ Dragons*
6ᵉ Régiment du Dauphiné became *7ᵉ Dragons*
7ᵉ Régiment de Monsieur became *13ᵉ Dragons*
8ᵉ Régiment d'Artois became *12ᵉ Dragons*
9ᵉ Régiment d'Orléans became *16ᵉ Dragons*
10ᵉ Régiment de Chartres became *14ᵉ Dragons*
11ᵉ Régiment de Condé became *2ᵉ Dragons*
12ᵉ Régiment de Bourbon became *5ᵉ Cavalerie*
13ᵉ Régiment de Conti became *4ᵉ Dragons*
14ᵉ Régiment de Penthièvre became *8ᵉ Dragons*
15ᵉ Régiment de Lorraine became *9ᵉ Dragons*
16ᵉ Régiment de Noailles became *15ᵉ Dragons*
17ᵉ Régiment de Schomberg became *17ᵉ Dragons*
18ᵉ Régiment d'Angoulême became *11ᵉ Dragons*

Under the terms of the regulation new uniforms were issued. The regiments distinctive lace was abolished as the uniforms were nationalised:

The *1ᵉ Dragons dit Colonel-General* wearing the uniform according to the regulations of 1786. It became the *5ᵉ Dragons* in 1791.

Regimental Number				Pockets	Revers	Collar and Cuff Flaps	Cuffs
1	7	13	19	Horizontal	C	C	C
2	8	14	20		C	C	
3	9	15	21		C		C
4	10	16		Vertical	C	C	C
5	11	17			C	C	
6	12	18			C		C
Scarlet	Crimson	Rose	Yellow				

*C means colour.

The *19ᵉ Dragons* was formed 27 February 1793, as was the *20ᵉ Dragons*. The *21ᵉ Dragons* was formed in April 1796. Under the re-organisation of *1 Vendémiaire AnXII* (24 September 1803), the *7ᵉ Hussars* became the *28ᵉ Dragons*, the *11ᵉ Hussars* became the *29ᵉ Dragons* and the *12ᵉ Hussars* became the *30ᵉ Dragons*.

In theory, dragoons could operate equally as well as light cavalry or as battle cavalry for charges. Under the regulations of 1791, we remember a dragoon was issued a helmet and *bonnet de police*, a double-breasted stable coat with a stand and fall collar, a *surtrout*, a pair of knee breeches (*culottes de peau*) with 2 pairs of knee guards (*manchettes du botte*), a pair of black gaiters, a pair of shoes, *sabre* belt, *giberne* and belt, as well as his large *manteau*. The list of clothing and its service life was not affected by any further regulations until 1802 in the mid-years of the Consulate period and it was the first major uniform reform of the era. The King's Livery for trumpeters was abolished in favour of white lace and the *fleur-de-lys* emblem was to be removed. Trumpeters retained blue for their clothing, and did so until well into the mid-years of the *1ᵉ Empire* as explored in the author's companion volume on *dragons* and lancers, *Napolèon's Dragoons and Lancers*, also available from Frontline Books.

1ᵉ Dragons

The oldest of the *dragon* regiments was created in 1656, it was known as the *Dragons Etranger du Roi* as it was raised in Germany. It became the *1ᵉ Dragons* in 1792. The regimental paperwork is very incomplete when it comes to regimental clothing.

The inspection of *23 Pluviôse AnVII* (11 February 1799) reported the following:[1]

The 2ᵉ Dragons dit Mestre de Camp wearing the uniform according to the regulations of 1786. It became the *10ᵉ Dragons* in 1791.

The *3ᵉ Dragons dit Royal* wearing the uniform according to the regulations of 1786. It became the *1ᵉ Dragons* in 1791.

Item	Total Items	Items Missing	In Good Condition	In Need of Repair	To Be Written Off	To Be Replaced	Total
Habits	582	323	582			323	905
Vestes	518	387	518			387	905
Culottes de Peau	520	385		93	427	812	905
Manteaux	470	435	351	101	18	453	905
Surtrouts	520	385		93	427	812	905
Stable Coats	172	733	172			733	905
Chapeaux							
Helmets	504	401	345	113	46	447	905
Bonnets de Police	471	434			471	905	905
Stable Trousers	463	442			463	905	905
Waistbelts	506	399	360	121	25	424	905
Gibernes	443	389	313	94	36	425	832
Porte-Gibernes	443	389	313	94	36	425	832
Musket Slings	442	390	307	112	33	423	832
Porte-Manteaux	516	389	357	123	36	425	905
Pair of Boots	475	430	264	113	98	528	905
Musketoons (*mousquetons* – short muskets)	409	423	310	81	18	441	832
Sabres	502	403	342	131	26	431	905
Pairs of Pistols	414	554	324	75	15	569	968
Selles Complete (saddles with bridles, girths and stirrups)	452	448	310	101	41	489	900
Schabraques	453	447	312	136	5	452	900
Housses	The regiment had none						

* Please note that the figures shown in the table are taken directly from the source, but some of the totals appear to have been calculated incorrectly.

The inspector, General François Antoine Louis Bourcier, reported the regiment was well turned out, and commented that the *habits* and *gilets* made in broadcloth and *manteaux* were all in good condition, everything else except the helmets was to be written off and replaced. The men's equipment was incomplete and not a single *housse* existed for the horses. The inspector in his list of the regiment's failings, remarked that the *habits* were neatly cut, but were either too small or too large, the sleeves were too long and the *habit* not ample enough to close well across the chest, and the tails stopped at the mid-thigh. Both the *surtrout* and *habit* were worn over the sleeved *veste* or *gilet* and restricted the dragoon in his movement. The *surtrouts* were to be totally replaced as were the *vestes*

Dragons 191

The *4ᵉ Dragons dit du Roi* wearing the uniform according to the regulations of 1786. It became the *18ᵉ Dragons* in 1791.

with new examples made according to the model. Bourcier furthermore remarked that new stable coats were to be made along with *pantalons*, and the colonel was to ensure each man had a pair of spurs. Bourcier also castigated the officers for their ignorance at the changes ordered in accordance with the regulations of 1786, which replaced the cloth *chaperons* with a sheepskin *schabraque*. He also questioned why the officers still had *chaperons* and wondered where the *housses* for the other ranks were. Bourcier suggested that the officers had better acquaint themselves with the regulations on this matter and get *housses* made.[2]

The next report we have is dated *10 Nivôse AnX* (31 December 1801). The reviewing officer, General Jean-Baptiste-Camille de Canclaux, remarked that the regiments buff work was all of the *Chasseur à Cheval* pattern and the regiment was armed with light cavalry *carbines*! The regiment also had 'many *sabres* to be exchanged for the dragoon pattern'. How did the regiment become so equipped? Further, the men had no *habits*, 534 *surtrouts* being in use along with 55 white *vestes*. The men only had their stable trousers for legwear and broadcloth *pantalons* reinforced with leather to the inner leg worn with boots. The regiment had *culottes de peau*, but clearly these had never been replaced. In addition, 505 stable coats were in use, 235 *manteaux*, 469 helmets and 435 *bonnets de police*. For the horses, 361 *housses* were in use, 65 pairs of cloth *chaperons* and 332 sheepskin *demi-schabraque*. De Canclaux authorised the immediate production of 243 *habits*, 300 *surtrouts*, 111 *manteaux*, 243 *gilets*, 243 stable coats, 874 pairs of *culottes de peau*, 582 pairs of stable trousers, 111 helmets and 394 *bonnets de police*. The regiment's leatherwork was, despite being the wrong model, in good condition. Only 73 *gibernes* with belts, *sabre* belts, sword knots and other items being authorised for production as replacements, along with 111 *porte-manteaux* and 205 pairs of boots. He also authorised the purchase of 57 saddles, 113 saddle blankets, 183 *housses* and 183 pairs of *chaperons*. For the saddles 28kg of best quality leather was purchased, 20 shoulders of buff to make the belt part of the *sabre* belts – presumably, the light cavalry slings were retained or were new slings made? – and also to make the straps needed to carry the dragoon musket off the saddle.[3] The regiment must have presented a very unique sight – *Chasseur à Cheval sabres* and leatherwork, light cavalry style *pantalons à cheval* worn over boots, a single-breasted *surtrout* and helmet. Lack of regulation items clearly resulted in a high degree of divergence from the regulation.

Inspected on *19 Vendémiaire AnXIII* (11 October 1804), the regiment mustered 590 other ranks who were wearing 843 *habits*, of which 450 needed repairs, 946 *surtouts* of which 419 needed repairs and 133 total replacement, and the elite company had 107 bearskins. We note a huge shortfall in harness, as well as 404 *housses* and 296 pairs of *chaperons* for 478 horses, which had just 337 saddles! The *manteaux* the inspector noted were made from *blanc piqué de bleu* (cloth made from 1 blue to 8 parts white thread) broadcloth.[4] This cloth was made from a mix of 7 white threads to 1 blue, giving a very light shade of blue.

Reviewed on *19 Thermidor AnXIII* (7 August 1805), since the previous inspection 181 *habits* had been made, but despite these 189 needed repairs and 175 total replacement.

The *5ᵉ Dragons dit de la Reine* wearing the uniform according to the regulations of 1786. It became the *6ᵉ Dragons* in 1791.

We note 787 *surtouts* were in use, of which just 10 were in good condition – all brand new and issued since the last inspection. Were these for trumpeters? There were 489 that needed repairs and the remainder were 'worn out'. Purchases included 707 pairs of *culottes de peau* and 150 helmets. Furthermore, 250 pairs of boots, 530 *housses* and 700 sets of *chaperons* now existed. The men were issued 807 dragoon muskets and 1,011 pairs of pistols, 830 *sabres* and for some odd reason 844 *bayonets*.[5]

2ᵉ Dragons

Created in 1693 and given the title of *Enghien-Cavalerie*. In 1746, the regimental title was changed to *Cavalerie de Condé*, and was reformed as *dragons* in 1776. It became the *2ᵉ Dragons* in April 1791.

Inspected in Verdun on 26 November 1794, the men's dress was considered very bad indeed. Of the 508 men under arms, the review notes that 44 men stood just 4ft, and 34 men stood 5ft 8, the average height, some 201 men, being 5ft 5. Of these, 25 men were veterans, serving over 21 years, 18 men had served over 15 years, 35 men had served for 7 years and the vast majority for less than 4 years. For the 508 men we note, 78 *habits* had been issued in 1787, 78 in 1788, 78 in 1789, 78 in 1790, 174 in 1791 and 130 in 1792. We note 111 of the white *vestes* had been issued in 1786 and were a decade old, as were 118 smocks,186 helmets and 284 *manteaux*.[6]

Inspected again on *29 Pluviôse AnVI* (17 February 1798), we observe of the 822 men under arms, just 61 had a *habit*, 92 a *veste*, 695 a pair of *culottes de peau*, 574 men had a *manteau*, 697 men a *surtrout* and 678 men a stable coat. Every single helmet – 529 examples – had to be replaced as life expired. No *bonnets de police* or stable trousers existed. Likewise, the leatherwork was in shambolic condition: 662 *sabre* belts existed. Of which, 126 needed repairs and 162 total replacement. Only 217 *gibernes* and belts existed, and there were 711 *porte-manteaux* and 577 pairs of boots in varying degrees of repair. No man had his regulation-issue clothing and equipment. So, what were the men wearing to make up for the lack of army issue kit?[7]

Reviewed on *10 Floréal AnX* (30 April 1802), the inspector noted the men's leatherwork was in bad condition and the greater part needed total replacement. The same was true of the *schabraques*, *housses* and *chaperons*. All of the 735 *habits* were in good condition, no *surtouts* existed, every man had a pair of *culottes de peau*, but only 594 men had a *manteau*. Stores held a wide array of cloth: 1,395m 45 green broadcloth, 18m 56 scarlet broadcloth, 385m 20 white broadcloth, 4m 20 blue broadcloth – 24m having been used – and 70m 52 of *blanc piqué de bleu* broadcloth to make *manteaux*. The blue broadcloth may have been destined for trumpeters.[8]

4ᵉ Dragons

The regiment was reviewed 10 December 1791, the men's clothing and equipment was either new or worn out. We note from the report that 173 *manteaux* and 160 helmets

The *6ᵉ Dragons dit du Dauphiné* wearing the uniform according to the regulations of 1786. It became the *7ᵉ Dragons* in 1791.

had been issued in 1786, issued in 1787 were 7 blue trumpeters' *habits* adorned with the King's Livery, 67 *manteaux* and 27 helmets. We find 61 helmets issued in 1788 and 90 in 1789 with a further 116 *manteaux*. Roughly, 2/3 of the *habits* had been issued in 1790 – 262 examples – the remainder in 1791 – 111 examples. For renewal in the course of 1792 were 130 *habits* with the same number of *vestes* and *gilets*, 173 linen smocks and *bonnets de police* – the only ones the unit had – and 65 helmets. Armament wise, 28 *fusils de dragon* needed replacement, so too did 36 pistols and 30 *sabres*. The unit had no allocation of pickaxes, sickles, shovels or bill hooks. Of the 390 men under arms, the overwhelming majority were all former soldiers of Louis XVI. There were 19 men who had served for over 21 years, 36 for over 14 years, 50 for over 7 years and 130 for 4 to 8 years. The majority – 161 – came from Picardie, 30 from the Isle de France, 23 from Alsace, 28 from Franche-Comté and 39 from Normandy. In terms of background, 231 were unemployed agricultural labourers seeking food and a roof over their head, so too did 104 unemployed town labourers. The remaining men previously had a trade in civilian life. We note 3 bakers, 10 carpenters, 8 shoemakers, 12 farriers, 3 masons, 4 wood turners, 3 hairdressers, 3 saddlers, 1 knifemaker and 8 tanners. The shoemakers, saddlers, farriers, knifemaker and hairdressers would all have found ready employment in the regiment.[9]

Reviewed on *1 Vendémiaire AnVI* (22 September 1797), roughly 50 per cent of the unit was missing their regulation-issue uniform. For example, in the fourth squadron, for 112 men, 38 *habits* existed, 19 pairs of *culottes de peau*, 67 *surtrouts*, 47 helmets, no man had a pair of stable trousers and just 12 had a *bonnet de police*. Again, 50 per cent of the men's leatherwork was missing. This was true across the regiment.[10]

Inspected again on *22 Ventôse AnVII* (12 March 1799), the unit's clothing situation was worse than before. For the 622 men under arms, 299 *habits* existed, of which 182 needed repairs and 88 replacing. We note 270 *gilets* existed, just 128 pairs of *culottes de peau*, 316 *manteaux*, 175 *surtrouts* and 415 helmets. No stable coats, *bonnets de police* or stable trousers existed. We note furthermore, 389 *sabre* belts were in use, 274 *gibernes* and belts and 268 pairs of boots. Incredibly, for a regiment with 622 men under arms, only 396 had a *sabre*, 318 had a *fusil de dragon* and 47 *sous-officiers* carried a pistol. We are at a loss to imagine how *ad hoc* and improvised the unit must have looked. Clearly, a vast array of civilian and non-regulation clothing was in use.[11]

The report on *1 Germinal AnVIII* (22 March 1800) tells us that for a regiment musting 770 men, chronic shortages were the established pattern of the unit's clothing. Again, we note for 770 men, just 397 *habits* existed, and of these 105 needed repairs and 207 total replacement. Some kit had been issued since the previous review, as 377 pairs of *culottes de peau* were now in use, but 77 pairs needed repairs and 215 pairs needed replacement. The number of *surtrouts* had dropped to 92, and helmets to 308, but we note 242 stable coats, 168 *bonnets de police* and 327 pairs of stable trousers had been issued: all very laudable, but such garments did not solve a chronic lack of more essential items such as helmets, *sabre* belts, *gibernes* (just 207 in use) or boots (387 pairs in use) and tellingly 445 *sabres*.[12]

General Nicolas Oudinot, future marshal, reviewed the regiment on *8 Pluviôse AnX* (28 January 1802) and noted the regiment mustered 632 men with 517 horses. Again,

The *7ᵉ Dragons dit de Monsieur* wearing the uniform according to the regulations of 1786. It became the *13ᵉ Dragons* in 1791.

as in earlier years, the unit had huge shortages of clothing and equipment, and what did exist was simply 'knackered'. For example, 569 *habits* were in use, 269 having made since *1 Vendémiaire AnIX* (23 September 1800), but 186 were in need of repairs and 189 were life expired. We note 602 *surtrouts* were in use, 200 needed repairs and 202 total replacement, despite 397 being issued over the previous year. Oudinot recorded 573 helmets in service, 191 needed repairs and the same number replacing. Rather than carrying *fusils de dragon*, the unit was issued 512 *banderole-porte-mousquetons* (a shoulder belt from which the musketoon is slung) and 510 light cavalry *mousquetons*. Oudinot ordered the purchase of substantial amounts of cloth and materials:[13] 5m white *serge* to line 78 *surtrouts* and 224 sable coats at 1 for every 2 garments; 732m 50 scarlet broadcloth to make facings for 293 *manteaux* at 2m 56 per *manteaux*; 75m 50 linen 7/8 to line stable coats and *surtrouts* at 0m 25 per garment; 79.50 linen 7/8 to line 135 *porte-manteaux* and 183 *housses* at 0m 25 per item to repair 391 helmets; 2 dozen large buttons for 78 *surtrouts*; 6 dozen small buttons for 78 *surtrouts* and stable coats; 2m 50 silver lace for rank stripes of 8 sergeant majors; 12m 50 silver lace for rank stripes of 40 sergeants and *fourriers*; 475m white linen lace for *bonnets de police*; 732m white linen lace for repair of 183 *housses* and production of 162 at 5m per item; 450 plumes as replacements, and for recruits and 73m 44 worsted lace for 72 corporals' stripes. Did the *surtrouts* had white tail facings? Or was it just the upper body in white *serge*? Again, we see, contrary to regulations, the *bonnets de police* had white lace decoration.

Reviewed once more on *19 Vendémiaire AnXII* (12 October 1803), the unit's manpower stood at 581 men with 415 horses. For the first time since 1790, every man had his full allocation of kit, but 1/3 needed replacing and 1/3 repairs. Out of 614 *habits*, 204 needed repairs and 205 replacing. All the *surtrouts* – 614 in use – were brand new and in good condition. A mix of white *manteaux* – 438 in use – and the new model *manteaux-trois-quatre* with shoulder cape, reported as *capouchon* – 438 of these – were in use, made from *blanc piqué de bleu* broadcloth (1 blue thread for every 8 white) as were 56 bearskins for the recently formed elite company. The war squadrons had 382 light cavalry *mousquetons* and 65 *fusils de dragon* for sentry duty in the barracks. The unit was to receive an additional 475 of these.[14]

5ᵉ *Dragons*

Inspected on *22 Ventôse AnVII* (12 March 1799), the unit's clothing and equipment was shambolic. The regiment had 644 *sous-officiers* and men, none of whom had the full regulation-issue clothing and equipment. For example, just 257 *habits* were in use of which 147 were 'knackered', not a single pair of *culottes de peau* existed. Likewise, no *surtrouts* or stable trousers. Only 249 men had a helmet. We are left to speculate as to how the regiment actually appeared. Again, only 263 *sabre* belts existed and 241 *gibernes* and belts; every single weapon in use needed total replacement.[15]

The *8ᵉ Dragons dit d'Artois* wearing the uniform according to the regulations of 1786. It became the *12ᵉ Dragons* in 1791.

The *9ᵉ Dragons dit d'Orléans* wearing the uniform according to the regulations of 1786. It became the *16ᵉ Dragons* in 1791.

The *10ᵉ Dragons dit de Chartres* wearing the uniform according to the regulations of 1786. It became the *14ᵉ Dragons* in 1791.

General Michel Ney inspected the regiment on *26 Ventôse AnX* (17 March 1802) and reported every item of clothing and equipment had to be replaced. He did not bother to review the men's clothing or the contents of the regimental stores.[16]

Reviewed again on *10 Thermidor AnXI* (29 July 1803), since the last review 330 *habits* had been issued, 344 white *vestes*, 56 bearskins and 590 *surtrouts*. Also issued were 2 *manteaux* bringing the total *manteaux* to 474 and 173 *capuchons* (capes with a shoulder cape) – bringing the total *capuchons* to 527. We also note 588 stable coats had been made, as well as 635 pairs of stable trousers and 593 pairs of *culottes de peau*. Also in use were 353 pairs of *gauntlets*, 529 helmets and 325 sword knots. Stores held 72 pairs of shoes, 47 pairs of grey gaiters, 86 black stocks with 58 spare buckles. Almost all the new items had come from central government stores, as regimental stores report the use of just 32m 64 green broadcloth and 74m white broadcloth.[17]

On *19 Brumaire AnXIV* (10 November 1805), every man had a *habit* and a *surtout*, 806 of each being in use, and the elite company had 106 bearskins. We also note 518 *blanc piqué de bleu manteaux* were in service accompanied by 413 pairs of green *pantalons à cheval* reinforced with leather. Some 504 *housses* were in service, with 549 *chaperons*. The inspector ordered 217 *habits* to be made which required 440m 50 green broadcloth, 49m scarlet broadcloth and 7m 22 white broadcloth. There were 60 *manteaux* were to be made, lined in scarlet *serge*, and 433 *surtouts*, which were entirely green. The trumpeters were all armed with light cavalry *mousquetons* as were 9 dragoons who potentially were *sapeurs*. There were 56 tools were in use.[18] The elite company wore bearskins, and had white *contre-epaulettes* and *aiguillettes* on the right shoulder.

6ᵉ Dragons

A report on 24 November 1791 tells us that the unit's clothing was in poor shape, and needed a lot of repairs, the men's equipment 'is in pitiable condition the equipment for the horses has degraded to a point beyond use'.[19] How much of this was replaced we simply do not know.

Reviewed on 28 May 1793, we learn from this the regiment needed 480 *carabines* and *banderole-porte-mousquetons* in whitened buff leather, 412 pistols and 340 *sabres*. In addition, 519 pairs of *culottes de peau* were needed, 360 helmets, 370 *bonnets de police*, 364 stable cloaks and 399 *manteaux*. Also needed were 258 *sabre* belts, 223 *gibernes*, 361 sword knots, 448 pairs of boots, 351 *housses*, 306 *porte-manteaux* and 210 saddles. The unit was ordered to make clothing and equipment for the 519 men under arms, the inspector adding that unit administration was chaotic and negligent. Scarlet broadcloth and scarlet *serge* was needed with much urgency the inspector noted.[20]

We know nothing more until *13 Germinal AnX* (3 April 1802). Interestingly, the inspector noted that the men's white *vestes* were cut too short, which meant when the men were mounted, the *sabre* belt sat on the top of edge of the *culottes*, with an expanse of shirt before the bottom of the *veste*. For the 522 men under arms, no man had a *habit* and 437 *surtrouts* were in use, only 396 pairs of *culottes de peau* existed and 415

The *10ᵉ Dragons dit de Chartres* wearing the uniform according to the regulations of 1786. It became the *14ᵉ Dragons* in 1791.

General Michel Ney inspected the regiment on *26 Ventôse AnX* (17 March 1802) and reported every item of clothing and equipment had to be replaced. He did not bother to review the men's clothing or the contents of the regimental stores.[16]

Reviewed again on *10 Thermidor AnXI* (29 July 1803), since the last review 330 *habits* had been issued, 344 white *vestes*, 56 bearskins and 590 *surtrouts*. Also issued were 2 *manteaux* bringing the total *manteaux* to 474 and 173 *capuchons* (capes with a shoulder cape) – bringing the total *capuchons* to 527. We also note 588 stable coats had been made, as well as 635 pairs of stable trousers and 593 pairs of *culottes de peau*. Also in use were 353 pairs of *gauntlets*, 529 helmets and 325 sword knots. Stores held 72 pairs of shoes, 47 pairs of grey gaiters, 86 black stocks with 58 spare buckles. Almost all the new items had come from central government stores, as regimental stores report the use of just 32m 64 green broadcloth and 74m white broadcloth.[17]

On *19 Brumaire AnXIV* (10 November 1805), every man had a *habit* and a *surtout*, 806 of each being in use, and the elite company had 106 bearskins. We also note 518 *blanc piqué de bleu manteaux* were in service accompanied by 413 pairs of green *pantalons à cheval* reinforced with leather. Some 504 *housses* were in service, with 549 *chaperons*. The inspector ordered 217 *habits* to be made which required 440m 50 green broadcloth, 49m scarlet broadcloth and 7m 22 white broadcloth. There were 60 *manteaux* were to be made, lined in scarlet *serge*, and 433 *surtouts*, which were entirely green. The trumpeters were all armed with light cavalry *mousquetons* as were 9 dragoons who potentially were *sapeurs*. There were 56 tools were in use.[18] The elite company wore bearskins, and had white *contre-epaulettes* and *aiguillettes* on the right shoulder.

6ᵉ Dragons

A report on 24 November 1791 tells us that the unit's clothing was in poor shape, and needed a lot of repairs, the men's equipment 'is in pitiable condition the equipment for the horses has degraded to a point beyond use'.[19] How much of this was replaced we simply do not know.

Reviewed on 28 May 1793, we learn from this the regiment needed 480 *carabines* and *banderole-porte-mousquetons* in whitened buff leather, 412 pistols and 340 *sabres*. In addition, 519 pairs of *culottes de peau* were needed, 360 helmets, 370 *bonnets de police*, 364 stable cloaks and 399 *manteaux*. Also needed were 258 *sabre* belts, 223 *gibernes*, 361 sword knots, 448 pairs of boots, 351 *housses*, 306 *porte-manteaux* and 210 saddles. The unit was ordered to make clothing and equipment for the 519 men under arms, the inspector adding that unit administration was chaotic and negligent. Scarlet broadcloth and scarlet *serge* was needed with much urgency the inspector noted.[20]

We know nothing more until *13 Germinal AnX* (3 April 1802). Interestingly, the inspector noted that the men's white *vestes* were cut too short, which meant when the men were mounted, the *sabre* belt sat on the top of edge of the *culottes*, with an expanse of shirt before the bottom of the *veste*. For the 522 men under arms, no man had a *habit* and 437 *surtrouts* were in use, only 396 pairs of *culottes de peau* existed and 415

The *11ᵉ Dragons dit de Condé* wearing the uniform according to the regulations of 1786. It became the *2ᵉ Dragons* in 1791.

helmets, of which 185 needed repairs and 230 total replacement. Every single *sabre* belt and *giberne* needed replacement, as did all 333 *banderole-porte-mousquetons*, and only 272 *carabines* were issued. Only 2 pairs out of 387 pairs of boots were in a serviceable condition. Basically, everything was 'knackered'.[21]

Little change had taken place by *27 Prairial AnXII* (16 June 1804). No *habits* existed, 1,255 *surtrouts* had been issued, 286 new *manteaux-trois-quatre* were made from *blanc piqué de bleu* broadcloth, 74 *vestes* and 980 pairs of *culottes de peau* had been made. For headdress, 194 helmets and 56 bearskins had been issued. The *gibernes* with belts and *banderole-porte-mousquetons* all still needed replacing, but 77 *carabines* had been issued. The report also shows that despite 490 pairs of boots being issued, 139 pairs still needed replacing and 122 pairs repairing.[22]

7ᵉ Dragons

Organised as the *7ᵉ Dragons*, created from the *Dragons du Dauphiné* on 17 March 1791,[23] the regiment was reviewed on 28 November the same year. The inspector noted the dress of the men was superb, discipline was excellent, equitation conformed to the regulations of 1788, Colonel Claude de Guibert being noted as an outstanding example of an officer. Of the 401 men, 8 had 3 service *chevrons* denoting over 21 years' service. In terms of background, 151 men were unemployed town labourers before volunteering, no doubt for a hot meal and a roof over their head. Indeed, 120 men were unemployed farm workers. Of the other men, they had all had trades before enlistment. We note 12 bakers, 15 carpenters, 6 surgeons, 15 shoemakers, 10 farriers – useful trade for the cavalry! – 12 masons, 17 wood turners, 8 wigmakers or hairdressers, 4 saddles, 15 knifemakers, 12 tailors and 4 tanners.[24]

Inspected on *16 Pluviôse AnVI* (4 February 1798), of all the 622 men under arms, no man had a stable coat or stable trousers, nor did any man have a pair of *culottes de peau* or a *surtrout*. What actually was the men's legwear? The inspector merely assured the colonel that the state would supply *culottes de peau*.[25]

Reviewed once more on *14 Germinal AnX* (4 April 1802), the unit had no *habits* whatsoever, 529 *surtrouts* were in use, but 410 of these were life expired. By the time of the review, 462 pairs of *culottes de peau* now existed but all bar 53 pairs were destined for the rubbish heap, to be joined with 362 stable coats, leaving just 24 in use. Also needing to be replaced were 315 *bonnets de police*, 159 *sabre* belts, 95 *porte-manteaux* and 68 pairs of boots. No man had a pair of stable trousers. The inspector ordered 452 saddles, bridles, *housses*, *chaperons* and saddle blankets produced, as they were beyond use. He also ordered 233 helmets repairing.[26]

The *12ᵉ Dragons dit de Bourbon* wearing the according to the regulations of 1786. It became the *3ᵉ Dragons* in 1791.

The *13ᵉ Dragons dit de Conti* wearing the uniform according to the regulations of 1786. It became the *4ᵉ Dragons* in 1791.

The *14ᵉ Dragons dit de Penthièvre* wearing the uniform according to the regulations of 1786. It became the *8ᵉ Dragons* in 1791.

Item	Total Items	Items Missing	In Good Condition	In Need of Repair	To Be Written Off	To Be Replaced	Total
Habits	237	668	96	44	97	743	905
Vestes	125	780	88	22		680	905
Culottes de Peau	515	390	236	40	62	424	905
Manteaux	299	611	465	124	40	651	900
Surtrouts	338	577	285	43	10	587	905
Stable Coats	114	284	64	35	15	799	8981
Chapeaux	100	796	28		72	822	896
Helmets	485	411	453	20	12	381	896
Bonnets de Police	172	733	44		128	842	905
Stable Trousers	172p	733	74	26	57	690	905
Waistbelts	286	719	205	81		619	905
Gibernes	397	499	307	30	6	499	896
Porte-Gibernes	397	499	307	30	6	499	896
Musket Slings		896				896	896
Porte-Manteaux	434	466	235	190	22	490	900
Pair of Boots	101	799	53	44	7	806	900
Musketoons		896				869	896
Sabres	220	686	68	113	54	634	905
Pairs of Pistols	118	812	110	2		812	900
Selles Complete	102	798	35	80		793	900
Schabraques	107	793	53	48	6	794	900
Housses							

* Please note that the figures shown in the table are taken directly from the source, but some of the totals appear to have been calculated incorrectly.

9ᵉ Dragons

The oldest inspection return we can find for the regiment dates from *20 Prairial AnIV* (8 June 1796).[27] The inspector noted the dress of the regiment was mediocre, virtually every item needed to be replaced, the *serge* used by the regiment was very low quality, and the depot had virtually no other materials to make new garments or any ready-made garments to issue.[28]

The *16ᵉ Dragons dit Lorraine* wearing the uniform according to the regulations of 1786. It became the *9ᵉ Dragons* in 1791.

Reviewed on *18 Prairial AnV* (6 June 1797), clothing and equipment was as follows:[29]

Item	Total Items	Items Missing	In Good Condition	In Need of Repair	To Be Written Off	To Be Replaced	Total
Habits	467	438	413	23	31	469	905
Vestes	597	308	527	22	48	356	905
Culottes de Peau	641	264	547	18	76	340	905
Manteaux	445	455	440	2	3	458	900
Surtrouts	423	482	394	10	19	501	905
Stable Coats	574	331	524	25	25	396	905
Chapeaux							
Helmets	583	317	504	49	30	347	900
Bonnets de Police	626	279	567	10	49	328	905
Stable Trousers	487	418	227		260	678	905
Waistbelts	587	318	547	24	16	334	905
Gibernes	515	381	475	40		381	896
Porte-Gibernes	515	381	484	31		381	896
Musket Slings		896				896	896
Porte-Manteaux	580	320	580			380	900
Pair of Boots	473	427	370	60	38	465	900
Musketoons		896				896	896
Sabres	586	319	533	20	33	352	905
Pairs of Pistols	427	473	411	13	3	476	900
Selles Complete	446	454	428	18		454	900
Schabraques	427	473	334	47	46	519	900
Housses	420	480	420			480	900

* Please note that the figures shown in the table are taken directly from the source, but some of the totals appear to have been calculated incorrectly.

Since the earlier inspection, the regiment had been issued 493 *habits*, 1,350 *vestes*, 344 *surtrouts* made in *tricot*, 44 *surtrouts* in broadcloth, 786 stable coats, 372 *manteaux*, 394 pairs of *pantalons* made from *treillis* (herringbone weave hemp canvas), 786 *bonnet de police*, 350 *housses*, 550 *sacs à distribution* and 400 *porte-manteaux*.[30]

We have a regrettable gap of 5 years in the regiments preserved paperwork. General Nicolas Oudinot inspected the regiment on *11 Ventôse AnX* (2 March 1802). The inspection was far from thorough – he made no record on clothing and equipment other than '*bon*', which tells us virtually nothing. The depot had issued 496 plumes and 4 remained in the depot along with 9 *habits*, 46 *manteaux*, 160 pairs of stable trousers, 18 waistbelts and 198 *porte-gibernes*. The depot had used since 1800, 772m *blanc piqué de bleu* broadcloth to make 150 *manteaux*, 424m 58 white broadcloth to make 584 *vestes*, 2,242m 80 green broadcloth, 136m 97 crimson broadcloth, 913m 38 green *tricot*, 26m 75

The *18ᵉ Dragons dit La Rochefoucauld*. The unit was disbanded in March 1788 and was replaced by the *Angouléme* regiment, which intern became the *11ᵉ Dragons* in 1791.

The *24ᵉ Dragons dit de Schomberg* wearing the uniform according to the regulations of 1786. It became the *17ᵉ Dragons* in 1791.

crimson *tricot*, 13,698m 87 crimson *serge*, 1,989m 64 white milled *serge*, 1,307m 64 *treillis* and 1,783m 90 linen. The depot furthermore had made 225 *housses* and 252 *schabraques* from sheepskin that had a crimson *tricot festoon*. The depot had also produced 575 black stocks with buckles and had issued 314 pairs of black gaiters.[31]

11ᵉ *Dragons*

The regiment was reviewed on 23 November 1791. The unit mustered 386 other ranks, 23 officers and 9 men on the regimental staff (*etat-major*). The position of unit chaplain was vacant. We note 3 men had been promoted to officer status. The regiment was fortunate that it had been re-clothed over the past 18 months: 411 *habits* and *vestes*, and 205 smocks had been issued along with 58 helmets in 1790, and during the course of 1791, 110 *habits*, 103 *vestes*, 206 smocks, 66 *manteaux*, 120 *bonnets de police* and 48 helmets. The majority of the *manteaux* – 312 – and *bonnets de police* – 282 – had been issued in 1788,

An excellent example of a trooper's pattern helmet reflecting the regulations of 1786. (*Private Collection UK*)

and we note 58 helmets were issued new in 1786. Every sheepskin *schabraque* (decorative saddle cover) – 398 of them – were to be replaced, yet at the same time 398 *housses* and 402 pairs of *chaperons* were in use. Armament wise, 425 *fusils de dragon* were in use, 475 pistols, 435 *sabres*, as well as 49 sickles, 119 hatchets, 106 shovels and 80 picks.[32]

Inspected on *18 Pluviôse AnVI* (6 February 1798), the unit mustered 594 other ranks, 4 master workmen, 2 surgeons and 43 officers. No man had his regulation allocation of clothing or equipment. We note for 594 men, 105 men had no *habit*, 85 had no *gilet*, 128 lacked a pair of *culottes de peau*, 153 had no *manteau*, 153 men had no *surtrout* and of the 429 in use, 325 needed total immediate replacement. No man had a stable coat or a pair of stable trousers and just 162 *bonnets de police* were in use, of which 126 needed replacing. We note 534 helmets were in use, 43 needed repairs and 61 replacing. Furthermore, we report 54 men had no *sabre* belt, 97 had no *giberne* and belt, 164 men had no boots and of the 418 pairs in service, 76 pairs needed replacing and 23 repairing. Regarding horse equipment, 472 saddles were in use, but only 347 sheepskin *schabraques* and *housses*. Clearly, men rode to war with a lot of their clothing and equipment simply missing with civilian items pressed into use out of necessity.[33]

Reviewed again on *5 Frimaire AnVII* (25 November 1798), the inspector wrote, 'the men's dress is terrible … the clothing is exceptionally bad, the broadcloth in use if of exceptionally poor quality.' He added the leather used to make *gibernes* and boots was badly tanned and prepared, the sewing was also far from accurate, and in consequence nearly every pair of boots needed to be replaced. The harness and saddlery the inspector lamented was 'very incomplete, and what exists, is in a very bad condition'. He added that 'the men's armament is very incomplete but is well maintained'.[34]

The regiment was reviewed on *12 Pluviôse AnX* (1 February 1802) by General Jean-Joseph Ange d'Hautpoul. He found little wrong with the clothing, but a lot wrong with the regiment's equitation, drill and discipline and referred the officers and *sous-officiers* to the cavalry regulations of 1788 and the police regulations of 1792 for the internal discipline of a regiment. He stressed the regiment's tailors needed to study better the model items, and that the captain clothing officer needed to be more rigorous in quality control and checking the master tailor had exactly copied the model item and regulation. Many old *vestes* needed whitening, as did the buff work. General d'Hautpoul comes across as a very thorough, well read and informed officer, very magnanimous in his approach to shortcomings – all in all an excellent officer. The elite company had not yet received any items to mark out their status. One oddity in the inspection is that the regiment was armed with light cavalry style *carbines* and no dragoon muskets and possessed not a single *bayonet*.[35]

21ᵉ *Dragons*

Formed in April 1796, it was disbanded in April 1797. For a regiment with such a short existence, we have located an inspection return of the regiment dated *17 Vendémiaire AnV* (8 October 1796):[36]

Dragons 215

A sumptuous officer's helmet reflecting the regulations of 1786. (*Musee de l'Armée*)

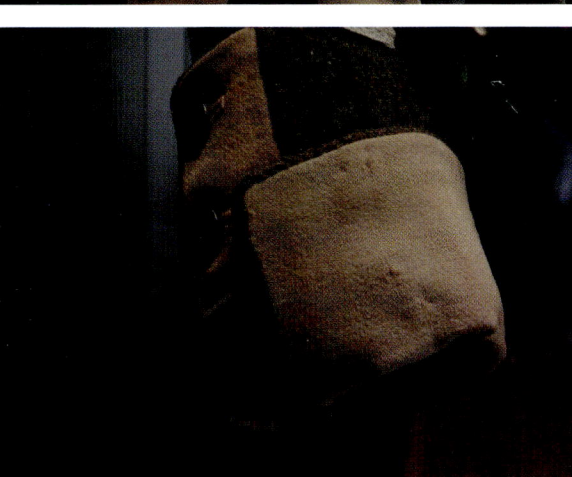

This *habit* reflects the regulations of 1791. It belonged to a corporal of the *16ᵉ Dragons*. The facings of the garment are made in a much finer cloth than the body. (*Musee de l'Armée*)

Item	Total Items	Items Missing	In Good Condition	In Need of Repair	To Be Written Off	To Be Replaced	Total
Habits	845	60	724	121		362	905
Gilets in Broadcloth	845	60	728	117		362	905
Culottes de Peau	845	60	602	136	107	150	905
Manteaux	762	143	722	40		150	905
Surtrouts	835	70	537	203	95	452	905
Stable Coats	813	92	423	252	138	362	905
Chapeaux	845						
Helmets	825	80	556	167	102	150	905
Bonnets de Police	826	179	587	155	84	603	905
Stable Trousers	800	105	200	325	275	905	905
Waistbelts	842	63	636	161	45	90	905
Porte-Manteaux	835	70	773	58	4	150	905
Pairs of Boots	845	60	444	260	141	301	905
Gibernes	845	60	845			90	905
Saddles	789	112	669	114	6	113	905
Schabraques	770	131	457	208	105	150	905
Sabres	832	73	558	201	73		905
Pairs of Pistols	786	119	678	85	23		905

* Please note that the figures shown in the table are taken directly from the source, but some of the totals appear to have been calculated incorrectly.

The clothing was passable, the equipment and saddlery needed attention, reported the inspector.

The regiment was created again in 1801 from the *1ᵉ Régiment de Piedmontese Dragons* with the annexation of Piedmont. It served with the *Grande Armée* from 1805 to 1807 and Spain from 1808 to 1813. It fought at the Battle of Leipzig and the campaign of France.

The regiment was inspected on 16 March 1802, its quite remarkable that of 441 *habits* in service for 447 men, 122 *habits* needed repairs and 98 were to be written off! The regiment's clothing was either life expired or totally missing. Yet despite the acute shortages, the regiment had 163 newly issued bearskins in use. Despite 441 *habits* being in use, just 156 *manteaux* were issued and a mere 200 pairs of *culottes de peau*. No helmets had been issued, and the men had to make do with 109 *bonnets de police* as their headdress. The depot had literally nothing – no cloth, no materials, no clothing or equipment. The inspector, General Jean-Baptiste-Camille de Canclaux, ordered 617 *habits* and *surtrouts* were to be made, 462 *manteaux* and 617 *gilets*, stable coats, pairs of stable trousers and *culottes de peau*, helmets, *bonnets de police* and sets of buff equipment.[37]

Presumably, the *1ᵉ Dragons circa* 1796 wearing the uniform according to the regulations of 1791.

Reviewed on *1 Nivôse AnXI* (22 December 1802), the regiment had no *habits* in use, and was wearing 424 *surtrouts*, with 36 more in the depot accompanied by 60 *manteaux*. Some 391 pairs of stable trousers were in use, with 27 more in the depot, 369 brand new helmets with 109 more in the depot and 59 bearskins with 16 in the depot. The depot also held 1,254 hides to make *culottes de peau*, 1,227m 40 *blanc piqué de bleu* broadcloth to make *manteaux*, 848m 33 green broadcloth, had used 95m 10 yellow broadcloth, and held 495m 74 green *tricot*, 858m 22 white milled *serge*, 1,588m 36 yellow milled *serge*, 762m 82 linen, 1,492m 35 *treillis*, 689 dozen large buttons and 34m 18 yellow *tricot*. *Tricot* was used either for legwear or *porte-manteaux*. So, did the trumpeters have yellow

The *7e Dragons* wearing its new regulation uniform. (*Collection KM*)

porte-manteaux? The inspector noted that the regiment was impeccably dressed, the elite company being noted for its imposing demeanour.[38]

General Nicolas Oudinot inspected the regiment on *9 Messidor AnXI* (28 June 1803). The regiment's account reveals that 1,159 francs 61 centimes had been spent on lace for *sous-officiers* and other distinctions – presumably, *epaulettes* for the elite company, plumes, bearskin cords etc. – and what else? – since 1 September 1802 along with 2,355 francs 36 centimes on repairing clothing, as well as 2,750 francs 25 centimes on cloth and 9,678 francs 5 centimes on making new clothing. The regiment mustered 427 rank and file and had 339 new *habits* in service. Oudinot commented that 400 blue *habits* that had existed at the previous review. Of these, 133 had been 'carried away' with deserters, 110 were in use, the rest had been converted into *surtrouts* or had been cut up to make *bonnets de police*. Some 442 *surtrouts* were in use, just 201 *manteaux*, 339 *gilet*s, 359 stable coats, 411 pairs of *culottes de peau* and 344 helmets. We note 56 bearskins were in use with the re-organised elite company, as well as 409 *bonnets de police*. It is clear that the regiment was still in the process of harmonising its uniform with the French model from that of Piedmont. For the horses, 200 saddles and sets of bridles existed, 200 *housses* and oddly 253 pairs of *chaperons*! The depot held 79 brand new unissued *habits*, 18 *surtrouts* that were likewise brand new and 41 needing repairs, 138 new *manteaux* and 91 old *Piedmontese* ones needing repairs, 49 new *gilets* and 61 needing repairs, 101 new stable coats and 8 needing repair, 7 new pairs of *culottes de peau*, 74 helmets and 91 *bonnets de police*. Oudinot authorised 149 *habits* to be made for new arrivals to the regiment, along with 597 pairs of *culottes de peau* and stable trousers, 597 *bonnets de police* and 199 pairs of dragoon boots to replace the *Piedmontese* boots that were in service. Since the previous inspection the regiment had received 698 dragoon muskets, 253 pairs of pistols and 716 *sabres*.[39]

Chapter 9

Hussards

The most flamboyant regiments of the French army after the imposing *cuirassiers* must surely have been the gaudily dressed *hussards*. At the time of the Revolution, 6 regiments existed: *Régiment du Colonel-General*, *Régiment de Bercheny*, *Régiment de Chamborant*, *Régiment de Salm*, *Régiment de Saxe* and *Régiment de Lauzun*. On 1 January 1791, the *Régiment de Bercheny* became the *1ᵉ Hussards*, the *Régiment de Chamborant* became the *2ᵉ Hussards*, *Régiment d'Esterhazy* the *3ᵉ Hussards*, *Régiment de Saxe* became the *4ᵉ Hussards*, the *Régiment du Colonel-General* became the *5ᵉ Hussards* and the *Régiment de Lauzun* became the *6ᵉ Hussards*.

The basic building block for the *hussards'* clothing regulation was that of 1 April 1791, which allowed *hussards* a *surtrout*, as well as *dolman* and *pelisse*, trumpeters were to wear dark blue with the King's Livery, authorised since 17 March 1788, each regiment was distinguished by its own unique colour combination:

- *1ᵉ Hussards* – *bleu de ciel* (sky blue) and scarlet, white buttons, lace and braid
- *2ᵉ Hussards* – brown faced *bleu de ciel*, white buttons, lace and braid
- *3ᵉ Hussards* – *gris-argentin* (silver-grey) faced *rouge-garance* (madder red) white buttons, red lace and braid
- *4ᵉ Hussards* – green faced scarlet, yellow buttons, lace and braid
- *5ᵉ Hussards* – *bleu* national, faced scarlet, yellow buttons, lace and braid
- *6ᵉ Hussards* – white, faced *bleu celeste* (celestial blue), yellow buttons, lace and braid

On 4 May 1792, the *4ᵉ Hussards* emigrated entirely, and the existing regiments adjusted their designation accordingly, the former *Régiment du Colonel-General* taking the *4ᵉ* position and *Régiment de Lauzun* taking the *5ᵉ* position. Created as the *7ᵉ Hussards* by decree on the 23 November 1792, from the *Hussards Defenseurs de la Liberté et Hussards de l'Egalitié*, it was renumbered as the *6ᵉ Régiment de Hussards* by the decree of 4 June 1793. The famous *7ᵉ Hussards de Marbot* were formed on 21 February 1793 along with the *8ᵉ*; the *9ᵉ*, *10ᵉ* and *11ᵉ* came along on 28 July 1793; the *12ᵉ* was raised on 9 February 1794; the *13ᵉ* in February 1795 and was disbanded on 21 April 1796.

The *dolman* and *pelisse* were the trade mark uniform of the *hussards*. The name '*dolman*' was also given to the uniform coat worn by *hussards*. The tight-fitting, short-cut coat was heavily braided. The *dolman* was a short cut coat, with a single piece back and single piece sleeves. It had a standing collar. The front was decorated with either 3 or 5 rows of buttons, up to 18 rows deep down the front of the jacket. The seams on the back of the coat were covered with flat braid. The pointed cuffs, collar, false pockets, leading and

The *1ᵉ Hussards dit Colonel-General* wearing the uniform according to the regulations of 1786. It became the *5ᵉ Hussards* in 1791 and then the *4ᵉ* in June 1793. The *4ᵉ* retained the scarlet and sky blue uniform until *1 Vendémiaire AnXI* (23 September 1802). The change to dark blue took time, and was perhaps not completed until after the Jena campaign or even later.

bottom edge were also covered in flat braid either 10 or 12mm wide. They were lined internally with linen. Around the bottom edge of the *dolman*, on the side, appeared a band of red *basane* (Moroccan leather). This reinforced the lining and stopped the *sabre* waistbelt rubbing through the lining. Over the duration of the *1ᵉ Empire*, the cut of the *dolman* changed – the bottom or leading edge increasingly moved up the torso as the waistline of civilian garments did the same. At the start of the *1ᵉ Empire*, the bottom of the *dolman* was just below the natural waist, by 1815 the *dolman* often finished above the natural waist. It was complemented by a *pelisse*.

A *pelisse* was originally a short fur-lined or fur-trimmed jacket that was usually worn hanging loose over the left shoulder of *hussards'* light cavalry soldiers, ostensibly to prevent sword cuts. The name was also applied to a fashionable style of women's coats worn in the early nineteenth century. The style of uniform incorporating the *pelisse* originated with the *hussards'* mercenaries of Hungary in the seventeenth century. In appearance the *pelisse* was characteristically a very short and extremely tight-fitting jacket, the cuffs and collar of which were trimmed with fur. The front of the jacket was distinctive and featured several rows of parallel frogging and loops, and either 3 or 5 lines of buttons. For officers, this frogging was either gold or silver bullion lace to match either gold (*glit*) or silver buttons. Other ranks had either yellow lace with brass buttons or white lace with 'white metal' buttons. The *pelisse* was usually worn slung over the left shoulder, in the manner of a short cloak. It was held in place by a shoulder cord. It was cut to be longer than the *dolman*. It was never worn over the *dolman*. In the winter it was worn over the *veste*, the *dolman* being placed into storage. In foul weather the *pelisse* or *dolman* would be covered by the *manteau*.

The *hussards* were issued a green *manteau* with shoulder cape, a *bonnet de police*, stable coat, stable trousers, boots, as well as tight-fitting *culottes hongroise* decorated with yellow or white braid. The regulations of April 1791 left the dress of the *hussards* unchanged, except that regimental lace and other distinctions for the *Régiment du Colonel-General* were abolished. The decree also allowed for a *surtrout*, the same colour as the *dolman*, plumes were officially to be black with the regiment's facing colour displayed at the very top. The *Régiment d'Esterhazy*, *Régiment de Saxe* and *Régiment de Lauzun* were allowed black felt *schakos*.

With the creation of new regiments of *hussards* – a total of 14 (although 2 regiments were numbered 7) – new guidelines were issued on 9 February 1795. It sought to harmonise the newly created regiments with the rest of the *hussards* as a branch of the service and authorised the adoption of the *hussards'* dress across all units.

1ᵉ Hussards

Demoted in 1783 to *2ᵉ* following the creation of the *Régiment du Colonel-General*, it regained its number *1ᵉ* during the reform of 1791. We know almost nothing about its dress during the Revolutionary epoch.

An officer of *2ᵉ Hussards dit Bercheny*, which became the *1ᵉ Hussards* in 1791.

Reviewed on *23 Pluviôse AnVI* (11 February 1798), most of the unit's clothing was either falling to bits or missing: just 56 *pelisses* existed, 36 of which were 'knackered', for the 796 men just 381 *dolmans* were in use, accompanied by the 153 *vestes*, 241 *surtrouts*, 487 *manteaux*, 311 pairs of *culottes hongroise*, 33 stable coats and 315 pairs of stable trousers. No *bonnets de police* or barrel sashes existed. We note 587 *schakos* were in use, 135 being 'knackered', leaving 204 men with no headdress. Equipment wise, 516 *sabre* belts and *sabres* were in service. There were only 119 *gibernes* and belts, 445 *banderole-porte-carabines* (shoulder belts to carry a *carbine*) and 412 *carbines*, but not a single *sabretache* (large, flat leather pouch). Furthermore, 148 men had no boots, and of the boots in use, 49 pairs needed repairs and 137 were 'knackered'.[1]

Inspected again on *16 Germinal AnX* (6 April 1802) by General Emmanuel de Grouchy, he reported that for the 741 men under arms, 967 *dolmans* existed, but of these, 400 needed repairs and 97 were life expired. Of the *pelisse*, 695 existed and 269 needing repairs or replacement. De Grouchy reported 769 *surtrouts* were in service, 574 *manteaux*, 786 *vestes*, 781 stable coats, 704 pairs of *culottes hongroise*, just 158 pairs of stable trousers, 704 pairs of underwear and 534 barrel sashes. Not every man had a *sabre* belt – 658 existing for the same number of *sabres* – 651 *banderole-porte-carabine* existed for 579 weapons. For headdress, 787 *schakos* were in use. The bulk of the regiment's clothing and equipment was life expired and needed urgently replacing de Grouchy ordered.[2]

2ᵉ Hussards

Created in Strasbourg on 25 January 1735 from Hungarian volunteers. The *2ᵉ Hussards*, latterly the *Régiment de Hussards de Chamborant* was reviewed on 28 March 1791. The report makes no mention of clothing, we have to wait until *1 Messidor AnVI* (19 June 1798) for any detail. The report tells us that the stable trousers rather than being made from canvas, were made from *tricot* reinforced with leather, 724 pairs being in use for 731 men. Only 446 *pelisse* were in service and just 390 *dolmans*, but we note the difference was partly made up with the use of *surtrouts*, 154 being in use. Only 96 men had a barrel sash, and 541 men had a *schako*; we are ignorant of the headdress used by 190 men. We note just 246 *sabretaches* were in use, 228 men had no *sabre* belt – 222 men had no *sabres* – 267 had no *giberne* and belt. The inspector, General François Antoine Louis Bourcier, ordered 240 *dolmans* made, 80 of each of the 3 regulation sizes.[3]

Reviewed again on *1 Vendémiaire AnIX* (23 September 1800), most men were not equipped according to the regulations. We note 743 *dolmans* were in use for 781 men, 601 *pelisse*, 332 *gilets*, 592 pairs of *culottes hongroise*, 75 *surtrouts*, 600 pairs of *pantalons à cheval*, 700 *schakos*, 64 barrel sashes, 195 *sabre* knots and 380 *sabretaches*. Again, we note 202 pairs of gloves were issued, 250 regulation shirts, 1,142 pairs of linen underpants and 1,185 pairs of stockings. Rather than black regulation stocks, black linen cravats were used. The inspector ordered 96 *dolmans* made, which required 14m 40 chestnut brown broadcloth and 6m *bleu celeste* broadcloth. We also note 80 stable coats needing 14m 40 *bleu celeste* broadcloth were ordered to be produced, along with 24 pairs of *pantalons à*

A trooper of *2ᵉ Hussards dit Bercheny*, which became the *1ᵉʳ Hussards* in 1791.

cheval, again made from *bleu celeste* broadcloth. These 2 garments between them required 12m 48 chestnut brown broadcloth. Presumably, collar and cuffs of the sable coats, and the button stands of the *pantalons à cheval*. We also note 130 green *manteaux* were ordered and 150 *schakos*.[4]

3ᵉ Hussards

The *3ᵉ Hussards* were made famous by the film *The Duellists*. The regiment was dressed in *gris-argentin* or at least that is what we are told by Lucien Rousselot and others. This may have been the case in the early 1780s, but cloth samples dating from 1788 reveal the colour was sky blue melange cloth and definitely not grey! The regiment's facings were *rouge-garance*. No archive documentation has survived that tells us why this change took place, or when. In fact, we know nothing until near year 1796 about the dress of the regiment.

We are fortunate that some of the regiment's standing orders have come down to us:[5]

[*19 Nivôse AnIV*] 9 January 1796
Sous-officiers and hussars who have been issued shell harnesses will hand them to the master saddler, who will repair them or give others.

[*15 Pluviôse AnIV*] 4 February 1796
The non-commissioned officers will be dressed in the future, on parade days in *fracs* and hats without plumes.

[*17 Pluviôse AnIV*] 6 February 1796
The brigade leader noticed that there were still white shoulder belts. They are to be blackened with wax.

[*7 Ventôse AnIV*] 26 February 1796
The *sous-officiers* will ensure that all *giberne* and *carbine* belts are blackened and that all hussars have their hair tied with weights.

[*12 Ventôse AnIV*] 2 March 1796
Officers who have not complied with the prescribed model for the uniform are asked to comply with it as soon as possible. They must not have *franches* [it is unclear how to understand this other than as fringing] to the *sabretaches* and the non-commissioned officers must not wear *ganse* on their *chapeaux*.

[*11 Germinal AnIV*] 31 March 1796
Ordinary instruction on foot tomorrow. The *sous-officiers* will have their *carbines sabres* and buff belts at the place of exercise.

An officer of *3ᵉ Hussards dit Chamborant*.

[14 Germinal AnIV] 3 April 1796
The hussars are remined that they must wear the cockade on the side of their *schako* with the *ganse* and button and not attached to the *schako* cords.

[? Floréal AnIV] [?] May 1796
Distribution of black *schakos* with wing [*flamme*].

[19 Floréal AnIV] 8 May 1796
7 musicians who are mounted are to ride grey or white horses.

[18 Prairial AnIV] 6 June 1796
For the parade tomorrow, the officers will all be in uniform, they will wear their red or white *gilet*s. The non-commissioned officers, will wear their *surtrout*, breeches and *veste*. Sunday, they will wear their *dolman* closed with the barrel sash over it.

[25 Prairial AnIV] 13 June 1796
The officers according to the order that I received, are requested to obtain by the 19 June [1796], black plumes surmounted by red to wear on their *schako*. Their *schabraques* will conform to the model which is found with the captain of clothing. They will be free to put a white worsted lace or silver lace on it.

[18 Messidor AnIV] 6 July 1796
Tomorrow at 8 am, the assembly will be called and at 8:30 am the regiment will be on horseback. The men will be in turned *schako* [i.e. the *flamme* rolled up], plume deployed, closed *dolman* and barrel sash over it, new breeches and boots.

[23 Fructidor AnIV] 9 September 1796
Officers henceforth can only wear a scarlet vest with a row of 18 buttons. Breeches with blue lace for non-parade days. On parade days, silver laced breeches and red uniform *gilet*.

For the troop, they are not permitted to wear yellow breeches or coloured waistcoats. For the troop … on parade days the *dolman* only on the 3 buttons at the top are fastened, white vest and the barrel sash worn over it, the plume without case.

As soon as they arrive back at the depot, the plume will be put back in its case.[6]

The regiment was reviewed on *6 Thermidor AnIV* (24 July 1796) and the resulting report provides clarity to the regimental standing orders, as well as a broader context for how the regiment was dressed. For 1,051 men, 438 men only had *pelisse*, well over 50 per cent lacked this characteristic feature of the *hussards*' dress. We note 43 *dolmans* were needed to equip every man, and of the 1,008 in use, 347 were life expired. Not every man had a pair of *culottes hongroise* as 17 men lacked these, or barrel sashes with 77 needed to equip each man. No man had his full allocation of clothing or equipment. Indeed, 242 *sabretaches*

A trooper of *3ᵉ Hussards dit Chamborant*, which became the *2ᵉ Hussards* in 1791.

were missing and of those in use 309 needed replacing. Remembering the cloth sample from 1788, which shows a light blue broadcloth for the uniform, we find confirmation that blue was indeed the regiment's colour. Stores reported 36,163 *aunes* blue broadcloth had been used to make *culottes hongroise, dolmans, pelisse, surtrouts,* 'stable caps' and *gilet*s. The stable coats and *dolmans* had red broadcloth for piping and the *manteaux* were made from dark green broadcloth. Issued since *4 Frimaire AnIV* (25 November 1795), we note 1,330 pairs of *culottes hongroise*, 661 *dolmans* and of interest 120 *pelisses* for *sous-officiers* and trumpeters trimmed in fox fur.⁷ Clearly, the scarlet *vestes* mentioned in the orders were an innovation as none existed at the time the order was written.

Regimental orders reported that in '1797 the officers are authorised to start again to use *gris-argentin* cloth for their uniforms [but not the troops]'.⁸ A receipt dated *3 Vendémiaire AnVI* (24 September 1797) confirms that the unit's cloth was still blue. We note that to make 359 *pelisses*, 356 *dolmans*, 699 *gilet*s, 182 stable coats and 96 *manteaux* the unit needed 116 *aunes bleu celeste* broadcloth, 31 *aunes rouge-garance* broadcloth, 18 *aunes* green broadcloth and 60 *aunes bleu celeste tricot* – for the stable coats – as well as flat white braid, square braid, flannel and Morrocco leather for the *dolmans*, 25 olives for the *pelisse*, 15 sheep hides and 592 dozen buttons.⁹ The sample in A.S.K. Brown's collection can easily be described as *bleu celeste*, so we have 2 sources corroborating the absence of *gris-argentin*. The regimental orders re-commence 4 years later:

[*5 Floréal AnVIII*] 25 April 1800
Leather helmets are prohibited.

[*1 Fructidor AnVIII*] 19 August 1800
The hussars will no longer carry their plumes on the *scabbards* but in the *porte-manteaux*. Their hair will be combed and powdered.

[*2 Sansculottides AnV*] 19 September 1800
The captains who will make visors for the *schakos* of the hussars will take care that they are wider than those which had been made by the saddler Sohn and instead of attaching them with hooks and eyes they will have them sewn to the *schakos*.

[*2 Frimarie AnIX*] 23 November 1800
The brigade chief recommends the production of *manteaux* and visors.

[*29 Frimarie AnIX*] 20 December 1800
Officers can wear *redingotes* with *gris[-]argentin* collar, *pelisse*s and *dolmans* in the field, either in silver or in goat hair, the *surtrout* with *revers* with 6 buttons. The officer's *pelisse* edges must be in fox fur.¹⁰

The leather helmets we assume to be the 1791 types.

Hussards 231

An officer of *4ᵉ Hussards dit de Conflans*, becoming *de Saxe* in 1788, emigrating during June 1793.

Reviewed on *11 Pluviôse AnX* (31 January 1802), the other ranks were still dressed in blue 2 years after the officers switched to *gris-argentin*. Stores held on *1 Vendémiaire AnIX* (23 September 1800) 2,102m 18 blue broadcloth, and purchased a further 2,869m 86 and used 3,955m 19 blue broadcloth to make 652 *dolmans*, 472 *pelisse* and 106 *surtrouts*.[11] Any change of the regiment's colour would take time.

The regiment was inspected on *30 Messidor AnXI* (19 July 1803), shortly before the regulation of *1 Vendémiaire AnXI* (23 September 1802), which authorised the use of *gris-argentin* broadcloth mentioned in the regimental orders 3 years earlier, but this time in the context of clothing the rank and file of the regiment. We note some 2,312m 36 of this cloth had been used to make 255 *dolmans*, 104 *pelisse* and 82 *surtrouts*; 917m 89 *gris-argentin tricot* had been used to make *culottes hongroise*. The unit had changed its pattern of *schako* by this date as we note 516 pairs of *schako* cords were in use, and 65 colpacks (a round bearskin hat usually with a bag or flap on top) for the elite company. The adjutant majors had 2 *redingotes* made and issued for them, and rather than regulation stocks, the men were allowed to use black linen cravats.[12]

4ᵉ Hussards

Created on 29 July 1792 from *the Légion de la Nievre*. There were also men in the regiment who had remained in France from the *Hussards de Saxe* and *Régiment du Colonel-General* – they had not emigrated to serve in the *Armée du Condé* against the French Republic.

Reviewed on *4 Messidor AnVI* (22 June 1798), the inspector ordered 138 scarlet *pelisses* to be made, along with 152 blue *dolmans*, 119 stable coats made in *bleu tricot* accompanied by 94 pairs of *pantalons à cheval* and 145 *porte-manteaux* made from the same material.[13]

Inspected on *8 Ventôse AnVII* (26 February 1799), the inspector noted the men's uniforms were very incomplete and replacement items were urgently needed. The situation existed as the clothing registers and depots were in administrative chaos: the clothing officer was given 3 months to audit the accounts, identify clothing and equipment needing repairs or replacement, procure materials and begin production of the required clothing and equipment. No inventory of the unit's stores existed. The exasperated inspector noted, 'great irregularities exist in the book keeping'. He was not suggesting the officers were committing fraud, but implied incompetence was allowing officers to get away with financial irregularities. The inspector, General François Antoine Louis Bourcier, strongly urged the officers to learn their trade in giving orders and how to administer and manage their regiment. Bourcier ordered 15m scarlet cloth to repair 49 *pelisse*, and 34m blue broadcloth was needed to repair 116 *dolmans*. Bourcier also authorised blue *tricot* to be purchased to repair 50 stable coats, 171 pairs of *pantalons* à *cheval*, 171 *porte-manteaux* and 27m blue broadcloth to repair 87 *manteaux*. In theory, these were green, not so in the 4ᵉ *Hussards*![14]

At the time of the review on *15 Floréal AnXI* (5 May 1803), we note 56 brand new stable coats made from regulation blue *tricot* had been made and 61 pairs of regulation stable trousers produced from 138m 21 of *treillis*. We note the unit's *manteaux* were still blue as not an inch of green broadcloth existed.[15]

A trooper of *Hussards de Conflans* wearing the uniform according to the regulations of 1786.

5ᵉ Hussards

Raised in 1783 with the *Ordonnance* of 14 September 1793, from the cavalry of the *Légion de Lauzun*, which had been formed in 1778. The *Légion de Lauzun* had served in America and had recently returned when it was re-christened the *Hussards de Lauzun*. In 1791, it became the *6ᵉ Hussards* and then in 1793 the *5ᵉ Hussards* with the decree of 4 June. Dressed in white and *bleu de ciel* with yellow lace and trim, the uniform of the *5ᵉ Hussards* was one of the most elegant of the epoch.

History has not been kind to the regimental archive of the *5ᵉ Hussards*, nothing exists between 1791 and 1803 concerning its uniform and equipment. General Michel Ney had inspected the regiment in summer 1802 when he commented that the *surtrouts* and *schakos* were 'all detestable' and the government was being slow in issuing new uniforms. The *manteaux* were clearly green as Ney noted, 1,168m 66 green broadcloth had been used to make 377 *manteaux*. Ney also records that 1,798m 48 blue *tricot* had been employed to make 1,022 pairs of *culottes hongroise*.[16]

General Marc-Antonie de Beaumont, whose actions in 1815 over shadowed his entire military career, reviewed the regiment in summer 1803. The regiment's manoeuvres were good, the men overall rode well and cared well for their horses. Discipline in the regiment was good. In fact, everything about the regiment met his satisfaction. Clothing in use was as follows:[17]

Item	In Good Condition	In Need of Repair	To Be Written Off	Total	Total Made Since 1802
Barrel Sashes	409	77	166	652	363
Dolmans	131	80	298	509	114
Pelisses	187	120	282	589	263
Surtrouts	57		1	58	57
Manteaux	200	98	289	587	9
Gilets	18			18	14
Stable Coats	101	70	256	427	149
Culottes Hongroise	24	34	297	355	33
Stable Trousers	378	50	270	698	571
Schakos	160	105	323	588	296
Bonnets de Police	222	32	390	644	233
Underwear			772	772	
Gloves			386	571	

* Please note that the figures shown in the table are taken directly from the source, but some of the totals appear to have been calculated incorrectly.

From the returns of the depot, 860 black plumes existed in 1802, 386 were issued after this, making 1,246 plumes delivered to the regiment of which 860 were in use. The depot held 867m 17 blue broadcloth and 1m 75 white broadcloth – no red broadcloth existed

An officer of *5ᵉ Hussards dit de Saxe* wearing the uniform according to the regulations of 1786, dressed in the famous *gris-argentin*.

in 1802 or had been purchased. The depot also held 1,069m 36 *serge*, 26m 35 white *tricot*, 636m 27 white flannel and 1,960m 31 linen. Over 1,000m *serge* had been used since the previous inspection – in theory, this was used to line *vestes* and *habits*. What else was it being used for? The *5ᵉ* only had 58 *surtrout*, and just 14 *gilet*s were made, which would have required far less than the 1,000m cloth to line these garments with. The only use for the white *tricot* was to make the 14 *gilet*s. Were these for trumpeters? The *surtrouts* were arguable for *sous-officiers* and were clearly cut so as not to need a *gilet* under them i.e. they closed to the waist. The regiment was armed with 816 musketoons of which 103 had been lost, 602 pairs of pistols and 878 *sabres*.[18]

8ᵉ Hussards

Created as the *Régiment des Éclaireurs de Fabrefonds* by Colonel Joseph Fabrefonds on 23 November 1792, it became the *9ᵉ Hussards* on 26 February 1793 and the *8ᵉ* only a matter of weeks later on 4 June the same year.

Inspected on 6 January 1793, not a single piece of *hussards'* kit was in use. We note *habits*, *vestes*, *pantalons à cheval*, and, presumably, *mirlitons* (conical *shakos* with a cloth wing in distinctive colour) as headdress listed as '*bonnets de parade*'. We may be wrong about this assertion. Clothing was either in good condition or 'past its best'. There were 72 of the 111 *habits* that needed to be replaced. Every single pair of *culottes hongroise*, 43 pairs of boots out of 93 in use also needed replacing, and 17 men had no regulation issue boots. Due to shortages, for 111 men, just 90 pairs of *culottes hongroise* and 55 pairs of *pantalons à cheval* existed, as well as 52 *bonnets de police* and 89 *sabres*. No doubt the unit was still dressed as *éclaireurs*, the colours of which we are totally ignorant.[19] The *habits* were, in fact, cut like a *surtrout*, complete with long tails, and had a stand and fall collar. The front of the garment was decorated with braid like a *dolman*.

Inspected on *1 Vendémiaire AnVI* (22 September 1797), the regiment was wearing little more than rags, if the men had regulation clothing and equipment. Looking at *4ᵉ* squadron as an example, for 112 men we note 29 *pelisse*, 65 *dolmans*, 8 pairs of *culottes hongroise*, 80 *gilet*s, 13 *surtrouts*, 30 stable coats, 45 pairs of *pantalons* à *cheval*, 13 barrel sashes, 17 *manteaux* and 44 *schakos* were in use. Of those items that existed, a quarter needed total replacement. Equipment was likewise missing or worn out: 30 *sabre* belts existed, 51 *gibernes*, 23 pairs of boots and 24 *sabretaches*. One is left wondering as to the bizarre appearance of the regiment.[20]

Inspected on *11 Germinal AnX* (1 April 1802), we note 2,909 sheepskins had been used to make *pelisse*, 912 *houpettes*. Were these tassels for the *bonnets de police* or plumes for the *schako*? The word is used confusingly for both items depending on the context that is missing here.

The next review that has survived is from *2 Prairial AnXI* (22 May 1803), which reports 26m 72 scarlet *tricot* had been used to make trumpeters' legwear, which implies they were dressed in reversed colours by this date.[21]

A trooper of *5ᵉ Hussards de Saxe*. In March 1788, the regiment became *d'Esterhazy* and adopted *bleu celeste*. It became the *4ᵉ Hussards* in 1791 and the *3ᵉ Hussards* in summer 1793.

9ᵉ Hussards

Formed on 2 September 1792 as the *2ᵉ Régiment des Hussards de la Liberté*, at which point the regiment carried – confusingly – the number 8. The *1ᵉ Régiment des Hussards de la Liberte* became the *6ᵉ Hussards*.

Inspected on 6 January 1793 not a single piece of *hussards'* kit was in use. We note *habits, vestes, pantalons à cheval*, and, presumably, *mirlitons* as headdress listed as '*bonnets de parade*'. Clothing was either in good condition, or 'past its best' with 72 of the 111 *habits* needing to be replaced reported as being Prussian blue with *aurore* lining and facings, the *culottes hongroise* were noted as Prussian blue with *aurore* braid and scarlet facings, and they had scarlet triple breasted waistcoats. Leatherwork was blackened cowhide.[22]

On conversion to the *hussards*, a document from the Ministry of War, ordered the following specification for clothing: *bleu de roi* (dark blue) broadcloth for *habits*, *gilets* and *pantalon de drap* garnished with leather; *bleu celeste* broadcloth for *pelisses* lined with black sheepskin; *sabretaches*; *chapeaux*, plumes, cockades and pompoms; *sabres* and *scabbards*; *sabre* belts; sword knots; *gibernes*; *pantalons* and *gilets* for stable duties; *bonnets de police*; *musettses* (nose bags that doubled up to contain grooming kits) and black stocks with buckles and card liners.

The new unit was to have 8 companies each of 60 men. It is interesting to note no *dolmans* are noted and a mix of two different shades of blue.[23] The *pelisse* was to be worn in the winter in lieu of the *habit*, and in essence was a very flamboyant overcoat.

A more detailed specification reports the *habits* were Prussian blue, the *gilets* were scarlet rather than *aurore* – but the two colours were extremely close in hue – the *culottes hongroise* were to be Prussian blue, the *manteaux* were *bleu de ciel*, so too were the *pelisses*, which had a black fur trim, the *chapeaux* were actually detailed as the *schakos*, which were presumably black and had a red summit. Clearly, the body of the *schako* was two colours and carried a black *flamme*. The unit's leatherwork was made from blackened and polished cowhide, and the sword knots were tricolour. The document also tells us that trumpeters were to be dressed in a scarlet *habit* with *aurore* epaulettes and lace. The *veste* and *culottes hongroise* were to be Prussian blue like the troopers.[24]

We note the second squadron became the cadre of the *10ᵉ Hussards* on 25 March 1793.

Inspected on 5 June 1793, the unit – the *Hussards de la Liberté dit 8ᵉ Hussards* – was still in the process of adopting *hussards'* rig. For 523 men, 139 *schakos* existed, 140 *manteaux*, 77 *habits*, 139 *vestes*, 142 pairs of *culottes hongroise*, 108 pairs of boots, as well as 139 *sabre* belts. No man was fully equipped. Stores held 100 *aunes bleu de ciel* broadcloth, 700 *aunes* flat *aurore* braid, 450 *aunes* square *aurore* worsted braid, 95 *pelisses* need repairs, 8 new *pelisses*, and 80 cut out and waiting to be sewn together.[25] A document dated 2 September 1793, tells us that the unit was to be dressed in *dolmans*. We are ignorant of their colour. On 1 May 1794, the first squadron of the *Hussards de la Liberté* became the *7ᵉ Régiment bis de Hussards*. Weeks later, on *14 Prairial AnII* (2 June 1794), the *8ᵉ* became the *10ᵉ Hussards*, but almost immediately was renumbered as the *9ᵉ* on *16 Prairial AnII* (4 June 1794).[26]

An officer of *6ᵉ Hussard dit Lauzun*, which retained is designation in January 1791, becoming the *5ᵉ Hussards* in summer 1793.

Inspection returns only give us a 'snap shot' of how a unit was dressed. Discovered at the French Army Archives by the author are the regimental orders of the *9ᵉ Hussards*, starting in *AnVII* (1798 to 1799), they offer a unique insight into the regiment's dress. We know nothing from 1793 to 1799, by which time the *hussards*' rig was fully adopted – we assume.

The *chef du brigade* (unit commanding officer) requested Captain Merge (the clothing officer), on *23 Nivôse AnVII* (12 January 1799), to begin the process to 'write to the bureau of the Artillery Equipment of the 3rd Military Division, to ensure that the arsenal of Paris sends us 200 *sabres* of the hussar pattern'. The order continued,

> will you please inform me as to the progress concerning foot wear, of the *basane* [oiled cowhide leather] to garnish our stable trousers, the red and black leather to garnish the *dolmans* and the *culottes hongroise* ... inform me when the broadcloth and *tricot* that the minister authorised has been received and of the purchase of *schako*s, the *sabretaches* and the barrel sashes.[27]

Towards the close of the same month, the captain was asked where the regiment's reimbursement was from buying new *manteaux*: 940 francs. The *chef du brigade* added, 'we still have not received authorisation to replace the majority of the clothing of our veteran *hussards* which almost entirely needs replacing'. Clearly, the process whereby inspectors of review and the minister of war authorised the production of clothing and the release of funds was frustratingly slow.[28]

The put-upon clothing officer was also asked where the uniforms were for 500 new recruits, the commanding officer noted some men had *dolmans*, others had *pelisses*, but no man had both items due to shortages. Every single pair of stable trousers needed to be exchanged for new he continued, the broadcloth being of Lyon quality (made locally to that region), and most men still lacked *manteaux*.[29] Clearly, the stable trousers were actually *pantalons à cheval* and were made from blue broadcloth and to be made using the braid and buttons in the regimental stores. The clothing officer was also ordered to buy 355m green broadcloth for *manteaux*, and was prompted about the expected delivery time of the *basane* for the stable trousers.[30] In the mid-February the regiment was still waiting for the delivery of bits, saddle blankets, *schabraques* and *basane*.[31]

The clothing officer was again questioned on *2 Ventôse AnVII* (20 February 1799) about when he expected the green broadcloth for *manteaux* to be delivered: he was reminded that the regiment's administrative council had ordered that *bleu celeste* broadcloth was to no longer be used for *manteaux* and, therefore, it was important that green broadcloth arrived with all celerity so *manteaux* could be made. The commanding officer also enquired where the recently ordered 400 pairs of boots were, along with the recently ordered buttons, braid, *bonnets de police* and *schako* cords. He was also told to increase the order of *bleu celeste* broadcloth from 1,300 to 1,500m and to procure 1,700m linen.[32] A week later, on *11 Ventôse AnVII* (1 March 1799), the commanding officer informed the clothing officer to go ahead with the production of 300 pairs of blue broadcloth stable

Hussards

A trooper of the *4ᵉ Hussards*, dressed in sky blue and scarlet. This distinctive uniform is how the regiment appeared throughout the Revolutionary Wars and into *1ᵉ Empire*.

A trooper of the *9ᵉ Hussards* in 1793. We know from regimental accounts that the men wore a *habit* cut from Prussian blue broadcloth lined in scarlet with yellow braid. The *pantalons* were Prussian blue with scarlet trim. The triple-breasted waistcoat was also scarlet. Leatherwork was blackened cowhide. From February 1795, the regiment adopted *bleu celeste* with scarlet facings and yellow trim.

trousers with the cloth received from Lyon, to begin production of *dolmans* without their braid, leather and linen lining, which was hoped to arrive from Paris soon.[33] The same day 600 stable coats were ordered and a reminder about the speedy delivery of buttons, braid and linen needed – we assume – for these garments.[34] As April 1799 began, the green broadcloth for the *manteaux* had still not arrived with the unit, of the 500 stable coats, 300 had been made, but more materials were needed. Likewise, the stable trousers had been cut out, but without *basane* and other materials could not be completed. The body shells of the *dolmans* had been sewn together, but without buttons, braid, leather and linen could not be completed. Such delays the commanding officer note were intolerable and a-typical.[35]

The commanding officer passed orders for the regimental band to change its *bleu celeste* clothing for red with *bleu celeste* facings. Their clothing was to be made from whatever materials were in the regimental stores. Orders were passed to ensure they rode grey mounts.[36]

On *5 Germinal AnVII* (25 March 1799), we learn the musicians had not received their new *dolmans* and were ordered to adopt *bleu celeste manteaux*. The commanding officer also requested that he be informed of the progress on making the broadcloth stable trousers and noted not a single pair of *culottes hongroise* existed.[37]

On *16 Germinal AnVII* (5 April 1799), the green broadcloth was still missing, so too were lace and buttons. Some yellow worsted braid and *soutache* (decorative braid) had been delivered to complete the *gilets* and *porte-manteaux*. Due to the lack of flannel, linen and leather the *dolmans* had been lined in blue *serge* as a matter of economy to get them completed and into service.[38] Then 2 days later, the commanding officer noted 250 *dolmans* had been lined in blue *serge*, but there was still no sign of a delivery date for the linen to line the *gilets* or white *serge* for the same garments. These '*gilets d'ordonnance*' (single-breasted waistcoat) were to be cut from broadcloth in the same form as the *gilet tresse* (braided waistcoat) and cut square at the bottom i.e. flat and closed with a single row of buttons. The clothing officer was also prompted to send news about the delivery of flat braid, square braid and *soutache* for the *gilets tresse* and *dolmans*, as well as buttons in 3 sizes of small, medium and large, and round i.e. not half ball buttons, for the *gilets*, stable coats and *dolmans*. The *basane* for the stable trousers had still not arrived.[39]

The next document we have concerning the dress of the unit is dated *25 Ventôse AnX* (16 March 1802). The unit had now adopted hussards' dress in *bleu celeste* and scarlet, with green *manteaux*. We note trumpeters – possibly *sous-officiers* – had 14 *surtrouts*, the *schako a flamme* had been replaced with a *schako* with yellow worsted cords. We also note yellow leather in store. The only logical use for this material was to line the trumpeters' yellow *dolmans*.[40]

Reviewed again on *20 Prairial AnXI* (9 June 1803), we note the regiment had 624 *dolmans*, 620 *pelisses*, 581 *surtrouts*, just 102 barrel sashes, as well as 559 *schakos* with cords. The depot held yellow *basane* leather for lining trumpeters' *dolmans* and also red *basane* leather for lining troopers' *dolmans*. The elite company had 64 colpacks and 1 was left

A trooper of the *9ᵉ Hussards* wearing the uniform described in February 1795. (*Collection KM*)

in the depot. We note, as with the earlier review, black sheepskin trim for other ranks' *pelisses*, and grey fox fur for *sous-officiers* and white for trumpeters.[41]

10ᵉ Hussards

The *10ᵉ Hussards* had been formed on 26 June 1793 from a cadre drawn from the *Hussards de la Liberté* and a squadron from the *Guides de l'Armée du Rhin*. Some men also came from the *Hussards de la Montagne*; the new regiment was organised in the *Département du Nord* (Department of the North) as a free corps. The men were dressed in Prussian blue with *aurore* braid and lace, trumpeters wore *gris-argentin*.[42] Reviewed in summer 1797, the unit mustered 893 men. No member of the unit had a *pelisse*, trumpeters wore 23 *surtrouts* and *gilet*s, and we note 800 men were issued their regulation uniform, but equipment existed in use for just 600 men. The depot had obtained on *15 Pluviôse AnIV* (4 February 1796), 2,075 *aunes bleu celeste* broadcloth, 326 *aunes* green broadcloth to make *manteaux*, 565 *aunes* scarlet broadcloth and 2,837 *aunes bleu celeste tricot*.[43]

On *22 Ventôse AnX* (13 March 1802), the regiment's depot had used 352m 68 blue broadcloth but held none, and held 86m 78 scarlet broadcloth, 366m 83 green broadcloth for *manteaux*, as well as 37m 34 *gris-argentin* broadcloth, 16m 44 red *tricot*, 8m 14 *serge*, 275m 19 wool flannel, 1,419m 10 blue *tricot*, 368m 86 red leather, 2,295m flat white worsted braid, 5,880m white worsted square braid, and, remarkably, 324 plumes! Clearly, the regiment used blue – presumably, *blue de celeste*? – and *gris-argentin* side by side. The small amount of *gris-argentin*, 13m used in 18 months, implies that trumpeters retained this colour rather than reversed colours. The use of just 2m 70 red *tricot* to make 4 pairs of *culottes hongroise* and 13 *porte-manteaux*, implies these items were for trumpeters. If so, what colour were the trumpeters' *dolmans* and *pelisses*? Arguably, scarlet to match the *culottes hongroise*. A remarkable ensemble.[44]

When we look at the inspection return of *16 Thermidor AnXI* (4 August 1803), not an inch of *gris-argentin* or scarlet cloth is in the depot! Clearly, the trumpeters were now in reversed colours. The report furthermore reveals the regiment had 401 *dolmans* in use and had been issued 535 since 1802, not a single *pelisse* existed, and 54 *surtrouts* had been issued. Some 168 brand new *pelisses* were in the depot, and 3,369 had been issued. So, where were they that day in 1803?[45]

11ᵉ Hussards

Created in June 1793, we know almost nothing about the regiment's dress before it was converted to a dragoon regiment. On *30 Nivôse AnVII* (19 January 1799), no man of the 905 under arms had his regulation-issue clothing, and what existed was mostly life expired. For example, of 608 *pelisse*, 166 needed repairs, 126 were fit only for the rag merchants and 423 had to be immediately replaced. Just 78 *surtrouts* were in use with *sous-officiers* and trumpeters, only 103 barrel sashes existed and a mix of *culottes hongroise*

Contemporary image of the 9ᵉ *Hussards*. The image is problematical as it shows a scarlet rather than *bleu celeste pelisse*.

An officer of *9ᵉ Hussards* at the beginning of the Consulate period. (*Collection KM*)

– 511 pairs – and *pantalons à cheval* – 550 pairs – were used side by side: not enough existed for each man to have both, it was a case of as long as the men had legwear, no one really complained too much. Not every man had a *schako* – 592 in use. So, what did 313 men used for their headdress? We note only 402 *sabretaches* existed, and 355 men had no *sabre* belt, 376 no *giberne*, 357 men needed a *sabre*, only half of the men had a *mousqueton* and just *sous-officiers* and corporals carried pistols.[46]

12ᵉ *Hussards*

Formed on *16 Brumarie AnII* (6 November 1793) as the *Hussards de la Montagne*, it became the *12ᵉ Hussards* on *21 Pluviôse AnII* (9 February 1794), and was initially raised in 1792 from volunteers who had to be 18 years of age. Looking at the demographics of the volunteers, we count of the 37 officers, 7 were the sons of farmers and 10 were the sons of merchants or manufacturers. The others were the children of literate or well to do people, architects, doctors, collectors, judges, clerks, naval captains and landowners; 10 of the officers were sons of lawyers. Similarly, not all of these officers were career soldiers. Only 9 had begun their careers before the Revolution, the other 28 had taken up arms at different times during the Revolution; 11 of them were merchants or manufacturers before 1789. Only 2 were farmers and 8 were students. All had served in different corps before enlistment and 4 had begun their military careers in the infantry; 8 had begun it in the *dragons*, 2 in the *Chasseurs à Cheval* and the *hussards*, 1 in the engineers and 1 in the bodyguards of the king of Spain. But

A trooper of *10ᵉ Hussards* in 1793. Dressed in Prussian blue with yellow trim. The regiment's appearance was totally transformed in February 1795 with the use of *bleu celeste* clothing and white lace.

A superb example of a trooper's *mirliton* cap. (*Private Collection UK*)

An officer of the *12ᵉ Hussards* shortly before its disbandment and conversion into a *dragon* regiment.

A group of light cavalry, drawn from life *circa* 1800. On the left is a gunner of light artillery, and next to him a *chasseur*. Clad in yellow, is, presumably, a trumpeter of the *9ᵉ Hussards*. We see the back view of a brown clad *hussar* – either *2ᵉ* or *12ᵉ* regiment – and a mounted *chasseur*.

21 had served in the National Guard, the volunteers, or the free companies before joining what would be the *12ᵉ*.⁴⁷

Each of these *corps francs* (free legions) was placed in the rear of one of the armies of the Republic: the *Hussards des Alpes* at Vienne, Lyon, Mâcon and Bourg, the *Éclaireurs de Fabrefonds* at Nancy or the *hussards* of Jemappes in Hainaut.

A dismounted trooper of the *6ᵉ Hussards*.

General François-Étienne-Christophe de Kellermann, victor of Valmy, inspected the regiment on *11 Brumaire AnVII* (1 November 1798), roughly 50 per cent of the regiment's clothing was missing or needed replacing. For example, for 903 men, only 496 *dolmans* existed, 2 needed replacing, 409 repairing and 407 men lacked a *dolman*. The unit's *dolmans* were chestnut brown with *bleu de celeste* cuffs, decorated with white braid and lace. The *surtrout* was likewise chestnut brown, lined with brown flannel to the tails, with linen to the sleeves and centre back. The unit wore *pantalons à cheval*, these were made from *bleu celeste tricot*, with brown side stripes for the button stands. The *manteaux* were made from dark green broadcloth and the *schako* had *bleu celeste flammes*.[48]

The unit was converted to *dragons* in summer 1803. François Fournier-Sarlovèze, the colonel, refused to see his *hussards* become *dragons*. He reprimanded the Ministry of War for is decision and refused to comply. In response, he was called to Paris, where was reprimanded and replaced as the head of his regiment. In November 1803, an inspection revealed the new *dragons* were obliged to do the drill in their stable, or *dolmans*, with

Troopers of the *4ᵉ Hussards* and *6ᵉ Hussards* drawn from life by Wilhelm Kolbe.

their *carbines* instead of the *fusils de dragon*. A document from new year 1804 reports the *30ᵉ Dragons* was still dressed in *dolmans* due to a lack of green cloth to make *habits de dragon*. The men had swapped their *schako* for dragoon helmets. In April 1805, at Lyon, Napoléon noticed that 2 squadrons of the regiment that provided him with the escort were not in full uniform but in *frac*. Stationed in Lyon, the regiment was inspected in July 1805 by General Guillaume Philibert Duhesme, who found that only 300 dragoons wore the regulation uniform and that the rest of the men of the regiment were still dressed as *hussards*. They had only 342 dragoon saddles, the rest being in the *hussards*' style. As for the elite company, they proudly wore their colpacks.[49]

Chapter 10

Chasseurs à Cheval

The *Chasseurs à Cheval*, a distinctive force of light cavalry, had a slow gestation period in France. On 25 March 1776, 48 companies of *dragons* were formed into 24 squadrons of *chasseurs*. Each *dragon* regiment had attached to it a squadron of *chasseurs*: as with the *dragons* capable of fighting on foot or horseback. At the start of January 1779, these squadrons were detached from the *dragons*, and formed into 6 regiments of *chasseurs*. The 6 regiments had distinctive colour facings: *1ᵉ* – scarlet, *2ᵉ* – crimson, *3ᵉ* – *citron* (yellow), *4ᵉ* – *chamois*, *5ᵉ* – *aurore* and *6ᵉ* – white.

An idea of how these units were dressed comes from the inspection of the *chasseurs'* units themselves as we have been unable to find any definitive text concerning their clothing.

1ᵉ Chasseurs à Cheval

Reviewed on 2 September 1783, we note the unit was dressed very much as *dragons* – no real surprise given their origin as *dragons*.[1]

Inspected again on 26 August 1784, the men wore dragoon helmets with a feather plume, had *habits* and *vestes* for parade dress, a *surtrout* for other duties and a *gilet* for stable work worn with a *bonnet de police*. In wet weather they had a *manteau* for mounted duties and in wet weather when on sentry duty or other dismounted duties a hooded shoulder cape recorded as a *capouchon*. The men were issued a *ceinturon* to carry their *sabre*, a dragoon-pattern *giberne* and belt, as well as a *fusil de dragon*, and rode on dragoon saddlery, comprising a *housse* and a half-sheepskin *schabraque*.[2]

A trooper of the *Chasseurs de Flandre* wearing the uniform according to the regulations of 1788. (*Musee de l'Armée*)

2ᵉ Chasseurs à Cheval

Reviewed on 22 September 1783, a substantial amount of clothing was needed for the year 1784 as replacements, which included 67 *habits* and *vestes*, 134 *surtrouts* and stable coats, 37 *manteaux*, 161 *bonnets de police*, 54 *capouchons*, 42 helmets, 404 pairs of gloves and 404 white stocks. Needing repairs were 252 helmets and 381 pairs of *culottes de peau*. Other items needed were 67 sword knots, 464 *aigrettes* for the helmet and 170 *gibernes*, and 239 *ceinturons* needed repairs as did 268 saddles. The men were armed with a pistol, a *sabre* and a *fusil de dragon*.[3]

Regulations of 1784

In August 1784, 6 legions of '*chasseurs*' were created, to have a battalion of the *Chasseurs à Pied* and 2 squadrons of the *Chasseurs à Cheval*. The uniform was as outlined to be the same as the line infantry with the regulations of 1779: the *habit* was green, lined in white *serge*. The *veste* and *culottes* – actually cut to be ankle length *pantalons* – were likewise *chamois*. They wore a Corsican-style hat with a turned-up brim on one side. Drummers wore a blue *habit* with the King's Livery adornment, with battalion facing colour distinctives for the *revers*, collar and cuffs. Each of the 6 battalions had distinctive facings piped in green: *Chasseurs des Alpes* – scarlet, *Chasseurs des Pyrénées* – crimson, *Chasseurs des Vosges* – yellow, *Chasseurs des Cévennes* – chamois, *Chasseurs du Gévaudan* – aurore and *Chasseurs des Ardennes* – white.

Both mounted and dismounted men had a white stock, a pair of white linen parade gaiters, a pair in black linen and a third pair in black twill, a *ceinturon-baudrier* for the *sabre* to be worn over the shoulder or at the waist, and a goatskin *havresac*, as well as a *giberne* and belt.[4]

We now look at what was worn.

Chasseurs des Alpes

The *Chasseurs des Alpes* was reviewed on 30 June 1785. It mustered 228 *Chasseurs à Pied* and 420 *Chasseurs à Cheval*. The inspector noted the *Chasseurs à Pied* required 90 new *habits*, many in use were too short in the arm, and had to be extended, which was not ideal the inspector lamented. He noted 26 *habits* and *vestes* needed replacing, as did every single pair of *pantalons*. Equipment wise, the men needed 82 *baudriers* and 42 *gibernes*, and the inspector furthermore noted 54 *fusils de dragon* needed repairing to make them serviceable. For the *Chasseurs à Cheval*, 63 *habits* and *vestes* were needed, along with 186 *surtrouts*, 186 stable coats, 46 helmets and 35 *manteaux*. Equipment wise, 42 *gibernes* were needed, 14 *fusils de dragon* (in the foot company) needed repairs, and for the *Chasseurs à Cheval*, 20 waistbelts were needed, 20 *gibernes* and 35 *fusils de dragon* (in the mounted *chasseur* company) needed repairs. Needing replacing were 17 saddles, 35 *porte-manteaux* and 89 pairs of boots as they were damaged beyond repair. In addition, 328 tools listed as sickles, hatchets, shovels and pickaxes, along with their covers were needed.[5]

Chasseurs des Pyrenees

Sister regiment the *Chasseurs des Pyrenees* were given a shake down inspection on 24 August 1785. The inspector noted the *Chasseurs des Pyrenees* needed 90 *habits*, many

An officer of the *Chasseurs de Lorraine* wearing the uniform according to the regulations of the November 1789, coupled with the April 1791 regulation helmet. The single-breasted *surtout* was in theory replaced with a *dolman*, but change would have taken time, and we feel this is how most *chasseurs* were dressed until the mid-1790s. (*Collection KM*)

had white piping figuring the pockets on the tails, and were made to the regulations of 21 February 1779. The cuffs were to be changed to match the regulations. The inspector added the officers still not had received their firearms, *gorgets* (metal crescent shaped plate worn at the collar by officers to show when they were on duty), sword knots or gaiters. Many officers of the *Chasseurs* à *Cheval* had not adopted the regulation sword knots or spurs.

As could be reasonable supposed, large amounts of clothing and equipment were needed. The *Chasseurs des Pyrenees* required 106 *habits*, 212 *vestes*, 106 *bonnets de police*, 318 pairs of *pantalons*, 60 *houpettes* in wool for the *chapeaux*. They also required 159 *chapeaux*, 30 *ceinturons* – plus 144 *ceinturons* needed repairing – 30 *gibernes* – plus 68 *gibernes* needed repairing – and 30 musket slings. For the mounted contingent, the needs were somewhat greater: 59 *habits*, 117 *vestes*, 119 *surtrouts*, 39 *manteaux* – and 179 needed repairing. Also required were 89 *bonnets de police*, 36 *capouchons*, 45 helmets – and a further 155 needed repairs, as well as 356 helmet plumes, 356 pairs of leather wrist gloves, 20 new *ceinturons* – and 225 repairing – 18 new *gibernes* and a further 178 required repairs. Furthermore, 89 new pairs of boots were needed and the same number needed replacing, 17 saddles were life expired and 270 needed repairs.[6]

Regulations of 1788

However, the 2 elements were separated into distinctive arms on 1 October 1786. The units retained the same facing colours as 1784, but now adopted dragoon-style leatherwork, as well as *culottes de peau*.

On 17 March 1788, the arm of *Chasseurs à Cheval* was expanded with the disbandment of the *dragon* regiments *Boufflers, Montmorency, Deux-Ponts, Dufort, Segur* and *Languedoc*, the *cadres* becoming *chasseurs* occupying the first 6 numbers of the arm: *Régiment d'Alsace* – crimson, *Régiment des Evêchés* – crimson, *Régiment de Flandre* – aurore, *Régiment de Franche-Comté* – aurore, *Régiment de Hainaut* – aurore, *Régiment de Languedoc* – aurore, *Régiment de Picardie* – scarlet, *Régiment de Guyenne* – crimson, *Régiment de Lorraine* – yellow, *Régiment de Bretagne* – chamois (buff), *Régiment de Normandie* – aurore and *Régiment de Champagne* – white.

On 3 January 1789, the regiments adopted the Prussian-style *chapeaux* rather than the round hat the *chasseurs* had used since 1784. More change was to follow on 1 December 1789, with the replacement of the *habit* and *revers* with the single-breasted *surtrout*, closed at the centre front with 6 large uniform buttons. The *veste* became green rather than *chamois*. Also rather than *culottes de peau*, Hungarian breeches (*culottes hongroise*) in the manner of the *hussards* were adopted. Again, green with white or yellow braid decoration, depending on the brigade. The 1e and 12e *régiments* formed the first brigade with yellow buttons and braid, the 2e and 7e formed the second brigade with white buttons and braid, the 3e and 8e formed the third brigade, the 4e and 10e the fourth brigade, the 5e and 9e the fifth brigade, and the 6e and 11e the sixth brigade.

Chasseurs à Cheval 257

A trooper of the *Chasseurs des Alpes* wearing the uniform according to the regulations of 1786. In 1788, it became the *Chasseurs de Picardie* and in 1791 the *7ᵉ Chasseurs*.

Word count and an incomplete archive record prevents a complete discussion of the *chasseurs'* units under the regulations of 1788. What follows, I hope, gives a flavour of the units that existed without much change through to December 1793.

Chasseurs d'Alsace

Created on 10 March 1788 from the *Régiment de Dragons de Boufflers*, the unit was given a shake down review on 28 September 1788. The unit had 8 officers and men on the *etat-major*, and 587 rank and file, as well as 8 *enfants de troupe*. The majority of the men – 254 – were unemployed farm labourers, as well as unemployed urban workers – 158 men – followed by artisans, 20 of them being knifemakers, 25 tailors and 12 saddlers – a useful trade in a cavalry unit – 21 shoe or bootmakers and 22 farriers. At the time of the review, the new unit was still very much dressed as *dragons*: 122 *habits* and *vestes* were issued in 1783, 141 in 1784, 87 in 1785 and 80 in 1786, all made to the regulations of 1779. There were 71 *habits* and *vestes* made in 1787 and 93 during 1788, with 148 garments needed of the new pattern in 1789. Also needed were 255 smocks, 588 pairs of *culottes*, 80 *gibernes* and belts, 59 *ceinturons*, 173 pairs of boots, 87 *housses* and *porte-manteaux* and 57 saddles. A mix of sheepskin *schabraques* – 516 – and dragoon saddlery – 384 in good condition – were in use side by side. No man had a *bonnet de police* and *manteaux* were restricted to the *bas-officiers* and trumpeters. We note 47 *fusils de dragon* with *bayonets* were in use, as well as 113 *mousquetons*, 691 pistols and 688 *sabres*.[7]

Chasseurs des Evêchés

Raised from the *Dragons de Montmorency* on 12 March 1788, the unit was reviewed on 3 October 1788, the unit mustered 569 men. In terms of demographics, 25 men had served for over 21 years, with half of the men having served for less than 4 years, the majority of which were unemployed urban labourers – 240 men – or artisans amongst which we find 5 surgeons, 19 shoemakers, 16 farriers – a useful trade for cavalry outfit recruits – 2 saddlers, as well as 8 bakers, 18 tailors and 1 tanner amongst the different trades represented. We do note 208 men were unemployed (disposed?) agricultural labourers. Since the formation of the unit, 14 men had died and 26 had deserted. Almost every man was still dressed as a dragoon. We note 60 *habits* dated from 1783, 64 from 1784, 90 from 1785 and 167 from 1786, all made in accordance with the regulations of 1779. There were 80 *habits* made in 1787 and the same number since the creation of the regiment. Every man had a helmet, smock, *veste* and a pair of *culottes de peau*, but only *bas-officiers* had a *manteau* and no man had a *bonnet de police*. Horse equipment included 437 *housses* and 477 pairs of dragoon-model *chaperons*, as well as 365 sheepskin *schabraques*. Clearly, the unit was starting to transition to *chasseurs*, but a lot of the dragoons' kit remained in service. It is perhaps for this reason that the inspector noted, 'the everyday dress of the men is very negligent, and the parade dress is lacking in uniformity'.[8]

A trooper of the *Chasseurs des Pyrénées* wearing the uniform according to the regulations of 1786. In 1788, it became the *Chasseurs de Guyenne* and then in 1791 the *8ᵉ Chasseurs*.

Chasseurs des Flandres

At the time of the 22 September 1788 review, for immediate needs, 107 *habits*, 46 *manteaux*, 215 helmets, 51 *gibernes* and belts, the same number of sword belts, sword slings, musket slings, 181 pairs of boots, as well as 101 *housses*, and the same number of pairs of *chaperons*, *porte-manteaux*, 73 saddles and 151 sheepskin *schabraques*. Over 2/3 of the unit's clothing was made to the regulations of 1779, the oldest items being issued in 1783. Of the 571 men, the majority – 314 – were agricultural labourers, 94 were urban workers, the remainder artisans, amongst which we find 3 surgeons, 20 bootmakers, 15 farriers, 5 saddlers and 13 tailors, all of whom no doubt used their skills in their new profession. A mix of *fusils de dragon* and *mousquetons* were in use, and 150 sickles, hatchets, shovels and pickaxes with their cases were in use.[9] The regulations of 1756 stated that the tools were carried strapped to the *fusils de dragon*. During the course of 1788, the unit received 453 linen smocks, 456 *bonnets de police* – authorised the previous year – and in the course of 1790 they were issued 648 complete uniforms, which included the new pattern *surtrouts* and *culottes hongroise*, as well as *chapeaux*. All the unit's leatherwork was to be changed, but dragoon waistbelts remained in use as did dragoon-pattern boots, at least for the time being as only 306 pairs of the new *chasseurs'* boots were authorised and 600 *banderole-porte-mousquetons* were issued. Firearms were an incredible mix of *fusils de dragon*, *mousquetons* and light cavalry *carbines*. Every man was to be issued a pair of pistols.[10] The regiment was finally equipped as *chasseurs* by 21 July 1791, 3 years after the regulations of 1789 had been issued and ironically a few months after the regulations of April 1791 had been announced.[11]

Chasseurs de Franche-Comté

Inspected on 23 September 1788, a lot of the cloth was verging on totally worn out: 123 *habits*, 123 *vestes* and 383 *manteaux* had been newly issued in 1783, and a further 308 *habits* dated from 1784 to 1786. Just 83 *habits* had been made since March 1788, along with 83 *vestes*, 258 smocks, 42 *manteaux* and 100 *bonnets de police*. This still left for immediate needs, 107 *habits* and *vestes*, 155 smocks, 35 *manteaux*, 200 *bonnets de police*, 52 *gibernes* and belts, 60 musket slings, 100 sword knots, 151 pairs of boots, 154 pairs of *chaperons*, 51 *housses* and 63 saddles.[12]

Chasseurs de Languedoc

Reviewed on 30 September 1788, as could be expected from a disbanded *dragon* unit, the new *chasseur* unit was still dressed as its parent unit. We note just 76 new *chasseurs' habits* had been made and 155 were listed to be made in 1789. We note 81 *habits* and *vestes* dated from 1783. With a 3-year lifespan – at most – these garments must have been 'utterly knackered'. But with France verging on fiscal collapse, where was the money to come from to pay for the army's new uniforms? We note *bas-officiers* and trumpeters had

Chasseurs à Cheval 261

A trooper of the *Chasseurs des Vosges* wearing the uniform according to the regulations of 1786. In 1788, it became the *Chasseurs de Lorraine* and then in 1791 the *9ᵉ Chasseurs*.

manteaux and *bonnets de police*, rather than *chaperons*, *housses* and *demi-schabraques* were used on the horses. A mix of *fusils de dragon* and *mousquetons* were in use, alongside 443 *bayonets*, 644 pistols, 640 *sabres*, 142 sickles and the same number of hatchets, shovels and pickaxes.[13]

Chasseurs de Guyenne

Inspected on 19 September 1788, a lot of the unit's clothing was very much 'past its best'. We record the 244 *habits* in use had been issued between 1783 and 1785 and, in theory, these should all have been removed from use. Just 64 new *chasseurs' habits* and *vestes* had been made, but every man was wearing a *chapeau*. For the coming year, the unit needed 229 *habits* and *vestes*, 313 smocks, 397 pairs of *pantalons*, 146 *manteaux* and 229 *bonnets de police*. The unit was still riding on dragoon horse equipment. We note 600 light cavalry *carbines* were in use, as well as 112 *mousquetons*, 644 pistols and 640 *sabres*. There were also 368 hatchets and other small tools that were carried in the empty pistol holsters. When we look at the 496 men under arms, the majority – 269 – were unemployed farm labourers, second only to unemployed urban workers without a trade – 135. Of those with a profession in civilian life, but who had been forced to enlist for food, shelter and a wage, we find 10 carpenters, 4 shoemakers, 9 farriers, 12 wigmakers or hairdressers, 9 knifemakers, 6 tailors and 9 tanners. Of these men, 13 had served for over 21 years.[14]

Regulations of 1791

In April 1791, the *chasseurs'* regiments abandoned their names and became numbered once more. Each regiment was to have an *etat-major* and 4 squadrons – each squadron of 2 companies. Each regiment was to have a theoretical establishment of 36 officers and 580 men, with 556 troop horses and 48 officers' mounts.

In theory, the *surtrouts* were swept away in favour of a *dolman*-style garment, worn over a white sleeveless *gilet*, with green *culottes hongroise*. The *surtrouts* remained in use for barrack wear and in the stables. Rather than a *chapeau* – if they ever were adopted – the men were to adopt the infantry helmet – *casque* – all buttons were to be white, as was all braid. Gone went the dragoon saddle and harness in favour of the *hussards'* model – round *porte-manteaux*, sheepskin *schabraques*, as well as light cavalry *sabres*.

On 6 December 1791, each regiment was expanded to 6 squadrons – 2 of which were dismounted. At the same time, the *ad hoc* corps *francs* (irregulars) were converted to regular units and became 8 new regiments of *chasseurs*. All 23 regiments were dressed in *hussards'* manner and allowed the *mirliton* rather than the infantry helmet.

In July 1794, the number of regiments was reduced – with the disbandment of the *17ᵉ* and *18ᵉ*, which had been formed from Belgian recruits, making 21 regiments in total. The 2 dismounted squadrons were abolished on 17 January 1796: the experiment of once more combining mounted and dismounted elements in the same formation was over for the third time since 1774.

A trooper of the *Chasseurs des Cévennes* wearing the uniform according to the regulations of 1786. In 1788, it became the *Chasseurs de Bretagne* and in 1791 the *10ᵉ Chasseurs*.

From *AnX* (1801 to 1802), regiments were to replace the helmet with a *schako* with a *flamme* in the style of a *mirliton*. It was to measure 180mm tall, and 217mm in diameter. The peak was attached with 3 hooks and eyes. The *flamme* was made from *serge*, 758mm long and in the regiment's distinctive colour. A feather plume was allowed, 325mm long, to be black with the regiment's principal colour at the tip. In theory, the *schako* was decorated with a copper lozenge plate and had chin scales. The *surtout* was to be cut short, with the tails to extend to the mid-thigh and was officially to replace the *dolman*.[15] The building block for the uniform of the *chasseurs'* regiments during the course of the *1ᵉ Empire* came with the decree of *3 Ventôse AnX* (22 February 1802):

The Consuls of the Republic, on the report of the Minister of War

II. The effects of clothing and equipment to be distributed in year X [1801 to 1802], on the funds of the mass of clothing, are those named below, and they will not be renewed until the periods hereafter determined.

XIV. *Chasseurs à Cheval.*

Object	Duration
Dolmans:	4 years
Broadcloth *vestes*:	4 years
Culottes hongroises:	2 years
Surtrouts:	2 years
Manteaux:	8 years
Schakos:	4 years
Stable trousers:	1 year
Sabre belts:	6 years
Boots:	2 years
Giberne and belts:	20 years
Carbine belts:	20 years
Porte-manteaux:	8 years
Saddles, breastplates, cruppers, girth surcingles, stirrups and irons, bridle and head collars:	20 years
Wool saddle blankets:	8 years
Schabraques:	8 years

Non-commissioned officers (sergeant, *fourriers* and sergeant majors), corporals and *chasseurs* will provide, at their expense, the repair of their boots.

Each non-commissioned officer and soldier will receive, each year, a *veste* made from the old clothing.

A trooper of the *Chasseurs du Gévaudan* wearing the 1786 uniform. In 1788, it became the *Chasseurs de Normandie* and in 1791 the *11ᵉ Chasseurs*.

The provisions of Articles IV, V, VI, VIII, IX and X are common to the *chasseurs*, viz:

IV. Non-commissioned officers and soldiers will be required to provide *bonnets de police* at their expense.

VI. The clothes and jackets that will be replaced in year X [1801 to 1802], will belong to the regiment; the best will be kept for the clothing of the new soldiers, for the guard-house, the prison and the discipline room.

VII. Non-commissioned officers and soldiers will be allowed to provide white linen breeches for the summer, while complying with the provisions of the instruction which will be written and addressed to each regiment by the Minister of War.

VIII. The administrative council will take steps to procure for each ordinary or barrack room, a number of canvas smocks for the men to wear on fatigues.[16]

Interestingly, *dolman*s were still allowed, but the decree of *1 Vendémiaire AnXI* (23 September 1802) reverted back to their abolition. Given the confusion of what was and was not regulation, colonels were free to pick and choose what their regiment wore. Nothing official had been written down about the dress of trumpeters. We assume that the regulations of 1792 for dressing trumpeters in blue remained unchanged. The author's companion volume on *chasseurs* and *hussards*, *Napoléon's Hussars and Chasseurs*, follows the story of the dress of the *chasseurs* on from *AnX* (1801 to 1802) to 1815 and is also available from Frontline Books.

Word count precludes an in-depth study of every regiment. Therefore, we present a sample of the *chasseurs'* units that existed from 1791 to 1803.

5ᵉ *Chasseurs à Cheval*

Inspected on 26 March 1791, the hastily renumbered *Chasseurs de Hainaut*, mustered 36 officers and 544 other ranks. At the close of the year, the unit was reviewed again on 22 December 1791. Every man was wearing a *dolman* and new white *veste*, 538 smocks were in use, 324 pairs of *culottes hongroise* had been issued in 1790 and 269 pairs in 1791, along with 486 *manteaux* and 135 *bonnets de police*. Every man also had a *surtrout*, 46 of which dated from 1786 and were certainly 'well past their best'. Needed for 1792 were a further 136 brand-new *dolmans*. The horse equipment all dated from 1788 and 1789. The trumpeters were all dressed in blue *habits* with the King's Livery lace. Also needed were 182 smocks to compliment 538 issued in 1790, 267 pairs of *culottes hongroise*, 55 *manteaux* and 136 *bonnets de police*. Armament wise, 505 *carabines* were in use, 517 *sabres* and 504 pistols. Of the men themselves, 19 wore 3 service *chevrons*, 32 had served long enough to earn 2 *chevrons* and 92 had served over 8 years. In terms of background, 165 were former agricultural labourers, 106 were town labourers, 41 were shoemakers,

A trooper of the *Chasseurs des Ardennes* wearing the uniform according to the regulations of 1786. In 1788, it became the *Chasseurs de Champagne* and then in 1791 the *12ᵉ Chasseurs*.

6 were saddlers, 12 were tailors, 44 farriers, 42 masons, 17 tanners, 8 surgeons, 15 bakers and 12 were carpenters amongst other trades. We note 40 men were Parisians, 40 were from French speaking Lorraine, 15 from German speaking Lorraine and just 40 were from Hainaut.[17]

Reviewed on *19 Thermidor AnIV* (6 August 1796), the 5*^e* had fully embraced the 'hussar look'. We note 684 *sabretaches* were in service with 279 needed to give every man such an item strictly against regulation. We note 945 *dolmans* were in use, alongside 946 white *gilet*s, 962 *surtrouts* used for stable duties, 951 pairs of *culottes hongroise*, 962 pairs of stable trousers, 946 *schakos* and 962 *bonnets de police*. The unit was armed with 846 *mousquetons*, 891 *sabres* and 611 pistols. We know from partial regimental accounts that *sous-officiers* wore superfine fabric uniforms, the *manteaux* were made from a heavy-weight green broadcloth and the trumpeters wore blue: some 43 *aunes* 23 blue broadcloth had been purchased earlier in the year of which 41 *aunes* had been used in the production of clothing comprising 26 *surtrouts*, 8 pairs of *culottes hongroise* and 1 *gilet* for the *trompette* major.[18]

The regiment was inspected again on *18 Brumaire AnVII* (8 November 1798), the report merely telling us 715 men were completely clothed and equipped.[19]

General François-Étienne-Christophe de Kellermann reviewed the regiment on *14 Brumaire AnVIII* (5 November 1799), and notes the regiment had 801 *schakos* and required an additional 102 examples, which had been promised by the Batavian government.[20] More detail is to be found in the next review, dated *6 Frimaire AnX* (27 November 1801), which tells us stores had used 26m 68 blue broadcloth to make more trumpeters' clothing. We remember in September 1792 all trumpeters were to have blue *surtrouts* with regimental distinctive colour facing, here is proof positive that the decree was enforced for a decade and well into the *1^e Empire* period as our companion text on *chasseurs* and *hussards* shows. Interestingly, stores admits the production and issue of 16 *pelisses*. Were these for the trumpeters? The *sabretaches* that existed in earlier years had all been taken from use. One innovation that seems to have been 'still born' was issuing '*bouton de consul* … 10mm diameter' for clothing.[21]

9*^e Chasseurs à Cheval*

The former *Chasseurs de Lorraine* were reviewed on 23 November 1791. Inspection records that the regiment was dressed according to the pattern clothing and in accordance with the regulations of 1786, and had the yellow facings, as stated in the regulations of 1788. The regulations of 1 December 1789, ordering the removal of *habits* in favour of *surtrouts*, had not been full enacted, as just 17 *surtrouts* had been made in the course of 1790, along with 97 *vestes*, 412 stable coats, 345 pairs of *culottes hongroise*, 109 *manteaux* and 70 *bonnets de police*. Every man, however, had adopted the 1791 pattern helmet. No *habits* or *surtrouts* were made in 1792, but we do note 559 *vestes*, 202 stable coats, 578 smocks and 336 pairs of *culottes hongroise* were authorised to be made amongst other items, which also included 416 pairs of boots, 184 *porte-manteaux* and 214 sheepskin

A trooper of the *5ᵉ Chasseurs* wearing the uniform according to the regulations of 1791. (*Collection KM*)

schabraques. Trumpeters wore blue *habits* and *culottes hongroise*, and the *habits* were still adorned with the King's Livery.[22]

Inspected again on *20 Germinal AnVI* (9 April 1798), the regiment was now wearing *dolmans* – 634 in use and 172 needed – as well as *schakos*. The trumpeters had 16 blue *surtrouts* with rose facings, and wore blue *culottes hongroise*, the only ones within the regiment. Every man wore 'a type of stable trousers, made from *tricot* with leather to the seat which are not regulated'. These were the only items of legwear for the other ranks – they must have become very dirty and smelly indeed.[23] The report of *27 Germinal AnX* (17 April 1802) tells us categorically that the men had *dolmans* rather than '*habit-dolmans*' mentioned in the 1791 regulation which some like Lucien Rousselot and Michel Petard call a *caraco* (short coat). We know the *9ᵉ* had *dolmans* as we find stores used red Moroccan leather to line the bottom quarter of the *dolman*. The men had both *culottes hongroise* and what we understand to be *pantalons à cheval* for campaign dress and stable duties. The trumpeters were now dressed in reversed colours: this is an innovation of the Consulate period.[24]

13ᵉ Chasseurs à Cheval

Formed in 1792 from the *Légion des Americains* and the *Légion des Midi*, these 2 free corps were amalgamated as the *13ᵉ Chasseurs* on 11 March 1793.

Reviewed on 11 May 1793, the unit mustered 547 other ranks and 37 officers. Clothing needs for 1793 included 143 *habits* and *vestes*, 280 *manteaux*, 150 stable coats and pairs of stable trousers, 120 *bonnets de police* and remarkably 100 bearskins – recorded as *bonnets a poil*. Does this mean a grenadier's bearskin? Or does it mean a fur crested helmet? We are inclined to think a bearskin or colpack.[25] We assume the bearskins were inherited from a progenitor unit.

The *13ᵉ Chasseurs* was amalgamated with the *13ᵉ Bis Chasseurs* – raised from the *19ᵉ Dragons* – in December 1793.

Inspected on *23 Germinal AnIII* (12 April 1795), remarkably, we note the men were wearing *habits* – 824 in use – as were 554 *surtrouts*. The men also had 558 white broadcloth *vestes*, rather than *culottes hongroise*, the men wore instead 'a type of stable trousers, made from *tricot* with leather to the seat which are not regulated', some 926 pairs in use. Rather than helmets, the men wore infantry *chapeaux*, 670 being life expired, and 462 being in good condition. We also note 74 pairs of *culottes hongroise* were in use, presumably, with *sous-officiers* and trumpeters. Most surprisingly, 200 pairs of heavy cavalry *culottes de peau* were in use. The inspector ordered 1,108 stable coats producing as none existed, 1,008 pairs of stable trousers and 1,134 pairs of *culottes hongroise* made. Every single piece of leatherwork had to be replaced: what existed was life expired. Just 162 *gibernes* and belts were in use and needed repair, meaning 1,041 new *gibernes* and belts had to be made. Also needed were – and this is quite remarkable – 820 *sabre* belts as only 388 existed. So, how did the men carry their *sabres* as only 804 were issued?[26]

A trooper of the *24ᵉ Chasseurs circa* 1799, wearing a non-regulation *mirliton* and *sabretache*. (*Collection KM*)

Reviewed on *6 Fructidor AnIV* (23 August 1796), the unit was now dressed in *dolmans* – a full 5 years after the regulated adoption – were wearing helmets and had 1,039 *sabretache* in service. Trumpeters were dressed in reversed colours. We again note that broadcloth *pantalons à cheval* were in service, with 498 pairs to be made during the course of 1796, along with 775 pairs of *culottes hongroise*, 151 *surtrouts*, 474 *bonnets de police* and 257 white *vestes*. Rather than the expected orange facings, the unit had scarlet. The inspector ordered orange to be adopted. The *surtrouts* were to be fitted with orange cuffs and piping. New *bonnets de police*, to be entirely green with orange piping were made. We also note the sheepskin *schabraque* had a green festoon rather than in facing colour.[27] It would only be in 1797 and perhaps 1798 that the unit finally became dressed fully as *chasseurs*.

Reviewed on *24 Pluviôse AnX* (13 February 1802), 503 *dolmans* were in use, 613 having been made since *24 Germinal AnVI* (13 April 1798), in the same period the unit had transitioned from helmets to *schakos*, with 559 being in use. Again, we are sure *dolmans* proper were used as we note in stores red Morrocco leather, 12mm-wide white worsted lace and square worsted braid. One pair of *culottes hongroise* had been made since *AnVI* (1798 to 1799), every man wore *pantalons à cheval*. No *surtrouts* existed, so we assume the trumpeters wore reversed colour *dolmans*.[28]

15ᵉ *Chasseurs à Cheval*

Levied as the *21ᵉ Chasseur*s 7 March 1793, it became the *15ᵉ* on *8 Floréal AnIV* (27 April 1796) following amalgamation with the *Chasseurs de Cote d'Or*. At the time of disbandment, the *Chasseurs de Cote d'Or* were dressed in *habits* – 266 in service – with broadcloth *pantalons* as well heavy cavalry *culottes de peau*. The headdress was a cavalry *chapeau*, and footwear was dragoon boots and also shoes for stable duties. Again, for dismounted duties linen smocks were issued and linen *pantalons*. The men had the luxury of linen underpants, 2 shirts each in some cases – 186 shirts for 680 men – as well as a black and a white stock, a pair of stockings and another luxury, a pair of *pantalons à cheval*.[29] We are ignorant of the regiment's facing colour.

A regrettable gap in the regiment's archive means we know nothing more until *18 Germinal AnX* (8 April 1802), when the inspector noted the regiment had been newly dressed in *dolmans*. We note 519 *surtrouts* were in use, and rather than white, the men's *vestes* were made from orange broadcloth. The inspector added, 'the regiment has no *culottes hongroise*, to supply this deficit the regiment uses stable trousers made from broadcloth' i.e. they were wearing *pantalons à cheval*. For headdress *schakos* were in use, and the regiment had 25 *sapeurs* wearing what we assume to be colpacks. Elite companies had been created by *18 Vendémiaire AnX* (10 October 1801), yet nothing was said about *sapeurs* or even colpacks, but the regulations neither said that these distinctions were not allowed: colonels had a high degree of latitude in how they dressed their men. After the review the elite company were authorised to buy 100 colpacks. Every man was to receive new *culottes hongroise* the inspector ordered and canvas stable trousers were likewise to be

Troopers of the *5ᵉ Chasseurs* wearing the 1801 regulation uniform. (*Musee de l'Armée*)

made. The trumpeters were dressed in blue with orange facings: stores had used 91m 22 blue broadcloth for this purpose. Armament wise, 446 *banderole-porte-mousquetons* were issued for 327 firearms. Of these 120, were listed as non-standard and 70 as Austrian, so too were 72 pistols and 123 *sabres*. Clearly, 'make do and mend' was the mantra of the minister of war – so long as men had a *sabre* and a firearm, that was all that was needed. No one paid too close attention to origin of weapons, no doubt given the parlous state of the French economy.[30]

Inspected again on *18 Messidor AnXI* (7 July 1803), we note 674 pairs of stable trousers were in use, 623 pairs of *culottes hongroise* and 652 pairs of *pantalons à cheval*. These had been paid for by judicious accounting. The regimental fund allocated to pay for men to have underwear, was used to make these garments. We also find a reference to tricolour pompoms for the *schakos* being in use, and the men now had white and black stocks rather than black cravats, and had been issued shoes for stable duties. The trumpeters now sported reversed colours.[31]

17ᵉ Chasseurs à Cheval

Created on 16 April 1793, as the *Chevau Légère Belge de Westflandres*, we know very little about the dress of the unit. Inspected on *20 Ventôse AnX* (11 March 1802), our first surprise comes with the presence of 407 *dolmans* accompanied by 408 *pelisses* – these were strictly not regulation, yet clearly a lot were used by the regiment. We also note 506 *sabretaches* in service. We assume barrel sashes completed the 'hussar look'. For headdress, 397 *schakos* were in use. Stores were totally devoid of cloth, materials and clothing.[32] The unit was disbanded on *1 Vendémiaire AnXI* (23 September 1802), no regiment of this designation existed during the *1ᵉ Empire*.

19ᵉ Chasseurs à Cheval

Formed on 10 June 1793 for the *Chasseurs de la Légion de Rosenthal*, the regiment was inspected on *30 Prairial AnVI* (18 June 1798), and the unit was decked out in *dolmans* – 528 in use for 625 men. The trumpeters wore *surtrouts*, white *gilets* and *culottes hongroise*. The other ranks wore *pantalons à cheval*, of which 64 pairs were needed to equip every man, 19 pairs needed repair and 17 pairs total replacement. The headdress was the *schako*, 30 being needed to equip every man. The inspector noted 625 *sabretaches* were needed to equip every man, that *pelisses* and *sabretaches* were in use, lamenting no regulation sanctioned this.[33] General de Grouchy reviewed the regiment on *15 Ventôse AnX* (6 March 1802), by which time the *pelisses* and *sabretaches* had been taken from use or lost on campaign.[34]

21ᵉ Chasseurs à Cheval

Created as the *Hussards-Braconniers* on 9 September 1792 as mixed corps of light infantry and cavalry, the formation decree said nothing abouts its clothing. Almost a year later, on 14 August 1793, the unit became the *21ᵉ Chasseurs*, at which point the light infantry section was disbanded.

Reviewed on *19 Vendémiaire AnV* (10 October 1796), the unit was decked out in *dolmans*, of which 450 were in good condition, 128 needed repairs, 284 were life expired and 41 were needed to equip every man. Also, in service were white *vestes*, *surtrouts*, stable coats, *manteaux*, as well as helmets and *bonnets de police* for headdress. Cloth in the depot comprised white, green and *ganse* broadcloth, green *tricot* and white *serge*.[35]

An officer in the unit was Captain James Bartholomew Blackwell, who was born in Ennis, County Clare in Ireland. He was sent to Paris, France aged approximately 10, to study for the priesthood at the Irish College as his maternal grand-uncle, Dr Bartholomew Murray MD, had provided a bursary for him. However, after deciding

An officer of *6ᵉ Chasseurs* in parade dress *circa* 1800. (*Musee de l'Armée*)

to study medicine instead at the Hôpital la Bicêtre he qualified as a surgeon. He was keen for adventure and joined the French army's *Esterhazy Hussards*. Thereafter, he became a naturalised French subject in 1784. He joined the *Brigade Irlandais* in 1787, enlisted in the *Voluntaries de Paris* in 1791 and joined the *21ᵉ* on 13 April 1793. He was placed in command of the unit's infantry detachment on 14 August 1795. Before his departure to Ireland in 1796 with General Louis Lazare Hoche, Blackwell fought a duel with his lieutenant, Joachim Murat as Blackwell believed that Murat had tried to seduce his wife. In 1798, he served with Irish revolutionary James Napper Tandy in an aborted landing in Ireland.[36] Due to his absence, his commanding officer in the *21ᵉ* requested a new captain clothing officer.[37] Imprisoned until 1802, he served in the Irish Legion, before becoming a staff officer under (now) Marshal Charles-Pierre Augereau. He transferred to General Jean-de-Dieu Soult's staff in 1807 in time for the Battle of Friedland, and he joined Louis-Nicolas Davout's (sometimes known as d'Avout) staff in October 1808. He retired in February 1814 on half pay as a colonel and was appointed governor of the town of Bitche, northern France. He served under the Bourbons, being made governor of the town of La Petite Pierre in August 1816. Wounded 3 times, notably at the battles of Jena and Eylau. He was made officer of the legion of honour on 23 July 1809 on Davout's recommendation. He died in Paris in 1820 and is buried in Père Lachaise cemetery.[38]

The *21ᵉ* was reviewed again on *13 Pluviôse AnX* (2 February 1802) when the inspector, General François Antoine Louis Bourcier, lamented almost everything had to be replaced. Of 852 *dolmans*, 184 needed repairs and 302 total replacement, 196 *surtrouts* needed repairs and 539 replacing, as did every pair of *culottes hongroise*. The unit used non-regulation *pantalons à cheval*, 666 in good condition and 320 needed immediate replacement. Every man had a *schako* and *bonnet de police*, again in varying states of repair. We can be sure the *dolmans* were what Bourcier reported them to be, as red Moroccan leather was in stores to line the bottom part of the garments. The unit had the luxury of white *vestes*, green sleeveless *vestes* and *aurore gilets* braided *a la hussards*. The trumpeters wore reversed colours – *aurore* faced green – and had *aurore* cloth *schabraques* rather than sheepskins.[39]

23ᵉ Chasseurs à Cheval

Created from the *Hussards de la Légion des Ardennes*, the regiment was inspected on *1 Messidor AnIV* (19 June 1796), and the men were wearing *dolmans* and their 'hussar look' was compliment with 924 newly issued *schako* a *flamme* and 924 *sabretaches*, again newly issued. The inspector was at pains to note the unit had been re-dressed from new items from the regiment's stores and more items of equipment and harness had yet to arrive as replacement items from government stocks.[40]

Reviewed on *4 Fructidor AnV* (21 August 1797), we note the trumpeters were dressed in reversed colours i.e. *capucine* (red-orange) faced green.[41]

24ᵉ Chasseurs à Cheval

Created in 1793 and reviewed on *28 Frimaire AnIII* (18 December 1794), the unit was dressed in *dolmans* and helmets.

On *28 Messidor AnVI* (16 July 1798), the unit was again in *dolmans* and helmets. Most items were worn out or missing: 128 men had no helmet; the same number had no *dolman* and of those in use 47 needed repairs and 122 immediate replacement. The trumpeters were issued *surtrouts*. Under the *dolmans*, the men had scarlet braided *hussards'*-style waistcoats.[42]

At the time of next inspection on *22 Pluviôse AnX* (11 February 1802), the inspector noted that the dress of the men was very bad, the majority of the clothing needed to be replaced. For example, of 620 *dolmans*, 400 needed repairs. Of 564 *surtrouts*, 205 needed repairing, and 230 were 'knackered' and needed to be replaced. No *culottes hongroise* existed, nor stable trousers and instead *pantalons à cheval* were worn in all orders of dress: of these 135 pairs needed repairs and 422 total replacement. Every single white *gilet* needed to be replaced. By the time of this review, the regiment had replaced its scarlet facings with *capucine*.[43] The inspector ordered the regiment to be re-dressed at speed: by the time of the new review 704 pairs of *culottes hongroise* had been issued, 329 pairs of *pantalons à cheval* and 118 pairs of stable trousers proper. We also note 100 *dolmans* had been made and 6 repaired.[44]

25ᵉ *Chasseurs à Cheval*

Formed in 1795 from the *Legion des Montagnes*, the unit was inspected on *10 Prairial AnVI* (29 May 1798), when the unit was decked out in *surtrouts*, *schakos*, as well as *pantalons à cheval*. The inspector order 437 *dolmans*, braided waistcoats and *culottes hongroise* made.[45]

At the time of the *5 Ventôse AnX* (24 February 1802) review, the unit had scarlet facings, just over 100m scarlet broadcloth being used to make clothing, along with 6,401m green broadcloth. A little over 32m red *tricot* had been used as well since 1798. We remark that 1,150 *dolmans* had been made in this time frame.[46]

The review of *22 Prairial AnXI* (11 June 1803) has surprises for us. Rather than the expected *rouge-garance* facings stores note it had used 39m 32 rose (hot pink) facing cloth with just under 60m remaining in stores, 20m 23 rose *tricot* and 10m blue broadcloth. Was this all destined for trumpeters clothing? The blue certainly was, but what of the rose? No scarlet (or red) broadcloth or *serge* is listed, but 4 *dolmans* – for the trumpeters? – along with 28 *surtrouts* had been made since the last review. We also note 38 *dolmans* had been repaired as had 24 *surtrouts*. From this, our conclusion must be that the unit's facings were rose. Furthermore, the inspection return tells us 1,917m 33 green broadcloth had been used in the production of *manteaux* and a little over 431m white broadcloth had been used to make 395 white *gilet*s. Stores also reported 392m green *tricot* had been employed to make 170 pairs of *culottes hongroise*. The headdress for the regiment was the *schako*, and we note 51 *sabretaches*.[47]

Chapter 11

Conclusions

The archive material presented in the previous chapters are transcripts of the original material used by the author. The narrative for each regiments' clothing and equipment has been constructed from the sources available to the author. The starting point are the official Ministry of War decrees for what was to be worn, the Ministry of War decree detailing the specification of items, and lastly regimental purchase accounts and inspection returns. We have not written on the various Guard formations as these are covered in the author's respecting volumes concerning the foot troops and mounted troops of the Imperial Guard, *Napoléon's Imperial Guard Uniforms and Equipment*, also available from Frontline Books.

Official inspection returns and regimental standing orders are key primary documents. They document in minute detail what was being worn on the day of inspection, what the regimental depot contained, what was purchased and in the case of the standing orders says exactly what was worn, when and how. This data gives us a snap shot of the *Grande Armée* as it was at the very close of its existence. This incredible source of information, along with regimental account books for expenses made on clothing and equipment has been used to present the *Grande Armée's* appearance 'warts and all' for the first time. The data allows us to reconcile the realities behind the Bardin Regulation, and shows the army as it really was.

I have endeavoured to let the primary sources speak for themselves without having to fit what they say into a superficial construct, created by other authors. This approach has allowed a fresh, and revisionary narrative to be produced on the uniform of the period 1786 to 1802. However, the chaotic nature of the archive sources means, we cannot draw any solid conclusions. The regimental archives for the period 1791 to 1793 for the *ligne* are totally devoid of inspection returns or details on clothing. It was only with Bernadotte at the Ministry of War and he immediate predecessors Barthélemy Louis Jospeh Schérer and Louis Marie Antonie Destouff de Milet de Mureau, that any semblance of order was retrieved in clothing the army. The chaos of the *amalgame* and the threat of invasion, military failure and the terror all impacted the way in which the army operated. Only when some modicum of organisation was imposed with the appearance of the directory that regiments began to be inspected on a regular basis, and the *ad hoc* system of re-supply replaced with a formal system of management. Edmond Dubois-Crancé who succeeded Bernadotte as minister for war, embedded the earlier reforms, which the new consulate inherited.

It is our task as historian to acknowledge that it may never be possible to fully align iconographic and written sources. We should work from quantifiable data –

A trooper of *6ᵉ Hussard* with a dragoon from an unknown regiment *circa* 1800.

the regimental records – and work from there. Dress regulations, original items and iconography help us visualise what these items look like and how they were worn. Yet in many cases the iconography shows uniforms that simply cannot be reconstructed from official documents. Yet which is correct? Where more than one independent eyewitness iconographic source presents similar information, we can be sure that the iconography is

A trooper of the *8ᵉ Cavalerie-Cuirassier* observed by Wilhelm Kolbe during 1800.

reliable or where the iconographic source is backed up by eyewitnesses' written testimony. For the Revolutionary period, iconography and archive concur: hardly any regiment was dressed according to the regulations.

Many readers will be disappointed that we can say nothing about how most trumpeters and drummers were dressed, or if their favourite regiment had *epaulettes* and what colour they were. The archive sources do not answer these questions: the documents where the colonel wrote down in *facsimilia* exactly what was worn and when simply no longer exists. Under a dozen sets of regimental standing orders from the line and guard exists from 1791 to 1815 have come down to us. We have to admit that we will never know exactly what a regiment wore in the overwhelming majority of cases. Hence, we have to compare what records we have, with contemporary iconography and come to a conclusion based on facts rather than speculation.

This book needs to be seen as a springboard for further research. Word count alone prohibits a review of every regiment that existed between 1786 and 1802. I offer an overview of the subject, and not a *defacto* 'nuts and bolts' review.

Bibliography

Printed Works

Anon., *Instruction Provisore sur l'Habillement des Troupes 1 Avril 1791* (l'Imprimerie Royale, Paris, 1791)

Anon., *Instruction pour servir à expliquer les principes d'après lesquels on ete exécutes les différends modeles de coiffure, l'Habillement et l'Equipement envoyés à chacun des Régiments d'Infanterie* (l'Imprimerie Royale, Paris, 1786)

Anon., *Instruction pour servir à expliquer les principes d'après lesquels on ete exécutes les différends modeles de coiffure, l'Habillement et l'Equipement envoyés à chacun des Régiments d'Infanterie* (l'Imprimerie Royale, Paris, 1787)

Anon., *Les Guides des Sous-Officiers de l'Infanterie Francaise, 2ᵉ édition* (Leroy-Berge, Paris, 1809)

Anon., *Ordonnance Provisoire sur l'exercise de la Cavalerie AnXIII, troisieme édition* (Chez Magimel, Paris, 1815)

Anon., *Reglement Arête pour le Roi pour l'Habillement et l'Equipment dès ses Troupes* (l'Imprimerie Royale, Paris, 25 Avril 1767)

Anon., *Reglement Arête pour le Roi pour l'Habillement et l'Equipment dès ses Troupes* (l'Imprimerie Royale, Paris, 1779)

Anon., *Supplément a la décision du conseil de la Guerre du 24 Novembre 1788* (l'Imprimerie Royale, Paris, 1788)

Bardin, Étienne Alexandre, *Manuel d'Infanterie, ou Résumé de tous les règlements, décrets, usages, renseignements concernant l'infanterie, dans lequel se trouve renfermé tout ce que doivent savoir les sergents et caporaux* (Chez Magimel, Paris, 1808)

Bardin, Étienne Alexandre, *Manuel d'Infanterie, ou Résumé de tous les règlements, décrets, usages, renseignements concernant l'infanterie, dans lequel se trouve renfermé tout ce que doivent savoir les sergents et caporaux* (Chez Magimel, Paris, 1813)

Bertaud, Jean Paul, *The Army of the French Revolution: From Citizen-Soldiers to Instrument of Power* (Princeton Legacy Library, Princeton, 2019)

Connelly, Owen, *The French Revolution and Napoléon* (Routledge, London, 2012)

Crowdy, Terry, *Napoléon's Infantry Hand Book* (Pen & Sword Books, Barnsley, 2015)

David, 'Decorated Men: Fashioning the French Soldier, 1852–1914', in *Fashion Theory*, Volume 7 (Routledge, Abingdon-on-Thames, 2003)

Dawson, Paul Lindsay, *Napoléon's Imperial Guard Uniforms and Equipment: The Infantry* (Frontline Books/Pen & Sword Books, Barnsley, 2019)

Forrest, Alan I., *Conscripts and Deserters: The Army and French Society During the Revolution and Empire* (Oxford University Press, New York, 1989)

Galtier-Boissière, Jean, *Mysteries of the French Secret Police* (Stanley Paul & Co., London, 1938)

Lynn, John A., *The Bayonets of The Republic: Motivation and Tactics in the Army of Revolutionary France, 1791–94* (Routledge, London, 2021)

Malibran, *Guide à l'Usage des Artistes et des Costumiers Contenant la Description Des Uniformes de l'Armée Française de 1780 à 1848* (Combet & Cie., Paris, 1904)

Miller, Amy, *Dressed to Kill: British Naval Uniform, Masculinity and Contemporary Fashions, 1748–1857* (National Maritime Museum, London, 2021)

3. SHDDT, *Xs 525 Décret 29 Aout 1793*
 4. SHDDT, *Xs 525 Circulaire No. 512*
 5. SHDDT, *Xs 525 Arête 25 Ventôse AnII*
 6. Forrest, Alan I., *Conscripts and Deserters: The Army and French Society During the Revolution and Empire* (Oxford University Press, New York, 1989), p.31
 7. Forrest (1989), p.31
 8. Lynn, John A., *The Bayonets of the Republic: Motivation and Tactics in the Army of Revolutionary France, 1791–94* (Routledge, London, 2021), p.220
 9. Connelly (2012), p.43
 10. Bertaud, Jean Paul, *The Army of the French Revolution: From Citizen-Soldiers to Instrument of Power* (Princeton Legacy Library, Princeton, 2019), p.151
 11. Ibid., p.155
 12. Lynn (2021), p.230
 13. Connelly (2012), p.43
 14. Dawson (2019), pp.36–37
 15. Ibid., p.37
 16. Ibid., pp.37–38
 17. Bardin, Étienne Alexandre, *Manuel d'Infanterie, ou Résumé de tous les règlements, décrets, usages, renseignements concernant l'Infanterie, dans lequel se trouve renfermé tout ce que doivent savoir les sergents et caporaux* (Chez Magimel, Paris, 1808), p.335
 18. SHDDT, *Xs 525 Arête 2 Ventôse AnIV*
 19. SHDDT, *Xb 162 Dossier 2ᵉ Régiment de Ligne. 1791 à 1793. Folio AnIII. Rapport 12 Ventôse AnIII*
 20. SHDDT, *Xb 220 Dossier 13ᵉ Régiment de la Ligne. Folio AnII*

Chapter 4: *Demi-Brigades d'Infanterie de Ligne*
 1. SHDDT, *Xs 525 Etat Aperçue des Fonds*
 2. SHDDT, *Xb 365 11ᵉ de Ligne. Dossier AnIV*
 3. SHDDT, *Xs 525 Arête 14 Messidor AnVII*
 4. SHDDT, *Xs 525 Arête 11 Thermidor AnVII*
 5. SHDDT, *Xs 525 Devis des étoffes et doublures nécessaires pour la confection de l'habillement complet d'un volontaire d'Infanterie de Ligne et d'un volontaire d'Infanterie légère, avec les dimensions de chaque partie de l'habillement, et des effets de grand et petit équipement communs à chacun d'eux*
 6. SHDDT, *Xs 525 Arête 26 Fructidor AnVII*
 7. The National Archives [hereafter TNA] Foreign Office [hereinafter FO] *27/54 Otto a Londres 27 Septembre 1799*
 8. Galtier-Boissière, Jean, *Mysteries of the French Secret Police* (Stanley Paul & Co., London, 1938), p.118
 9. SHDDT, *Xs 525 Décret 9 Thermidor AnVIII*
 10. SHDDT, *Xs 525 Projet d'Arête Relatif à l'Habillement des Troupes pour l'an X*
 11. SHDDT, *Xb 225 1ᵉ Demi-Brigade. Dossier AnVI. Rapport 24 Prairial AnVI*
 12. SHDDT, *Xb 225 1ᵉ Demi-Brigade. Dossier AnVI. Rapport 13 Prairial AnXI*
 13. SHDDT, *Xb 342 1ᵉ de Ligne. Dossier AnXIII. Rapport 13 Fructidor AnXIII*
 14. SHDDT, *Xb 225 2ᵉ Demi-Brigade. Dossier AnVIII. Rapport 8 Germinal AnVII*
 15. SHDDT, *Xb 532 5ᵉ de Ligne. Dossier AnIX. Rapport 28 Floréal AnVI*
 16. Ibid., *Dossier AnIX. Rapport 8 Brum AnIX*
 17. Ibid., *Rapport 27 Floréal AnX*
 18. Ibid., *Rapport 27 Floréal AnX*
 19. Ibid., *Rapport 27 Floréal AnX*
 20. SHDDT, *Xb 365 11ᵉ de Ligne. Dossier AnXII. Rapport 1 Brumaire AnXII*
 21. SHDDT, *Xb 380 17ᵉ de Ligne. Dossier AnXII. Rapport 1 Brumaire AnXII*
 22. Ibid., *Dossier AnXIII. Rapport 23 Thermidor 13*
 23. SHDDT, *Xb 243 21ᵉ Demi-Brigade. Dossier AnV. Rapport 26 Fructidor AnV*
 24. SHDDT, *Xb 244 22ᵉ Demi-Brigade. Dossier AnIV. Rapport 19 Prairial AnIV*

25. Ibid., *Dossier AnV. Rapport 1 Fructidor AnV*
26. Ibid., *Dossier AnX. Rapport 10 Ventôse AnX*
27. Ibid., *Dossier AnXI. Rapport 26 Prairial AnXI*. See also *Rapport 24 Floréal AnXI*
28. SHDDT, *Xb 249 28ᵉ Demi-Brigade. Dossier AnVI. Rapport 24 Prairial AnVI*
29. Ibid., *Dossier AnX. Rapport 5 Messidor AnXI*
30. Ibid., *Dossier AnX. Rapport 1 Prairial AnX*
31. SHDDT, *Xb 251 30ᵉ Demi-Brigade. Dossier AnX. Rapport 27 Pluviôse AnX*
32. Ibid., *Dossier AnXI. Rapport 28 Floréal AnXI*
33. SHDDT, *Xb 418 35ᵉ de Ligne. Dossier AnXII. Rapport 1 Brumaire AnXII*
34. SHDDT, *Xb 261 40ᵉ Demi-Brigade. Dossier AnVII. Rapport 8 Floréal AnVII*
35. Ibid., *Dossier AnX, Rapport 18 Ventôse AnX*
36. SHDDT, *Xb 380 17ᵉ de Ligne. Dossier AnXII. Rapport 1 Brumaire AnXII*
37. SHDDT, *Xb 264 Dossier 43ᵉ Demi-Brigade. Folio AnVII. Rapport 13 Nivôse AnVII*
38. Ibid., *Dossier AnXI. Rapport 2 Thermidor AnXI*
39. SHDDT, *Xb 264 Dossier 44ᵉ Demi-Brigade. Folio AnIV. Rapport 21 Messidor AnIV*
40. Ibid., *Dossier AnX. Rapport 26 Pluviôse AnX*
41. Ibid., *Dossier AnXI. Rapport 12 Thermidor AnXI*
42. SHDDT, *Xb 280 59ᵉ Demi-Brigade. Dossier AnX. Rapport 16 Floréal AnX*
43. SHDDT, *Xb 290 70ᵉ Demi-Brigade. Dossier AnVII. Rapport 24 Frimaire AnVII*
44. Ibid., *Dossier AnX. Rapport 10 Ventôse AnX*
45. Ibid., *Dossier AnXI*. Rapport 6 Messidor AnXI
46. SHDDT, *Xb 418 35ᵉ de Ligne. Dossier AnXII. Rapport 1 Brumaire AnXII*
47. SHDDT, *Xb 292 73ᵉ Demi-Brigade. Dossier AnX. Rapport 11 Ventôse AnX*
48. Ibid., *Dossier AnXI. Rapport 21 Messidor AnXI*
49. SHDDT, *Xb 292 74ᵉ Demi-Brigade. Dossier AnV. Rapport 16 Prairial AnV*
50. Ibid., *Dossier AnX. Rapport 4 Pluviôse AnX*
51. SHDDT, *Xb 497 82ᵉ de Ligne. Dossier AnXII. Rapport 1 Nivôse AnXII*
52. SHDDT, Ibid. *Rapport 26. Vendémiaire AnXII*
53. SHDDT, *Xb 507 92ᵉ de Ligne. Dossier AnXII. Rapport 22 Brumaire AnXII*
54. SHDDT, *Xb 308 96ᵉ Demi-Brigade. Dossier AnVII. Rapport 11 Brumaire AnVII*
55. Ibid., *Dossier AnX. Rapport 4 Germinal AnX*
56. Ibid., *Dossier AnXII. Rapport 22 Brumaire AnXII*
57. SHDDT, *Xb 312 101ᵉ Demi-Brigade. Dossier AnIX. Rapport 1 Messidor AnIX*
58. Ibid., *Dossier AnX. Rapport 28 Pluviôse AnX*
59. SHDDT, *Xb 365 11ᵉ de Ligne. Dossier AnXII. Rapport 1 Brumaire AnXII*
60. SHDDT, *Xs 525 Armée du Rhine. Situation 1 Nivôse AnVIII*
61. SHDDT, *Xs 525 Armée du Rhine. Situation 1 Nivôse AnVIII*
62. Ibid., p.2
63. Ibid., p.3
64. SHDDT, *Xs 526. Rapport 6 Frimaire AnVIII*
65. SHDDT, *Xs 526. Rapport 6 Frimaire AnVIII*
66. SHDDT, *Xs 526. Rapport Augereau au Moreau 13 Frimaire AnIX*
67. SHDDT, *Xs 526. Rapport 1 Ventôse AnIX*

Chapter 5: *Chasseurs à Pied*

1. SHDDT, *Xc 76 Régiment des Chasseurs. Règlement Provisoire du Roi, 10 Aout 1784*
2. Anon. (1786), pp.96–98
3. Anon. (1786), p.98
4. Crowdy, Terry, pers comm, 8 February 2024
5. SHDDT, *Xb 123 Ordonnance du roi, portant Règlement sur la formation et la solde de douze Bataillons d'Infanterie Légère 17 Mars 1788*

6. Ibid.
7. SHDDT, *Xb 123 Bataillons Infanterie Légère. Dossier Bataillon de Chasseurs Royaux du Dauphiné. Rapport 18 Aout 1788*
8. Ibid., *Dossier Chasseurs Royaux de Provence. Rapport 20 Octobre 1788*
9. Ibid., *Dossier Chasseurs Royaux de Provence. Rapport 6 Octobre 1789*
10. Ibid., *Dossier Chasseurs Corse. Rapport 6 Septembre 1789*
11. Ibid., *Dossier Chasseurs Cantabres. Rapport 8 Septembre 1788*
12. Ibid., *Dossier Chasseurs Cantabres. Rapport 11 Aout 1789*
13. Ibid., *Dossier Chasseurs Bretons. Rapport 4 Octobre 1788*
14. Ibid., *Dossier Chasseurs Bretons. Rapport 24 Septembre 1789*
15. Ibid., *Dossier Chasseurs d'Auvergne. Rapport 3 Octobre 1788*
16. Ibid., *Dossier Chasseurs d'Auvergne. Rapport 25 Juillet 1789*
17. SHDDT, *Xb 124 Bataillons Infanterie Légère. Dossier Chasseurs des Vosges. Rapport 23 Septembre 1788*
18. Ibid., *Dossier Chasseurs des Cévennes. Rapport 26 Septembre 1788*
19. Ibid., *Dossier Chasseurs des Cévennes. Rapport 20 Septembre 1789*
20. Ibid., *Dossier Chasseurs du Gévaudan. Rapport 30 Septembre 1788*
21. Ibid., *Dossier Chasseurs du Gévaudan. Rapport 30 Septembre 1789*
22. Ibid., *Dossier Chasseurs des Ardennes. Rapport 25 Octobre 1788*
23. Ibid., *Dossier Chasseurs des Ardennes. Rapport 21 Juillet 1788*
24. Ibid., *Dossier Chasseurs des Ardennes. Rapport 21 Juillet 1789*
25. Ibid., *Dossier Chasseurs de Roussillon. Rapport 8 Septembre 1788*
26. Ibid., *Dossier Chasseurs de Roussillon. Rapport 24 Septembre 1789*
27. SHDDT, *Xb 200 Bataillons Infanterie Légère. Dossier 5e Bataillon. Rapport 24 Mai 1792*
28. Ibid., *Dossier 6e Bataillon. Rapport 31 Décembre 1791*
29. Ibid., *Dossier 7e Bataillon. Rapport 26 Décembre 1791*
30. SHDDT, *Xb 200 Bataillons Infanterie Légère. Dossier 8e Bataillon. Rapport 13 Fevrier 1792*

Chapter 6: The *Légère* is Born
1. SHDDT, *Xs 525 Décret de la Convention Nationales, 7 Septembre 1793*
2. Malibran (1904), pp.283–289
3. SHDDT, *Xb 384 18e de Ligne 1811 à 1815. Rapport 20 Vendémiaire AnXI*. This report has been misfiled amongst the papers of the *18e de Ligne* and not *18e Légère*.
4. SHDDT, *Xb 325 6e Demi-Brigade Légère. Dossier AnVII. 3 Frimaire AnVII*
5. SHDDT, *Xb 200 Bataillons Infanterie Légère. Dossier 7e Bataillon. Rapport 2 Germinal AnII*
6. SHDDT, *Xb 327 9e Demi-Brigade Légère. Dossier AnVII. Rapport 9 Prairial AnVII*
7. Ibid., *Dossier AnX. Rapport 18 Nivôse AnX*
8. SHDDT, *Xb 330 Dossier 13e Demi-Brigade Légère. Folio AnV. Rapport 6 Thermidor AnV*
9. Ibid., *Dossier AnX. Rapport 17 Thermidor AnX*
10. Ibid., *Dossier AnXI. Rapport 8 Prairial AnXI*
11. SHDDT, *Xb 330 Dossier 14e Demi-Brigade Légère. Folio AnX. Rapport 1 Ventôse AnX*
12. SHDDT, *Xb 384 18e de Ligne 1811 à 1815. Rapport 20 Vendémiaire AnXI*. This report has been misfiled amongst the papers of the *18e de Ligne* and not *18e Légère*.
13. SHDDT, *Xb 334 19e Demi-Brigade Légère. Dossier AnX. Rapport 28 Ventôse AnX*
14. Ibid., *Dossier AnX. Rapport 5 Germinal AnX*
15. Ibid., *Dossier AnX. Rapport 30 Floréal AnXI*

Chapter 7: *Cavalerie*, *Carabiniers* and *Dragons*
1. Anon. (1786), p.44
2. Ibid., p.46
3. Anon. (1786), p.44
4. Anon., *Supplément a la décision du conseil de la Guerre du 24 Novembre 1788* (Paris, l'Imprimerie Royale, 1788), p.1

5. Anon. (1786), pp.45–46
6. *Les Gupil No. 32 Devis de Dragons*
7. Anon. (1791), pp.9–11
8. Malibran (1904), p.414
9. Anon., O*rdonnance Provisoire sur l'exercise de la Cavalerie AnXIII, troisieme édition* (Chez Magimel, Paris, 1815), pp.64–65
10. Anon. (1791), pp.3–4
11. Malibran (1904), p.413
12. Anon., *Reglement Arête pour le Roi pour l'Habillement et l'Equipment de ses Troupes* (l'Imprimerie Royale, Paris, 1779), p.26
13. Anon. (1791), pp.4–5
14. Anon. (1791), pp.4–5
15. Malibran (1904), p.412
16. Ibid.
17. SHDDT, *Xc 94 1ᵉ Cavalerie. Dossier 1791. Rapport 1 Décembre* 1791
18. Ibid., *Dossier AnIV. Rapport 21 Fructidor AnIV*
19. Ibid., *Dossier AnVI. Rapport 23 Floréal AnVI*
20. Ibid., *Dossier AnX. Rapport 17 Germinal AnX*
21. SHDDT, *Xc 96 2ᵉ Cavalerie. Dossier 1791. Rapport 1 Décembre 1791*
22. Ibid., *Dossier AnV. Rapport 1 Germinal AnV*
23. Ibid., *Dossier AnVI. Rapport 8 Vendémiaire AnVI*
24. Ibid., *Dossier AnVII. Rapport 22 Ventôse AnVII*
25. Ibid., *Dossier AnVIII. Rapport 1 Vendémiaire AnVIII*
26. SHDDT, *Xc 98 3ᵉ Cavalerie. Dossier 1791. Rapport 5 Décembre 1791*
27. Ibid., *Dossier AnVII. Rapport 28 Germinal AnVII*
28. Ibid., *Dossier AnX. Rapport 15 Ventôse AnX*
29. SHDDT, *Xc 99 3ᵉ Cuirassiers. Dossier AnXI. Rapport 10 Fructidor AnXI*
30. SHDDT, *Xc 98 4ᵉ Cavalerie. Dossier AnVI. Rapport 3 Messidor AnVI*
31. Ibid., *Dossier AnVII. Rapport 2 Brumaire AnVII*
32. SHDDT, *Xc 107 8ᵉ Cavalerie. Dossier AnX. Merlin au Ministre de geurre 10 Frimaire AnX*
33. Ibid., *Dossier AnVI. Rapport 1 Vendémiaire AnVI*
34. Ibid., *Dossier AnVII. Rapport 13 Pluviôse AnVII*
35. Ibid., *Dossier AnXI. Rapport 17 Prairial AnXI*
36. Ibid., *Dossier AnXIII. Rapport 14 Vendémiaire AnXIII*
37. SHDDT, *Xc 109 9ᵉ Cavalerie. Dossier AnVI. Rapport 30 Vendémiaire AnVI*
38. Ibid., *Dossier AnVII*
39. Ibid., *Dossier AnX. Rapport 10 Nivôse AnX*
40. Ibid., *Dossier AnXI. Rapport 28 Prairial AnXI*
41. SHDDT, *Xc 113 11ᵉ Cavalerie 1796 à AnXII. Rapport 22 Vendémiaire AnXII*
42. SHDDT, *Xc 115 12ᵉ Cavalerie. Dossier 1791. Rapport 8 Décembre 1791*
43. Ibid., *Dossier AnVI. Rapport 20 Frimaire AnVI*
44. Ibid., *Dossier AnX. Rapport 12 Pluviôse AnX*
45. Ibid., *Dossier AnXI. Rapport 15 Prairial AnXI*
46. SHDDT, *Xc 116 12ᵉ Régiment de Cuirassiers. Dossier AnXIII. Rapport 24 Vendémiaire AnXIII*
47. Ibid., *Dossier AnXII*
48. SHDDT, *Xc 117 13ᵉ Cavalerie. Dossier 1793. Rapport 13 Mai 1793*
49. Ibid., *Dossier AnVII. Rapport 1 Prairial AnVII*
50. Ibid., *Dossier AnX. Rapport 23 Pluviôse AnX*
51. Ibid., *Dossier AnXI. Rapport 22 Floréal AnXI*
52. SHDDT, *Xc 171 22ᵉ Dragons AnXIII à 1814. Dossier AnII. Rapport 1 Vendémiaire AnXII*
53. Ibid., *Dossier AnII. Rapport 1 Vendémiaire AnXII*
54. SHDDT, *Xc 121 15ᵉ Cavalerie. Dossier AnV. Rapport 1 Germinal AnV*

55. SHDDT, *Xc 121 15ᵉ Cavalerie. Dossier AnVII. Rapport 1 Prairial AnVII*
56. SHDDT, *Xc 121 15ᵉ Cavalerie. Dossier AnX. Rapport 11 Germinal AnX*
57. SHDDT, *Xc 172 23ᵉ Dragons. Dossier AnXIII. Rapport 15 Vendémiaire AnXIII*
58. Ibid., *Dossier AnXIV. Rapport 2 Frimaire AnXIV*
59. SHDDT, *Xc 131 25ᵉ Cavalerie. Dossier AnVI. Rapport 18 Frimaire AnVI*
60. Ibid., *Dossier AnX. Rapport 27 Ventôse AnX*
61. SHDDT, *Xc 90 1ᵉ Carabiniers. Dossier AnV. Rapport 5 Nivôse AnV*
62. Ibid., *Dossier AnVII. Rapport 1 Vendémiaire AnVII*
63. Ibid., *Dossier AnX. Rapport 30 Germinal AnX*
64. Ibid., *Dossier AnXI. Rapport 5 Messidor AXI*

Chapter 8: *Dragons*
1. SHDDT, *Xc 132 1ᵉ Dragons 1792 à AnX. Rapport 23 Pluviôse AnVII*
2. Ibid., *Dossier AnVII. Rapport 23 Pluviôse AnVII*
3. Ibid., *Dossier AnX. Rapport 10 Nivôse AnX*
4. SHDDT, *Xc 133 1ᵉ Dragons AnXII à 1811. Dossier AnXIII. Rapport 19 Vendémiaire AnXIII*
5. Ibid., *Dossier AnXIII. Rapport 19 Thermidor AnXIII*
6. SHDDT, *Xc 134 2ᵉ Dragons. Dossier 1794. Rapport 26 Novembre 1794*
7. Ibid., *Dossier AnVI. Rapport 29 Pluviôse AnVI*
8. Ibid., *Dossier AnX. Rapport 10 Floréal AnX*
9. SHDDT, *Xc 137 4ᵉ Dragons. Dossier 1791. Rapport 10 Décembre 1791*
10. Ibid., *Dossier AnVI. Rapport 1 Vendémiaire AnVI*
11. Ibid., *Dossier AnVII. Rapport 22 Ventôse AnVII*
12. Ibid., *Dossier AnVIII. Rapport 1 Germinal AnVIII*
13. Ibid., *Dossier AnX. Rapport 8 Pluviôse AnX*
14. Ibid., *Dossier AnXII. Rapport 19 Vendémiaire AnXII*
15. SHDDT, *Xc 139 5ᵉ Dragons. Dossier AnVII. Rapport 22 Ventôse AnVII*
16. Ibid., *Dossier AnX. Rapport 26 Ventôse AnX*
17. Ibid., *Dossier AnXI. Rapport 10 Thermidor AnXI*
18. SHDDT, *Xc 140 5ᵉ Dragons. Dossier AnXIV. Rapport 19 Brumaire AnXIV*
19. SHDDT, *Xc 141 6ᵉ Dragons. Dossier 1791. Rapport 24 Novembre 1791*
20. Ibid., *Dossier 1793. Rapport 23 Mai 1793*
21. Ibid., *Dossier AnX. Rapport 13 Germinal AnX*
22. Ibid., *Dossier AnXII. Rapport 27 Prairial AnXII*
23. SHDDT, *Xc 143 7ᵉ Dragons. Dossier 1791. Rapport 17 Mars 1791*
24. Ibid., *Dossier 1791. Rapport 28 Novembre 1791*
25. Ibid., *Dossier AnVI. Rapport 16 Pluviôse AnVI*
26. Ibid., *Dossier AnX. Rapport 14 Germinal AnX*
27. SHDDT, *Xc 146 9ᵉ Dragons. Dossier AnIV. Rapport 20 Prairial AnIV*
28. Ibid., *Dossier AnIV. Rapport 20 Prairial AnIV*
29. Ibid., *Dossier AnV. Rapport 18 Prairial AnV*
30. Ibid., *Dossier AnV. Rapport 18 Prairial AnV*
31. Ibid., *Dossier AnX. Rapport 11 Ventôse AnX*
32. SHDDT, *Xc 149 11ᵉ Dragons. Dossier 1791. Rapport 23 Novembre 1791*
33. Ibid., *Dossier AnVI. Rapport 18 Pluviôse AnVI*
34. Ibid., *Dossier AnVII. Rapport 5 Frimaire AnVII*
35. Ibid., *Dossier AnX. Rapport 12 Pluviôse AnX*
36. SHDDT, *Xc 169 21ᵉ de Dragons An IV à 1814. Dossier AnV. Rapport 17 Vendémiaire AnV*
37. Ibid., *Dossier AnXI. Rapport 1 Nivôse An XI*
38. Ibid., *Dossier AnXI. Rapport 1 Nivôse AnXI*
39. Ibid., *Dossier AnXI. Rapport 9 Messidor AnXI*

Chapter 9: *Hussards*

1. SHDDT, *Xc 237 1ᵉ Hussards. Dossier AnVI. Rapport 23 Pluviôse AnVI*
2. Ibid., *Dossier AnX. Rapport 16 Germinal AnX*
3. SHDDT, *Xc 239 2ᵉ Hussards. Dossier AnVI. Rapport 1 Messidor AnVI*
4. Ibid., *Dossier AnIX. Rapport 1 Vendémiaire AnIX*
5. Croyet, Jerome, pers comm, 29 May 2020
6. Croyet, Jerome, pers comm, 29 May 2020
7. SHDDT, *Xc 241 3ᵉ Hussards. Dossier AnIV. Rapport 6 Thermidor AnIV*
8. Croyet, Jerome, pers comm, 29 May 2020
9. SHDDT, *Xc 241 3ᵉ Hussards. Dossier AnVI. Etat de draps 3 Vendémiaire AnVI*
10. Croyet, Jerome, pers comm, 29 May 2020
11. SHDDT, *Xc 241 3ᵉ Hussards. Dossier AnX. Rapport 11 Pluviôse AnX*
12. Ibid., *Dossier AnXIII. Rapport 30 Messidor AnXI*
13. SHDDT, *Xc 243 4ᵉ Hussards. Dossier AnVI. Rapport 4 Messidor AnVI*
14. Ibid., *Dossier AnVII. Rapport 8 Ventôse AnVII*
15. Ibid., *Dossier AnXI. Rapport 13 Floréal AnXIII*
16. SHDDT, *Xc 245 5ᵉ Hussards. Rapport 17 Pluviôse AnX*
17. Ibid., *Dossier AnXI. Rapport 30 Thermidor AnXI*
18. Ibid., *Rapport 30 Thermidor AnXI*
19. SHDDT, *Xc 254 9ᵉ Hussards. Rapport 6 Janvier 1793*
20. SHDDT, *Xc 252 8ᵉ Hussards. Dossier AnVI. Rapport 1 Vendémiaire AnVI*
21. Ibid., *Dossier AnXI. Rapport 2 Prairial AnXI*
22. SHDDT, *Xc 254 9ᵉ Hussards. Rapport 6 Janvier 1793*
23. SHDDT, *Xc 254 9ᵉ Hussards. Rapport 2 Septembre 1792*
24. Ibid., *Compte de la Levée du Corps*
25. Ibid., *Rapport 5 Juin 1793*
26. Ibid., *Historique du Corps*
27. SHDDT, *Xc 254 Registre d'Ordres du 9ᵉ Hussards*, p.4
28. Ibid., p.16
29. Ibid., p.17
30. Ibid., p.30
31. Ibid., p.45
32. Ibid., pp.51–52
33. Ibid., p.60
34. Ibid., p.62
35. Ibid., p.80
36. Ibid., pp.82–83
37. Ibid., p.86
38. Ibid., p.91
39. Ibid., pp.104–105
40. SHDDT *Xc 255 9ᵉ Hussards. Dossier AnX. Rapport 25 Ventôse AnX*
41. Ibid., *Dossier AnXI. Rapport 20 Prairial AnXI*
42. SHDDT, *Xc 256 10ᵉ Hussards 1793 à 1811. Dossier 1793. Rapport 30 Aout 1793*
43. Ibid., *Dossier AnV. Rapport 1 Vendémiaire AnV*
44. Ibid., *Dossier AnX. Rapport 22 Ventôse AnX*
45. Ibid., *Dossier AnXI. Rapport 16 Thermidor AnXI*
46. SHDDT, *Xc 257 11ᵉ Hussards 1793 à 1811. Dossier AnVII. Rapport 30 Nivôse AnVII*
47. SHDDT, *Xc 259 12ᵉ Hussards. Dossier AnVII. Dossier 1793*
48. Ibid., *Dossier AnVII. Rapport 1 Brumaire AnVII*
49. Ibid., *Dossier AnXIII*

Chapter 10: *Chasseurs à Cheval*
1. SHDDT, *Xc 77 Régiment des Chasseurs. Dossier 1ᵉ Régiment. Rapport 2 Septembre 1783*
2. Ibid., *Dossier 1ᵉ Régiment. Rapport 26 Aout 1784*
3. Ibid., *Dossier 2ᵉ Régiment. Rapport 22 Septembre 1783*
4. SHDDT, *Xc 76 Régiment des Chasseurs. Reglement Provisoire du Roi. 10 Aout 1784*
5. SHDDT, *Xc 77 Régiment des Chasseurs. Dossier Chasseurs des Alpes. Rapport 30 Juin 1785*
6. SHDDT, *Xc 77 Régiment des Chasseurs. Dossier Chasseurs des Pyrénées. Rapport 24 Aout 1785*
7. SHDDT, *Xc 76 Chasseurs à Cheval. Dossier Chasseurs d'Alsace Rapport 28 Septembre 1788*
8. Ibid., *Dossier Chasseurs des Evêchés. Rapport 3 Octobre 1788*
9. Ibid., *Dossier Chasseurs des Flandres. Rapport 22 Septembre 1788*
10. Ibid., *Dossier Chasseurs dse Flandres. Rapport 12 Septembre 1789*
11. Ibid., *Rapport 21 Juillet 1791*
12. SHDDT, *Xc 76 Chasseurs à Cheval. Dossier Chasseurs de Franche-Comté. Rapport 23 Septembre 1788*
13. Ibid., *Dossier Chasseurs de Languedoc. Rapport 30 Septembre 1788*
14. Ibid., *Dossier Chasseurs de Guyenne. Rapport 19 Septembre 1788*
15. SHDDT, *Xs 525 Circulaire 4 Brumaire AnX*
16. SHDDT, *Xs 525 Projet d'Arête Relatif à l'Habillement des Troupes pour l'an X*
17. SHDDT, *Xc 193 5ᵉ Chasseurs. Dossier 1791. Rapport 22 Décembre 1791*
18. Ibid., *Dossier AnIV. Rapport 19 Thermidor AnIV*
19. Ibid., *Dossier AnVII. Rapport 18 Brumaire AnVII*
20. Ibid., *Dossier AnVIII. Rapport 8 Brumaire AnVIII*
21. Ibid., *Dossier AnX. Rapport 6 Frimaire AnX*
22. SHDDT, *Xc 201 9ᵉ Chasseurs. Dossier 1791. Rapport 23 Novembre 1791*
23. Ibid., *Dossier AnVI. Rapport 20 Germinal AnVI*
24. Ibid., *Dossier AnX. Rapport 27 Germinal AnX*
25. SHDDT, *Xc 209 13ᵉ Chasseurs. Dossier 1793. Rapport 3 Mai 1793*
26. Ibid., *Dossier AnIII. Rapport 23 Germinal AnIII*
27. Ibid., *Dossier AnIV. 6 Fructidor AnIV*
28. Ibid., *Dossier AnX. 24 Pluviôse AnX*
29. SHDDT, *Xc 214 15ᵉ Chasseurs. Dossier AnIV*
30. Ibid., *Dossier AnX. Rapport 18 Germinal AnX*
31. Ibid., *Dossier AnXI. Rapport 18 Messidor AnXI*
32. SHDDT, *Xc 218 17ᵉ Chasseurs. Dossier AnX. Rapport 20 Ventôse AnX*
33. SHDDT, *Xc 219 19ᵉ Chasseurs. Dossier AnVI. Rapport 30 Prairial AnVI*
34. Ibid., *Dossier AnX. Rapport 15 Ventôse AnX*
35. SHDDT, *Xc 224 21ᵉ Chasseurs. Dossier AnV. Rapport 19 Vendémiaire AnV*
36. Ibid., *Dossier AnV Etat Nominatif*
37. Ibid., *Dossier AnV. Lettre, Duprez au Ministre de Guerre*
38. Archives Nationales [hereafter AN] LH/247/38
39. SHDDT, *Xc 224 21ᵉ Chasseurs. Dossier AnX. Rapport 13 Pluviôse AnX*
40. SHDDT, *Xc 227 23ᵉ Chasseurs. Dossier AnIV. Rapport 1 Messidor AnIV*
41. Ibid., *Dossier AnV. Rapport 4 Fructidor AnV*
42. SHDDT, *Xc 229 24ᵉ Chasseurs. Dossier AnVI. Rapport 28 Messidor AnVI*
43. Ibid., *Dossier AnVI. Rapport 10 Prairial AnVI*
44. Ibid., *Dossier AnXI. Rapport 16 Messidor AnXI*
45. SHDDT, *Xc 231 25ᵉ Chasseurs. Dossier AnXI. Rapport 22 Prairial AnXI*
46. Ibid., *Dossier AnXV. Rapport 5 Ventôse AnX*
47. Ibid., *Dossier AnXI. Rapport 22 Prairial AnXI*

Dear Reader,

We hope you have enjoyed this book, but why not share your views on social media? You can also follow our pages to see more about our other products: facebook.com/penandswordbooks or follow us on X @penswordbooks

You can also view our products at www.pen-and-sword.co.uk (UK and ROW) or www.penandswordbooks.com (North America).

To keep up to date with our latest releases and online catalogues, please sign up to our newsletter at: www.pen-and-sword.co.uk/newsletter

If you would like a printed catalogue with our latest books, then please email: enquiries@pen-and-sword.co.uk or telephone: 01226 734555 (UK and ROW) or email: uspen-and-sword@casematepublishers.com or telephone: (610) 853-9131 (North America).

We respect your privacy and we will only use personal information to send you information about our products.

Thank you!